D1093139

PROTECT AND SURVIVE

THE HOME OFFICE

CIVIL DEFENCE

MANUAL OF
BASIC TRAINING

PROTECT AND SURVIVE

THE HOME OFFICE

CIVIL DEFENCE

MANUAL OF
BASIC TRAINING

Edited by Campbell McCutcheon

TEMPUS

First published 1949, this edition 2007

Tempus Publishing
Cirencester Road, Chalford
Stroud, Gloucestershire, GL6 8PE
www.tempus-publishing.com

Tempus Publishing is an imprint of NPI Media Group

British Library Cataloguing in Publication Data.
A catalogue record for this book is available from the British Library.

ISBN 978 0 7524 4422 2

Typesetting and origination by NPI Media Group
Printed and bound in Great Britain

Contents

GENERAL PREFACE

The series of Civil Defence handbooks and pamphlets is produced under the authority of the Home Secretary by the Civil Defence Department of the Home Office with the assistance of and in co-operation with the Secretary of State for Scotland and other Ministers concerned.

Measures for safeguarding the civil population against the effects of war which these publications describe, have become an essential part of the defensive organisation of this country. The need for them is not related to any belief that war is imminent. It is just as necessary that preparations for Civil Defence should be made in time of peace as it is that preparations should be made for the Armed Forces.

The publications cover, as far as is possible, measures which can be taken to mitigate the effects of all modern forms of attack. Any scheme of Civil Defence, if it is to be efficient, must be up-to-date and must take account of all the various weapons which might become available. The scale of bombing experienced in Great Britain during the 1939-45 war might be considerably exceeded in any future war, and types of weapons and tactics which were not experienced in this country might conceivably be used against it in the future. It does not follow that any one of the weapons, e.g. the atomic bomb, will necessarily be used, and it is most important that a proper balance is held between what is likely and what is possible.

The use of poison gas in war was forbidden by the Geneva Gas Protocol of 1925, to which this country and all the other countries of the Western Union were parties. At the outbreak of a war, His Majesty's Government would try to secure an undertaking from the enemy not to use poison gas. Nevertheless the risk of poison gas being used remains a possibility and cannot be disregarded any more than can certain further developments in other scientific fields.

The publications are designed to describe not only precautionary schemes which experience in the last war proved to be extremely effective in preventing avoidable injury and loss of life, or widespread dislocation of national industries, but also the training, both technical and tactical, which will be required of the personnel of the Civil Defence Services if they are to be ready effectively to play their part if war should ever break out. The publications aim at giving the best available information on methods of defence against all the various weapons. Information is not complete in respect of some of these weapons and the best methods of countering them, but as results of experimental work and other investigations mature, they will be revised and added to from time to time so that the Civil Defence Services may be kept up-to-date and their training may be on the most modern and experienced lines.

Introduction

The Second World War ended, literally, in a bang. The largest explosions the world had ever seen destroyed the Japanese cities of Hiroshima and Nagasaki, along with almost 400,000 lives. Within a few days Japan had capitulated, but the world had changed forever.

Billions of dollars and 130,000 men and women from every Allied country, working in universities, factories and research establishments across the United States, had made the ultimate weapon – the Atomic Age had started. The political map of the world had also been redrawn. Europe had been war-ravaged for six years, much of its infrastructure damaged, with a major economic re-building required in every country involved in the war. The USSR, one of the successful Allied countries, was, of course, going to set itself on a course of isolationism, taking much of Eastern Europe into its sphere of influence. Winston Churchill realised the problems that would occur as the balance of power in Europe changed. In March 1946, he stated that: 'From Stettin in the Baltic to Trieste in the Adriatic an iron curtain has descended across the Continent.' He had warned of war throughout the 1930s and been ignored. This time, the world listened. He'd realised that the next threat to world peace was going to come from Russia and her new satellite states. With the advent of the nuclear age, the West had a short time while it was the dominant power, but Russia had spent the last few days of the war, and much time afterwards, searching out and removing Nazi nuclear secrets from the many universities and research establishments in its zone of Germany. Many German scientists were also removed to Russia and made to work for the benefit of the Russian people. It was thought that the Russians would be quite a few years behind the USA in developing the Bomb! The Americans hadn't assumed for the tons of information sent back to Russia from Germany and they certainly hadn't assumed for the actions of spies like Klaus Fuchs and Julius Rosenberg, who handed the Russians many nuclear secrets. Their information was enough to ensure that Stalin's Russia detonated 'Joe 1' on 29 August 1949. The nuclear arms race had begun in earnest and in 1952 the UK tested its first nuclear bomb.

The threat of war was now totally different from what had gone before! A whole new series of phrases entered the dictionary – mutually assured destruction, megaton, nuclear winter, Defcon, H-bomb – and the countries of the developed world started planning for the worst eventuality. The British Government looked seriously at civil defence again in the late 1940s and set up a series of regional and local command centres. Over 300,000 members of the public were recruited into the Civil Defence Corps and other voluntary groups like the Royal Observer Corps. Many were issued with the handbook you are reading now. However, this was just one part of the Civil Defence Manual, and a whole different set of pamphlets were issued to the Civil Defence centres, as well as many of the missing pages of this volume. No doubt, the Government considered some parts of the pamphlets simply too scary for general consumption and held the information back.

With the Cuban Missile Crisis the threat of nuclear war was at its most severe but by 1965 had dwindled greatly. By 1968, the perceived lack of a threat of war led to the stepping down of the Civil Defence Corps and civil defence had taken a back seat. With local government reorganisation in 1974, regulations were made which required local authorities to have contingency plans for war. Little happened in reality until the Conservatives came into power in 1979 and the start of the next phase of the Cold War started. With Ronald Reagan and Margaret Thatcher in power in the USA and UK, and Gorbachev in power in the Soviet Union, the arms race had begun again with renewed vigour.

In 1980, as a result of a review of 'civil preparedness for home defence', the Government sprang into action. The United Kingdom Warning and Monitoring Organisation was modernised, as were the Green Goddess fire engines and the Wartime Broadcasting Service. It was at this time that the 'Protect & Survive' leaflets were sent to every household and the BBC showed the drama *Threads*. It was a shocking portrayal of the effects of a nuclear war on two families in Sheffield and gave many in Britain their first taste of the true horrors of nuclear war. Meanwhile, huge nuclear bunkers had been built by many local authorities, some under their headquarters and others in the countryside. The Government had also constructed regional centres and plans were in place to remove artworks from museums and art galleries to safe stores in caverns buried deep in the hills of Wales and Scotland. New regional authority bunkers were built too and others modernised. The threat of all-out nuclear war was being taken very seriously and the Campaign for Nuclear Disarmament saw its membership numbers surge. The arrival of American cruise missiles at Greenham Common and Lakenheath saw the setting up of peace camps which were constantly in the news, as were CND's marches at Aldermaston.

By 1986, the Government had realised that its planning for war could be used for peacetime emergencies too and the Civil Protection in Peacetime Act came into force that year. Volunteers were again sought to help at grass roots levels, but perhaps only 30,000 volunteers came forward in the whole of the UK. London's Civil Defence Authority estimated it would need 50,000 volunteers just to man its food kitchens and emergency feeding centres. Mind you, the chances of many surviving the bombs that would rain down on London, or the effects of the fallout, were slim anyway.

By 1990, the civil defence planning in Britain was at its height, more sophisticated than at any time since the Cuban missile crisis, but the start of the 1990s was the period of glasnost and the fall of the USSR was imminent. By July 1991, all work on bunkers and other civil defence planning all but ceased. The Royal Observer Corps was stood down and the siren warning system so familiar to those of us who had lived through the 1970s and '80s was scrapped too. By 1993, everything was closed down, the bunkers sat mothballed and empty, some with water dripping down the now-abandoned sites. For the first time since the end of the Second World War, Britain was without a civil defence capability. The abandonment of the system was as quick as it had been at the end of the war, but this time, there was to be no attempt to have a new infrastructure in place.

Over the past decade, many of the bunkers have been sold to private developers, or just abandoned to the elements. However, at least one, at Kelvedon Hatch in Essex, has been re-opened as a museum to the longest non-war in British history. With the dismantling of the infrastructure, little now remains elsewhere of Britain's Cold War Civil Defence organisation, but it can be found in all sorts of places if you just look hard enough. A good place to start is Robert Clarkes' *Four Minute Warning: Britain's Cold War*, also published by Tempus. It is a great introduction to how the Cold War affected Britain and to the remains visible around the country today.

HOME OFFICE

CIVIL DEFENCE

Manual of Basic Training

VOLUME II

BASIC
CHEMICAL WARFARE

PAMPHLET No. 1

LONDON: HIS MAJESTY'S STATIONERY OFFICE
1949

ONE SHILLING NET

GENERAL PREFACE

The series of Civil Defence handbooks and pamphlets is produced under the authority of the Home Secretary by the Civil Defence Department of the Home Office with the assistance of and in co-operation with the Secretary of State for Scotland and other Ministers concerned.

Measures for safeguarding the civil population against the effects of war which these publications describe, have become an essential part of the defensive organisation of this country. The need for them is not related to any belief that war is imminent. It is just as necessary that preparations for Civil Defence should be made in time of peace as it is that preparations should be made for the Armed Forces.

The publications cover, as far as is possible, measures which can be taken to mitigate the effects of all modern forms of attack. Any scheme of Civil Defence, if it is to be efficient, must be up-to-date and must take account of all the various weapons which might become available. The scale of bombing experienced in Great Britain during the 1939-45 war might be considerably exceeded in any future war, and types of weapons and tactics which were not experienced in this country might conceivably be used against it in the future. It does not follow that any one of the weapons, e.g. the atomic bomb, will necessarily be used, and it is most important that a proper balance is held between what is likely and what is possible.

The use of poison gas in war was forbidden by the Geneva Gas Protocol of 1925, to which this country and all the other countries of the Western Union were parties. At the outbreak of a war, His Majesty's Government would try to secure an undertaking from the enemy not to use poison gas. Nevertheless the risk of poison gas being used remains a possibility and cannot be disregarded any more than can certain further developments in other scientific fields.

The publications are designed to describe not only precautionary schemes which experience in the last war proved to be extremely effective in preventing avoidable injury and loss of life, or widespread dislocation of national industries, but also the training, both technical and tactical, which will be required of the personnel of the Civil Defence Services if they are to be ready effectively to play their part if war should ever break out. The publications aim at giving the best available information on methods of defence against all the various weapons. Information is not complete in respect of some of these weapons and the best methods of countering them, but as results of experimental work and other investigations mature, they will be revised and added to from time to time so that the Civil Defence Services may be kept up-to-date and their training may be on the most modern and experienced lines.

CONTENTS

NOTE

*The pagination of this pamphlet is not continuous as it
may be necessary to introduce new pages at a later date.*

INTRODUCTION

The purpose of this pamphlet is to set out in simple form the basic principles of personal and collective protection against Chemical Warfare.

The information it contains should enable every member of the Civil Defence Organisation to understand the properties and effects of War Gases, and to appreciate the risks which these entail.

The pamphlet should also be of interest to the general reader since the protection of the civil population must depend largely on the action of individuals themselves. A knowledge of the basic principles and of the correct way of applying any available measures of personal protection should enable members of the general public to look after themselves, and thus ensure an effective national defence against gas warfare.

The Germans did not use gas during the 1939-1945 war, but on its conclusion it was found that they held large stocks of both new and old war gases and some of these were ready for use in bombs and shells.

Though we cannot be certain why they did not use this weapon, it is fair to assume that the knowledge that the population of this country all possessed efficient respirators and were trained in their use, together with the possibility of retaliation, was an important deterrent.

It should, however, not be assumed that gas will not be encountered in future wars.

New gases have been discovered, and the fact that gas was not used during the last war might well increase the possibility of its future use, in the hope of achieving the surprise upon which the success of any gas attack largely depends.

Gas warfare is, therefore, still one of the risks that the civil population must be prepared to face and gas training and provision of protection must continue.

A number of unused paragraphs have been left at the end of each chapter to permit of any additions that may be considered necessary from time to time. This, it is hoped, will avoid the necessity of renumbering paragraphs in Chapters which would otherwise have to be done.

A 2

CHAPTER I

1. WAR GASES

Gas is a chemical weapon relying on its poisonous effects and, like other weapons of war, its object is to kill or incapacitate. As its name implies it may be used as invisible vapour. It may be employed as minute solid particles or liquid droplets which are airborne and invisible ; or it may be used as liquid which evaporates to form invisible vapour—both liquid and vapour being dangerous.

War gases may be divided into two main categories :—

Non-persistent and persistent.

Non-persistent Gas

Non-persistent gases are those which will remain effective for only a short time, so that the locality in which they have been released quickly ceases to be dangerous. They are liberated in the form of airborne droplets of liquid, particles of a solid, or as a true gas. They are therefore at the mercy of the prevailing weather conditions and are quickly dispersed.

Persistent Gas

Persistent gases are liquids which evaporate slowly, giving off poisonous vapour and therefore " persist " or remain dangerous for some considerable time, unless something is done to destroy or neutralise the liquid.

2. CLASSIFICATION BY EFFECTS

The division of gases into the two main groups—non-persistent and persistent—is convenient because as soon as it has been determined to which category the gas belongs, it is possible to decide whether the area in which the gas has been liberated requires special treatment.

Gases may also be classified according to the effects they produce upon the human body, and such a system of grouping is more satisfactory when considering the subject of personal protection.

This method of classification is by no means rigid, for some of the gases possess the characteristics of more than one group, but the principal war gases may be divided into five main groups. These groups, placed in what is now considered to be their order of importance are as follows :—

(i) Nerve Gases
(ii) Blister Gases
(iii) Choking Gases
(iv) Tear Gases
(v) Nose Gases

For the purpose of personal protection it is important to know the general characteristics of these groups. In the sections which follow, therefore, the characteristics and effects of the above-mentioned gases are described in terms which are, as far as possible, applicable to each group as a whole. Those interested in the specific properties of individual gases will find particulars of the better known ones in the " Chart of War Gases " Appendix " A."

3. CHARACTERISTICS AND EFFECTS

The effects produced by any war gas depend on the amount of the gas and the length of time a person is exposed to it. The stronger the concentration, the greater will be the injury produced in a given time. It should not, however, be assumed that small quantities of gas will always cause injury.

(i) Nerve Gases

(a) Characteristics

The members of this group are persistent or semi-persistent liquids which give off invisible vapours. These vapours have practically no smell. They are absorbed only through the eyes and breathing passages and cannot be detected except by their effects.

The liquid can be absorbed through the skin and will penetrate clothing and may be absorbed by the skin underneath. Neither vapour nor liquid cause irritation or blistering.

(b) Effects

V A P O U R—Small doses absorbed in either vapour or droplet form cause contraction of the pupils of the eyes resulting in dimness of vision and difficulty in focussing on near objects. They also cause running of the nose, headache and tightness of the chest. These symptoms develop in 5—30 minutes, depending on the dose.

If larger doses are absorbed, the symptoms described above will be followed by twitching and convulsions of the limbs and then possibly death. These more serious symptoms develop in about 5 minutes to 6 hours depending again on the dose.

L I Q U I D—Splashes of liquid on the skin will be rapidly absorbed, even large splashes being absorbed in a few minutes. The symptoms are the same as those produced by exposure to vapour. If liquid Nerve gas is swallowed in contaminated food or water it will cause death.

There may be a delay between the initial symptoms and the onset of convulsions and possibly death, during which period it will be impossible to say whether or not a fatal dose has been received. Anyone, therefore, who shows the initial symptoms, contraction of the pupils, headache, etc., must be regarded as seriously ill and treated accordingly.

(c) Protection

The respirator, provided it fits properly and is in an efficient condition, will protect the eyes and breathing passages against Nerve gases, but will not, of course, prevent absorption of the liquid through the skin of other parts of the body.

(ii) Blister Gases

(a) Characteristics

The members of this group are liquids of varying degrees of persistence, giving off invisible vapour. They have great powers of penetration and there are few materials into which both liquid and vapour will not be absorbed.

Contact with the liquid will cause injury, as will exposure to the vapour, provided the period of exposure to the latter is sufficiently long.

Both liquid and vapour will attack any part of the body.

Some members of the group have pungent smells and irritant effects on the nose and eyes, and thus will give early warning of their presence.

6

Others have faint and indefinite smells which are unlikely to be recognised in air raid conditions.

(b) Effects

V A P O U R—Exposure of the eyes to vapour causes no immediate discomfort, but if prolonged, may result in closure of the eyes after some hours, with temporary blindness for one or two weeks.

Breathing of the vapour over long periods, may cause serious injury to breathing passages and lungs which may prove fatal.

Exposure of the skin to vapour causes no immediate discomfort or irritation. If the exposure is prolonged or the concentration of vapour is high, redness of the skin and severe irritation will develop in 2—24 hours. This redness may soon begin to show numerous small blisters which run together to form larger ones.

L I Q U I D—A small drop of liquid in the eye, unless treated immediately, will usually cause permanent blindness in that eye.

Liquid swallowed in contaminated food or water, and liquid in the form of minute airborne droplets which are inhaled, will both cause severe internal injury.

Liquid on the skin will be rapidly absorbed and may or may not cause a stinging sensation. Except for this, there will be no apparent effects until 15 minutes to about 2 hours afterwards, when redness and irritation of the skin will develop, and this will be followed by the formation of blisters within 1 to 8 hours.

(c) Protection

The respirator will protect the eyes, nose, breathing passages and lungs. Special clothing is required to protect other parts of the body.

(iii) Choking Gases

(a) Characteristics

The members of this group are true gases or liquids which evaporate quickly. They are therefore non-persistent or only slightly persistent.

Those which have been used in war have pronounced and offensive smells. When inhaled in large quantities they cause serious damage to the lungs which may prove fatal.

(b) Effects

Their effects are immediate and unmistakable. The initial symptoms are irritation of the nose and throat, causing coughing which may be violent. There is a feeling of tightness in the chest and a pain behind the breast bone. A certain amount of irritation of the eyes is common.

After exposure the initial symptoms may subside for a time, during which no ill effects are felt, but this may be followed by the appearance of the more serious symptoms. In consequence of this, no physical exertion should be undertaken in the 24 hours following exposure to Choking gases, if the initial symptoms have been severe.

(c) Protection

The respirator gives complete protection against Choking gases.

(iv) Tear Gases

(a) Characteristics

The gases in this group may take the form of invisible minute airborne solid particles, or invisible vapour from persistent liquids. They are effective even in low concentrations.

(b) Effects

The effects which are immediate, are smarting of the eyes and a profuse flow of tears. They cause no permanent injury to the eyes unless solid or liquid Tear gas enters the eye.

(c) Protection

The respirator gives complete protection.

(v) Nose Gases

(a) Characteristics

The gases in this group are solid arsenical compounds, which, when dispersed by heat or explosion, produce vast numbers of minute airborne particles. These are invisible and except when highly concentrated have no smell.

(b) Effects

When inhaled these gases are extremely effective even in very low concentrations, but the onset of symptoms is delayed for a few minutes.

They produce a burning pain at the back of the nose, in the throat and chest, a fullness of the head and a general feeling of discomfort. Sneezing, coughing, headache and aching of the gums are common.

The symptoms tend to increase after putting on a respirator or getting clear of the cloud, since the particles which have been inhaled remain in the nose, throat and chest. Though they cause much discomfort these symptoms pass off quickly leaving no ill effects.

(c) Protection

The respirator gives complete protection.

CHAPTER II

9. BEHAVIOUR OF GAS UNDER DIFFERENT CONDITIONS OF WEATHER AND GROUND

The effectiveness of gas may be considerably influenced by both the weather conditions at the time and the characteristics of the area in which it is released.

(i) Weather Conditions

The principal weather conditions affecting the behaviour of gas are wind, temperature and rain.

(a) *Wind*

Non-persistent gas will be carried along by the wind, being diluted and dispersed all the time. The stronger the wind, the more rapid will be this dilution and dispersal and hence the shorter the distance the gas will travel in effective concentration.

Persistent gas will evaporate more quickly under the influence of a strong, drying wind than in a calm, but there will be little increase in the danger from vapour on account of its more rapid dilution and dispersal.

(b) *Temperature*

In a high temperature and bright sunlight there is a tendency for upward air currents to develop, and in consequence non-persistent gas will be dispersed upwards and as it rises will also spread out sideways. Temperature chiefly affects persistent gas. In hot weather persistent gas evaporates more quickly than in cold and the vapour danger is correspondingly increased unless there is a strong wind blowing. In very cold weather some persistent gases may freeze and in this state they will give off little or no vapour until they begin to thaw. Contact with frozen blister gas, however, will still cause blistering of the skin. Persistent gases are more readily absorbed by some materials, e.g., tarmac road surfaces, when these have been warmed by the hot sun.

(c) *Rain*

Rain will have little effect on either non-persistent or persistent gases unless it is really heavy. Heavy rain tends to wash gas out of the air and may wash away liquid persistent gas on the surface to other places where, however, it may still be dangerous.

(ii) Ground Characteristics

In open country gas will drift with the wind, passing round or over obstacles such as hedges, small clumps of trees, etc.

Gas released in a built-up area will drift before the wind following the direction of the streets. Where the wind is at an angle to the line of a street some of the gas will travel down side streets. Thus a fairly wide area in a general downwind direction from the point of release of the gas will be dangerous. There will be a tendency for non-persistent gases or the vapour of persistent gases to form pockets in hollows or

13

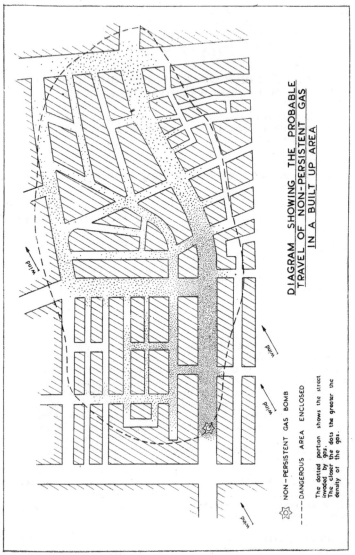

NON-PERSISTENT GAS BOMB

------ DANGEROUS AREA ENCLOSED

The dotted portion shows the street invaded by gas. The closer the dots the greater the density of the gas.

DIAGRAM SHOWING THE PROBABLE TRAVEL OF NON-PERSISTENT GAS IN A BUILT UP AREA

Fig. 1

sheltered places where there is little air movement. Dangerous concentrations may therefore remain in such places for some time after the main volume of the gas has been carried away by the wind (*see Fig.* 1). The fact that war gases themselves are heavier than air will not prevent dangerous concentrations from piling up against and passing over the top of any but the tallest buildings if they cannot find an easier way round them. Porous surfaces will more readily absorb liquid gas than hard surfaces. The gas thus absorbed being less effected by weather conditions will remain dangerous for a long period.

(iii) Summary

Gas will be most dangerous in mild weather with a light wind to drift it considerable distances in high concentration. Both non-persistent and persistent gases are likely to be more dangerous in built-up areas than in open country.

CHAPTER III

13. GAS ATTACK

If gas is used in attacks on the civilian population of this country, the gases most likely to be used are those of the Nerve, Blister and Choking groups. The possibility of a tear gas with a pronounced smell being used in conjunction with a blister gas to mask the latter's presence should not, however, be overlooked. Effective attacks could be made by aircraft dropping bombs or releasing liquid gases in the form of spray.

(i) Bombs

Bombs filled with Nerve and Blister Gases may be of large, medium or small capacity.

The fuzes used in large and medium type bombs may be such as to burst the bomb case on impact or to burst the bomb case at a pre-determined height above the ground.

With an impact fuze a part of the filling will be liberated in the form of small droplets and vapour, which will drift away with the wind.

The high explosive burster, which is initiated by the fuze, may be powerful enough just to open the bomb and splash its contents around the point of burst heavily contaminating everything in the vicinity. This contamination will continue to give off dangerous vapour which will drift downwind.

On the other hand the burster may be such as to open the bomb and disrupt the filling thus dispersing the liquid in a mixture of much smaller droplets and vapour which will drift with the wind, leaving little or no liquid contamination.

With the air burst fuze practically the whole of the liquid contents of the bomb will fall like rain over a limited area beneath. Drops of Nerve or Blister gas falling on exposed skin or entering the eyes are extremely dangerous and drops of liquid blister gas on clothing may cause injury by blisters unless the clothing is removed soon enough.

Small capacity bombs will normally be carried in containers designed to open in the air above the objective and to scatter their contents over an area in a similar manner to the containers filled with German 1Kg incendiary bombs in the last war.

The bombs will be opened on reaching the ground by a small fuze or by shattering of the casing on impact.

Bombs filled with Choking Gas

Large capacity bombs only will be used with this type of filling and will be fuzed to open on impact.

When such a bomb with a choking gas bursts, a very highly concentrated cloud of gas forms immediately in the vicinity. This will drift with the wind, being gradually diluted and dispersed as it travels. In weather conditions favourable to the use of gas the concentration may be sufficiently high over the first few hundred yards of its travel to kill unprotected persons in its path. For a further few hundred yards it is likely to remain sufficiently concentrated to cause serious injury to unprotected persons.

(ii) Spray

Persistent liquid gases of the Nerve and Blister groups released from containers carried in aircraft will split up into small drops which will fall like a short, sharp shower of rain over a fairly wide area. Whether from low flying or high flying aircraft the principal danger from this spraying method of attack lies in the fact that large numbers of people in the open are likely to be injured by drops of the gas falling on their exposed skin or clothing. There will be little danger from blister gas vapour, and blister gas contamination of the ground is unlikely to be heavy enough to call for special decontamination action. If, however, nerve gas is dropped by this method the vapour danger will be considerable.

CHAPTER IV

17. RECOGNITION OF THE PRESENCE
OF WAR GAS

In the past all members of the Civil Defence Services were taught to take certain steps to detect war gas and to recognise its type.

The Public, too, were encouraged to learn enough about simple methods of detection to enable them, at least, to realize the presence of war gas.

The recommended methods were well suited to the conditions which then prevailed. All known war gases could be readily detected by one, or a combination of, the tests advocated and, if these were properly carried out, there was no danger to the individual using them.

With the arrival of nerve gases as possible agents in gas warfare, however, these conditions have changed. Owing to the very insidious, rapid, and dangerous effects of these gases and, except in the liquid form, the absence of any means of recognising their presence until the initial symptoms (see Chapter I—Nerve Gases (b) Effects) show they have already attacked the body, protection can only be ensured by putting on the respirator immediately an enemy air attack takes place in the vicinity or the " gas warning " is given and, by keeping it on until the "gas clear" signal is given. *To use the sense of smell would be dangerous and should not be attempted.*

For members of the C.D. Services and for ordinary individuals this prohibition reduces the means of recognising the presence of war gases and identifying their type to what can be done while wearing the respirator, i.e., to what can be seen, what can be heard, what can be felt on exposed parts of the body and to chemical indicators.

It may be possible to see faint vapoury clouds of some non-persistent gases such as those of the " choking " group or the " nose " group but this is unlikely except near the source of the gas.

It will be possible, also, to see wet patches and splashes of liquid persistent gas except in wet weather when they may not be obvious.

Such liquid might be Nerve, Blister or Tear Gas.

As regards hearing, there may be a noticeable difference between the sharp crack of the explosion of an H.E. bomb and the duller sound of a gas bomb, which has a small bursting charge and contains a large quantity of gas, whether the latter bursts on the ground or in the air.

A loud, sharp explosion cannot, however, always be assumed to be an H.E. bomb because the large-capacity gas bomb, designed to produce a highly concentrated cloud of minute droplets and vapour, may sound much the same, but any suggestive indications may be useful if considered in conjunction with other observations.

With the eyes, nose and lungs protected by the respirator, recognition of the presence of gas by the sense of feeling will be confined to the appreciation of wetness on exposed parts of the body from liquid of the persistent Nerve, Blister and Tear Gases.

27

18. CHEMICAL DETECTORS

In addition to the above ways by which the presence of gas may sometimes be recognised, a special paint, known as Detector Paint, can be used for indicating the presence of LIQUID NERVE and BLISTER gases. It is usually greenish-yellow or brown in colour. When Liquid Nerve or Blister Gas comes into contact with it, the paint changes to a reddish colour. This colour change may not be easy to see if the liquid itself is of a dark colour or the paint is soiled with mud or dirt. Liquid Tear Gas will also give a reddish reaction on Detector Paint

The principal uses of detector paint are to give an immediate indication if droplets of Liquid Nerve or Blister gas have fallen and to test suspicious splashes, or wet patches on the ground.

The Spray Detector consists of a board about 18″ square painted with Detector Paint and set in the open at a slight slope, so that drops of liquid will tend to run and leave the red reaction easier to see. Existing surfaces, such as the tops of postal pillar boxes, can be painted with detector paint to serve as Spray Detectors. Numbers of Spray Detectors will be needed and they should be set up in a position fully exposed to the weather.

The Ground Detector consists of a strip of paper, painted with Detector Paint and fixed over the end of a stick such as a broom handle. The painted paper should be pressed, not rubbed, on the suspected ground and if Liquid Nerve or Blister gas is present, the red reaction will be seen on the paper. Apparatus is also available for determining the presence of BLISTER GAS VAPOUR and for assessing the degree of danger arising from such concentrations.

Other, more elaborate, apparatus for carrying out chemical tests to identify certain gases, not easily recognised, will be required by specially trained personnel.

19. SUMMARY

Recognition of the presence of Nerve Gas is a very difficult problem, and experiments and research are being undertaken to develop safe methods which can be adopted whether Nerve Gas is present or not. Full information will be issued to the Civil Defence Services at a later date.

Though the detection of gas has become more difficult, the giving of gas warnings will still be a responsibility of the Civil Defence Services, and all members of the public too must be continually on the look-out for unusual sounds of bursting bombs ; for symptoms in themselves and others ; for splashes of liquid ; suspicious smoke or other visible signs for which there is no natural explanation, and if there are any indications of the possible presence of gas, the respirator must be put on immediately, if it is not already being worn.

CHAPTER V

24. PERSONAL PROTECTION — I
RESPIRATORS

War gases attack by way of the eyes, nose and mouth and, in some cases, through the skin of any part of the body. Protection against gas is obtained, therefore, by preventing gas from gaining access to vulnerable parts of the body. In the case of the individual this can be done by wearing a respirator and, when necessary, special clothing, described in a later chapter.

The respirator in its simplest form consists of a covering for the eyes, nose and mouth with a canister attached, through which all air breathed in by the wearer must pass. This canister, known as the container, is filled with material which will remove all traces of war gas from air breathed through it, and is fitted with a non-return valve to prevent the moist used air passing out through it and causing damage to its contents.

25. PROTECTION AFFORDED

The respirators described in this chapter will give protection against all war gases in concentrations a great deal stronger than any likely to be met in the open and will remain effective even if worn repeatedly during successive gas attacks. It must be remembered, however, that they have not been designed to protect against some of the gases which may be met in industrial processes or in every day life. For instance, they will not protect against the deadly carbon monoxide gas, present in coal gas and the exhaust fumes of motor cars.

26. TYPES OF RESPIRATOR

Different kinds of respirator were produced to meet the special requirements of different types of wearers having regard to the risks they might have been called upon to face and the nature of their duties whilst exposed to gas. The three principal types were :—

Civilian types for the general public who were not expected to remain for long periods or undertake strenuous work in gas affected atmospheres.

They comprised the Civilian Respirator, the Small Child's Respirator, the Anti-gas Helmet for babies, the Helmet Respirator and the Hospital Respirator.

The Civilian Duty Respirator. A more robust type for those who had to remain at their posts and carry on with their normal duties whether gas was present or not.

The Service Respirator. A more elaborate type for those who might have been called upon to remain for long periods and to work hard in high concentrations of gas.

The wearer of any respirator must inevitably experience some slight resistance to breathing and be handicapped to a certain extent in his normal activities. Every effort has been made to reduce those drawbacks to a minimum by giving the clearest and widest field of view possible and, where necessary, fitting an outlet valve to allow easy escape of the air which is breathed out.

33   B

Side straps exerting a pull in line with the axis of the container. ⟶

T buckle not ⟶ too far down at back of the head.

Eye panel well clear of ⟵ nose.

⟵ Eyes about the middle of the eye panel

Snug fit under the chin.

Fig. 2
The Civilian Respirator being worn.

(i) The Civilian Respirator

This consists of a mask of thin sheet rubber with a large window of non-inflammable transparent material. The container fits into the facepiece and is secured by means of a stout rubber band. The rubber of the mask, being thin and flexible, makes a gas-tight contact with the skin of the face all round. The mask with container attached is held in place by three webbing bands which pass through a T-shaped buckle at the back of the head (*see Figs.* 2 *and* 3).

When the wearer breathes in, air is drawn through the container where all traces of war gas are removed. When he breathes out the valve at the inner end of the container closes to prevent his moist

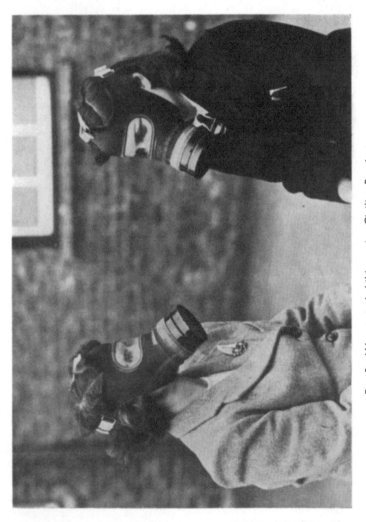

Fig. 3. Woman and child wearing Civilian Respirators

breath from going out through the container and it escapes from the facepiece past his cheeks.

Civilian Respirators were made in three sizes, large, medium and small.

A stout cardboard carton was issued with each respirator to contain it when not in use. (*See Figs.* 4 *and* 5.)

(ii) The Small Child's Respirator

This respirator was designed for children sufficiently developed to wear a respirator but not big enough to be satisfactorily fitted with the

Fig. 4.
Civilian Respirator with its carton.

Fig. 5.
Showing the correct way of packing the respirator in its carton

Fig. 6.
The Small Child's Respirator.

small size Civilian Respirator. As a rough guide it was suitable for children between the ages of about 18 months and 4 to $4\frac{1}{2}$ years. Some Children below the age of 4 years were fitted with the small size Civilian Respirator.

It consists of a thin, flexible moulded rubber facepiece with separate eye-pieces of non-inflammable transparent material and an outlet valve. A container is screwed into a metal mount on the front of the facepiece (*See Fig.* 6). This container, though smaller, gives the same degree of

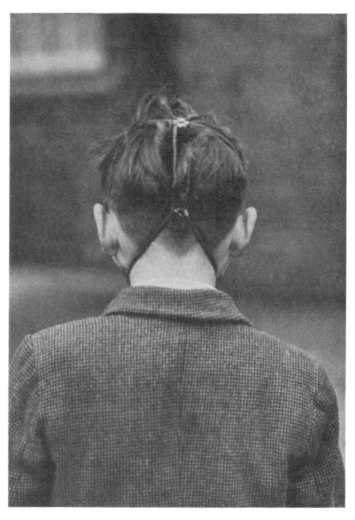

Fig. 7.
Back view of Small Child's Respirator showing bottom two springs
of head harness hooked together

protection as that fitted to respirators for adults. The respirator is held
in place by a head-harness formed of coiled springs enclosed in cotton
braid. The head-harness is not adjustable but the tension and flexibility
of the springs is such that the facepiece is held in firm but comfortable
contact with the face. A hook and eye attachment to the two lower
springs of the head-harness enable them to be hooked together at the
back of the neck which prevents easy removal of the respirator by the

Fig. 8.—The Baby's Anti-Gas Helmet.

child itself (*see Fig.* 7). A stout cardboard carton with a sling was supplied with the respirator to contain it when not in use.

(iii) The Baby's Anti-Gas Helmet

This was designed for children too small to wear the Small Child's respirator. It consists of a hood of impervious fabric, with a large window to cover the head, shoulders and arms of the baby and is tied by means of a draw tape round the waist. The hood is supported by a light metal frame with a back which can be adjusted in length to suit all sizes of babies and children up to the age of five years. (*See Fig.* 8.)

39

(iii) Keep respirators dry. Moisture is liable to cause deterioration of all parts. Moisture entering the container makes breathing more difficult and sets up internal rusting which may lead to perforations and leaks. Always dry all parts of the respirator, including the inside of the facepiece, after use and before packing it away in its carrier.

(iv) When not in use, keep the respirator properly folded in its carrier, so that it is not exposed to strong light, and place it in a cool, dry place. Strong sunlight and heat cause cracking and perishing of the rubber parts.

(v) Take the respirator out of its carrier periodically to air it and to allow it to resume its natural shape. When a facepiece has been folded for a long time it is liable to become creased and this may cause leaks.

(vi) Never hang a respirator by its head-harness. This causes stretching and loss of elasticity in the elastic straps and in the rubber of the facepiece of the Civilian Respirator.

33. SPECIAL PRECAUTIONS WITH CERTAIN TYPES

The transparent window is the most vulnerable part of the Civilian Respirator. Great care is needed to prevent folding, creasing, denting and scratching of this window. The respirator should always be packed in its carton in such a way that the window lies flat and at full length on top of the container. (*See Fig*. 5 *on page* 36).

The outlet valve of the Civilian Duty Respirator and those Civilian respirators so fitted is liable to be torn if the respirator is carelessly handled. Care is necessary, particularly in taking the respirator out of its carrier, to avoid this.

CHAPTER VI

41. PERSONAL PROTECTION—II ANTI-GAS CLOTHING

Though properly fitting respirators will adequately protect the eyes, the covered part of the face, the breathing passages and lungs from all forms of war gases, the rest of the body is vulnerable to liquid nerve gas and to either the liquid or the vapour of blister gases.

Ordinary clothing when contaminated, will be penetrated and can act only as a delaying agent. Moreover, unless promptly removed, it becomes a danger not only to the wearer, since it keeps the gas in close contact with his skin, but to others with whom he may come in contact.

Special anti-gas clothing and other protective equipment was therefore designed for men and women in the Civil Defence Services who might have needed them in the course of their duties.

The materials found most suitable for making these outfits are the oil-dressed fabric called " oilskin," and rubber. Both these are penetrated only slowly by the liquid gases and afford protection for periods which depend on the thickness of the materials. This duration of protection, is, however, long enough for the spells of duty normally required and longer, in fact, than they can be safely worn when performing manual work, as, being non-porous, they keep in the heat and perspiration of the body and so cause fatigue and exhaustion, particularly in hot weather.

42. TYPES OF OUTFIT

There are two types of oilskin clothing, the " heavy " and the " light." They differ only in the thickness, weight and strength of the material used.

Owing to its greater handicap the " heavy " suit is used only when the work to be carried out involves considerable risk of damage to the material by tearing and scratching. Rescue work is in this category and the men in this service therefore use the heavy outfit. All others normally have outfits of the light material.

A suit of oilskin of either kind consists of a jacket and trousers, but to protect those parts of the body still uncovered, the complete anti-gas outfit also includes boots and gloves of rubber or oilskin, canvas over-mittens to preserve the oilskin gloves, and an oilskin curtain to be worn on the helmet to protect the neck from spray. (*See Figs. 11 and 12.*)

These articles are in addition to the respirator, helmet and eye-shields, for all outdoor workers. The eye-shield is intended to protect the eyes from the sudden arrival of liquid gas in spray form and should be worn at all times in the open when the respirator itself is not in use.

There is an oilskin hood to protect those parts of the face, head and neck left uncovered by the respirator. When worn in addition to the rest of the anti-gas outfit it imposes great strain on the wearer and should be restricted to occasions when work has to be carried out in high concentrations of blister gas vapour as liable to be found in enclosed places.

The heavy outfit should be worn over special underclothing and socks only, but the light outfit can be worn over ordinary clothing or uniform.

Fig. 11.
The Heavy Anti-Gas Outfit.

43. DRESSING

In order to get the maximum protection and comfort whilst at work, the anti-gas outfit should be put on in a definite fashion and order, as follows :—

    (1) Attend to wants of nature
    (2) Remove own clothing, underclothing and socks
    (3) Put on official underclothing and socks

Fig. 12.

The Light Anti-Gas Outfit.

NOTE.—The webbing belt is not standard equipment but is useful in preventing " ballooning " of the coat in windy weather.

   (4) Put on trousers
   (5) Put on boots
   (6) Put on Jacket
   (7) Adjust respirator in " Alert " position
   (8) Put on eye-shield if required
   (9) Put on gloves and over-mittens if worn
  (10) Put on helmet with anti-gas curtain attached.

The rarely worn hood is not put on till the individual is just about to enter the vapour concentration that calls for it and after he has adjusted the respirator facepiece. Should helmet be needed as well as hood, this goes on last of all with chin-strap to back of head and curtain removed.

The above drill is for the " heavy " outfit, but is the same for the " light " outfit except that items (2) and (3) will not apply when the suit is worn over ordinary clothing.

It is desirable that some other person should assist at the dressing and particularly check its correctness when completed.

44. UNDRESSING

When work is over the anti-gas clothing may be contaminated and must be carefully removed, to avoid danger to the wearer, and carefully stored to prevent danger to others, till it is decontaminated.

Undressing, therefore, must be a drill.

It is done at specially fitted depots to which the worker returns and normally is carried out by another suitably protected person, though self-undressing is possible if hands are treated with anti-gas ointment immediately after removal of gloves, and again when outer garments have been removed.

All outer garments and equipment are removed out-of-doors in an open shed to avoid creating a vapour danger.

The order of undressing is as follows :—

(1) Gloves and over-mittens (if worn) removed
(2) Whipcord untied and sling of haversack brought over head with one hand while supporting haversack with the other
(3) Helmet pushed to back of neck
(4) Respirator complete removed*
(5) Helmet with curtain removed
(6) Jacket removed
(7) Trousers lowered
(8) Sits down on a form and boots removed ⎫ Feet kept off
(9) Trousers removed ⎭ floor

Man being undressed then swings over on form, stands up on clean side and then enters the building proper and himself removes the rest of his garments, washes, re-dresses in clean clothing and leaves by another route.

Each article, as removed, is placed in a metal bin with a lid, separate bins being provided for different types of article.

45. USE OF ANTI-GAS CLOTHING

Reference has been made to the handicap imposed on the worker by the wearing of anti-gas clothing. Such clothing, therefore, should be worn only when conditions render it essential and then only so much and in the fashion i.e. jacket inside or outside trousers, necessary for safety. It should be remembered that the principal use of anti-gas clothing is to protect against liquid. As the clothing cannot be made completely airtight, vapour will in time find its way inside.

* In the presence of Nerve Gas it will be necessary to keep the Respirator Facepiece on until he enters the building proper. This can be done by removing the container from the haversack.

The hood in particular should not be worn unless essential and when worn should be put on at the last moment and removed at the first opportunity.

Decisions on these points must be made by the officer-in-charge on the spot who should have the pocket vapour detector to help him. In the case of liquid, good training of the individual should enable him to avoid contamination in many cases.

CHAPTER VII

51. COLLECTIVE PROTECTION

Every individual can rely on his respirator for his own protection against war gas, and this is his primary defence, but the protection which is afforded against vapour, by buildings in sound condition, is of considerable value and against liquid and spray is complete.

Provided the doors and windows of the buildings are close fitting and are kept shut, only a very small quantity of gas in vapour form will find its way in from outside. More elaborate precautions can be taken by sealing up the doors, windows and any other openings of a room so that no gas can enter, but in this case neither can the air in the room be renewed and in consequence, the heat and moisture given off by the occupants; the products breathed out by them and the gradual using up of oxygen—which is essential to life—make conditions unbearable. Such a room can, therefore, only be used for a limited period which will vary according to the number of occupants.

While a raid is in progress members of the public should seek refuge in a shelter or indoors. Doors and windows should be kept closed during the attack and ordinary ventilation systems should be shut down. When a gas warning is given, respirators should be put on as, if the building is damaged by explosion, e.g. windows broken, the respirator will be the only protection against gas.

If therefore, members of the public take shelter indoors immediately on a gas alert and remain there until the gas clear signal has been given, the risk of becoming a gas casualty will be considerably reduced.

CHAPTER VIII

55. GENERAL ANTI-GAS PRECAUTIONS

To untrained and unprotected persons, gas could probably cause more casualties than most other weapons because of its stealthy approach and more widespread effects. The risks of injury by gas, however, are far easier for the individual to avoid than those by any other weapon, provided he makes proper use of the protective equipment available.

(i) Keeping under cover

Except when their duty demands that they should be in the open, people should keep under cover during " Alerts." The protection thus afforded has been outlined in the previous chapter.

(ii) Precautions when out of doors

Members of the Civil Defence Services whose duties compel them to remain out of doors and members of the public who are in the open when the " Alert " sounds must take every precaution to protect their eyes from drops of liquid gas from air burst bombs or aircraft spray. The steel helmets and eye-shields will prevent drops from entering the eyes. Members of the public also can get good protection for the eyes by pulling the brim of the hat or cap well forward. The natural temptation to look upwards when aircraft are heard must be resisted. If an overcoat or raincoat is being carried it should be put on. The collar of the coat, overcoat or raincoat should be turned up to protect the back of the neck. Gloves should be worn or if not available the hands should be kept thrust into the pockets. Should drops of liquid gas from air burst bombs or aircraft spray fall on people in the open they should come to little harm if the above precautions are observed, but they should remember that hats and coats must be removed before entering any building and this might also be necessary in the case of trousers, skirts, stockings, boots and shoes if any signs of droplet contamination is found on these garments. People who have been hit by drops of liquid gas should hang up their outer clothing to air, preferably under cover in a well ventilated out-building or open shed, and, with as little delay as possible, carry out the personal preventive cleansing procedure described in Chapter IX.

(iii) Use of the Respirator

Once it has been established that an enemy is using gas, there must be no hesitation on the part of anybody in using any protective equipment that has been made available. Many of the gases that might be used do not advertise their presence. Nobody should hesitate, through fear of appearing ridiculous, to put on a respirator at the slightest suspicion that gas may be present, or if other people are seen to be wearing theirs. Once respirators have been put on they must not be removed until the " Gas Clear " signal is given.

(iv) Keeping Upwind of the Source of Gas

As Non-persistent gases, which include the vapour given off by persistent liquid gases, drift with the wind, everybody should, as far as their duties allow, try to keep upwind of any sources of gas such as the places where gas bombs have burst or areas where gas spray has fallen. If overtaken by gas in the street the quickest way to get clear of the gas is to move at right angles to the direction of the wind. For this reason it is a good plan to note the direction of the wind in the vicinity at all times. (*See diagram on Page* 14.)

(v) Avoiding Contamination

Nobody should needlessly walk in liquid gas on the ground even when wearing suitable footwear as this will tend to spread the contamination and render elaborate decontamination of their footwear necessary. There will, of course, be occasions when walking through liquid contamination may be necessary, for example when the Leader of a Decontamination party is making a thorough reconnaissance of the area in which a blister gas bomb has burst. Members of the Civil Defence Services, whose duties demand that they should enter and work in an area contaminated by liquid gas, and members of the General Public who may have to be led through such an area, while being evacuated from buildings rendered temporarily uninhabitable by gas must be careful to avoid, as far as possible, touching, handling or brushing against anything which may have been splashed with liquid and treading on earth or debris on the ground which may be heavily contaminated. Should it be necessary to handle contaminated material e.g., in order to reach a casualty, the hands should be protected by anti-gas gloves, if available, or if not, by smearing them liberally with anti-gas ointment. Any stout material wrapped round the hands to prevent contact between the bare skin and the contaminated material will give a certain amount of temporary protection in an emergency.

People who have walked through a contaminated area should remove their boots or shoes. They must be left outside until they have been properly decontaminated.

Clothing which has been contaminated by liquid gas must be removed as soon as possible otherwise the contamination will penetrate to the skin and cause injury. As in the case of boots, contaminated clothing must not be taken inside any building. The outer clothing, at least, must be taken off and left outside. It will not be safe to wear again until it has been collected and put through the process of decontamination appropriate to its degree of contamination.

It is important that everybody should know and understand what can be done in the way of First Aid and Preventive Cleansing for people who have been affected by gas. Chapter IX should be studied and such preparations, for carrying out the treatments described therein as lie within the scope of the ordinary householder, should be made.

CHAPTER IX

59. FIRST AID AND PREVENTIVE CLEANSING

Speed of action is the key-note of First Aid in gas contamination of any part of the body.

The method of First Aid employed will vary in detail according to the type of gas and the way in which it attacks the body but the first and immediate object is to prevent or lessen injury by getting rid of all traces of the gas as quickly and effectively as possible.

In order to do this, clothing which has been contaminated by liquid or vapour must be promptly removed and affected skin rapidly cleansed. It is obvious that the affected individual must first be protected from further exposure by putting on a respirator and by removal to a place free from the gas. In the following paragraphs the war gases are taken in the order in which they appear in Chapter I with the appropriate First Aid in each case.

(i) Nerve Gas

V A P O U R . Put on respirator, and if possible, get out of the gas area and change clothing, keeping respirator on until this is done.

L I Q U I D . Owing to the rapidity with which liquid Nerve gas is absorbed by the skin, it is essential that any visible liquid should be dabbed off with a handkerchief, rag or other swab as quickly as possible—it must not be wiped off as this may spread contamination. Care must be taken to dispose of whatever material is used as a swab, so that it will not endanger others. The affected individual, with a respirator on, must be removed to a place free from the gas and all contaminated clothing immediately taken off and contaminated skin areas scrubbed thoroughly with soap and water. If any injury has occurred in the contaminated area of the body leaving the skin broken, the wound must be scrubbed with soap and water before any other contaminated part is treated.

Onset of Symptoms

Immediately the initial symptoms of dimness of vision, running of the nose, and tightness of the chest appear, the case must be treated as seriously ill and kept lying down because it is impossible at this stage to say whether or not the more dangerous symptoms of twitching and convulsions will eventually appear. Early medical supervision is essential.

Contaminated Food

In the event of contaminated food being swallowed, vomiting should be produced at the earliest possible moment either by tickling the throat or giving a large quantity of salt and water to drink.

(ii) Blister Gas

V A P O U R . Put on respirator and get out of gas atmosphere. As soon as possible contaminated clothing should be removed and at least the skin which has been exposed, and if practicable the whole body, thoroughly washed with soap and water, preferably warm.

LIQUID.

Eyes. If liquid gas has entered the eyes they must be washed out at once with plenty of water (or salt and water if available). A good stream of water from a water bottle or other vessel should be directed for at least one minute into each eye. Should only one eye be affected, care must be taken not to contaminate the sound eye when washing out the injured one.

SKIN. Visible liquid must be immediately removed from the skin in the same way as in Nerve Gas contamination, followed by the application of anti-gas ointment* or bleach cream well rubbed into the contaminated areas, with the fingers. Bleach cream must be washed off with water after two minutes. If anti-gas ointment or bleach is not available, the affected part should be thoroughly washed with soap and water.

Contaminated clothing must be promptly removed and, if practicable the whole body washed with soap and water, preferably warm.

Anti-gas ointment or bleach cream should not be applied to the skin when reddening has developed. Blisters should not be opened.

(iii) Choking Gas

People who have breathed in Choking Gas may sometimes be able to carry on their work with only mild discomfort or slight cough and tightness of the chest, and yet after an hour or more may suddenly get worse and collapse with severe lung symptoms. Anyone who shows signs of having breathed in Choking Gas, or who is suspected of having done so, should therefore be removed as soon as possible to a place free from the gas. He should be made to lie flat on the back and be kept warm until seen by a doctor. Early medical treatment may save his life. Contaminated clothing must be removed. Artificial respiration must not be attempted.

(iv) Tear Gas

In the majority of cases the symptoms will rapidly subside when the respirator has been adjusted. If they persist the individual affected should be moved to a place free from gas and the eyes bathed with warm water or salt solution (one teaspoonful to a pint of warm water).

If actual liquid enters the eyes they should be treated on the lines laid down for Blister Gas.

If the skin is irritated it should be washed with soapy water.

Liquid contaminated clothing will have to be removed.

(v) Nose Gas

No special first aid treatment is necessary as a rule. Symptoms will usually subside fairly soon if the respirator is put on promptly.

Sometimes the symptoms may be delayed and may not be felt until a few minutes after the respirator has been put on. Any tendency to remove the respirator in such a case must be checked while in the presence of the gas.

An exceptionally severe case may need removal to fresh air where treatment in the form of a gargle and washing out the nose may be given.

---

* *Anti-gas ointment* contains a substance which counteracts the poison. Bleach cream is a mixture of tropical bleaching powder and water. It is made by adding the bleach to the water in small quantities while stirring until the mixture has the consistency of thick cream.

CHAPTER X

63. PRINCIPLES OF DECONTAMINATION

If bombs filled with persistent liquid gases are dropped there will be an appreciable amount of liquid on the ground in and around the craters and everything within a limited area will be splashed with liquid, the amount depending on the distance from the crater. Each bomb will produce an area of " contamination " varying in extent with the size of the bomb.

This contamination will be dangerous in two ways—from the liquid and the vapour.

The liquid may be picked up on shoes or boots ; smeared on to clothing by brushing against contaminated objects ; or may get on to the hands by handling anything on which there is liquid gas. As the liquid gases of the Nerve and Blister groups have great powers of penetration, casualties are likely to occur from any of the above causes.

The danger does not arise from the liquid only. The vapour which comes off the liquid is also damaging to unprotected people who remain exposed to it. This vapour danger will remain all the time there is free liquid on the ground, on walls of buildings and other objects. In the case of contamination inside buildings, it may still persist from liquid which has soaked in, even after the free liquid has dried up on the surface.

The continued presence of contaminated areas in a town or city cannot be allowed and urgent action is required to deal with the two-fold danger—in other words, they must be " decontaminated." An area or an object of any sort is said to be decontaminated when it has been rendered safe for all normal uses, but this does not necessarily mean that all traces of gas have been destroyed or removed. An open area in a town or city, for instance, would be considered to be decontaminated when the streets are safe for wheeled or pedestrian traffic ; when there is no danger from brushing against or handling anything in it and when there is no appreciable danger from vapour. There may still be a certain amount of liquid which has soaked into road surfaces, pavements, walls of buildings and other objects, but it will not be picked up on boots, clothing or hands and any vapour from it will be coming off so slowly and be so rapidly dispersed that it will not constitute a danger.

Decontamination work will be carried out by specially trained parties, but some knowledge of the principles of decontamination should be useful to everybody.

64. DECONTAMINATION METHODS

Contamination may be REMOVED, DESTROYED, SEALED, or it may be left to the action of the weather in certain cases.

(i) Removal

Free liquid on the ground or other surfaces can be removed by washing it away with water from a hose. This merely moves the contamination from one place to another but this method should only be adopted in cases where it can do no harm especially bearing in mind its final destination. The removal by hosing should be assisted by scrubbing. The method is laborious and, moreover, will only deal with liquid on the surface. Unless it is undertaken within a very short time of the contamination occurring, some further treatment of the liquid which has soaked in will be needed.

Free liquid can also be removed by mopping it up. Rags or cotton waste may be used for this purpose, but it must be remembered that they will become contaminated and must be safely disposed of after use. Moistening the rags or cotton waste with a suitable solvent of the gas will render this method more effective. In the case of contamination on hard and impervious surfaces such as glass or clean metal, careful and thorough mopping up by " the solvent " method may be all the de-contamination necessary.

Free liquid on a flat horizontal surface can be mopped up by sprinkling dry earth, sand, sawdust, ashes or other similar materials over it and allowing time for the liquid to be soaked up. The mopping material is then shovelled up and, being contaminated, must be buried or otherwise disposed of safely. This method, although seldom sufficient by itself, is often a useful preliminary to further treatment.

(ii) Destruction

Liquid contamination can be destroyed by applying a chemical which will react with it and change it into a harmless substance. In the case of blister gases the most useful chemical for this purpose is chloride of lime, commonly known as bleach. The bleach may be applied dry in the form of powder in which case it will react violently and the mixture may burst into flames. The decontamination will be rapid and effective. Where a fire is undesirable the bleach may be mixed with sand or earth or made into a cream or paste with water.

Dry bleach is ineffective with Nerve gases and a bleach cream or other alkaline solution should be used.

Liquid Blister and Nerve gases which have soaked into clothing and other similar materials can be destroyed by boiling the contaminated articles if they will stand it. Certain precautions must be taken by the specially trained people, who will undertake this work, to safeguard themselves and to avoid damaging the fabrics. This decontamination process should not therefore be attempted at home.

(iii) Sealing

Contamination can be covered up so that no one can come into contact with it and no vapour can escape from it. On a horizontal surface an even seal of three inches of earth, sand or ashes, must be spread over the whole contaminated area. This is a laborious method and will only be effective so long as the seal remains undisturbed. Painting the Blister gas contamination on a vertical surface with bleach cream will not only destroy any free liquid but also seal that which has soaked in.

(iv) Weathering

In certain circumstances it may be possible to leave decontaminating action to the sun, wind and rain, but the affected area must be roped off to prevent access to it, until there is no further danger from contact with the liquid and insufficient vapour is coming off to constitute a danger. This method may take a considerable time. Weathering is also adopted for dealing with clothing which is contaminated with small droplets only or vapour.

CHAPTER XI

69. OTHER DANGEROUS GASES

A list and description of the gases most likely to be used as offensive agents in war have been given in Chapter I.

There are, however, a number of other dangerous gases which might be encountered in war or peace, either deliberately used by an enemy or occurring accidentally. Some knowledge of these is highly desirable and the more important are considered here.

(i) Prussic Acid

This is a colourless, very volatile, liquid with a smell of bitter almonds.

When inhaled in high concentrations the vapour can cause rapid death by paralysing the respiratory centre in the brain and thereby stopping breathing.

Luckily, however, the vapour is somewhat lighter than air and is rapidly diluted in the open to harmless strength. Prussic acid can also be absorbed through the skin, but the danger is slight unless the contamination is heavy or evaporation is retarded by a covering of clothing.

Shells filled with prussic acid, used in the open field in the 1914-1918 war, proved useless, but in enclosed spaces, such as tanks, an effective and deadly concentration might be rapidly built up. The Japanese had a prussic-acid bomb designed for this purpose.

The respirator gives protection against concentrations likely to occur in the open.

Treatment must be immediate and consists of rapid removal of the victim to fresh air and artificial respiration. Free liquid must be removed at once from the skin, and clothing which has been contaminated should be taken off and hung in the open air until it no longer smells of gas.

(ii) Arseniuretted Hydrogen (Arsine)

This is a colourless, inflammable, gas. In high concentration it smells like acetylene but in lower concentrations has no appreciable smell. It does not cause any irritation of eyes, breathing passages, lungs or skin, so for the detection of its presence, white test papers which turn yellow are used.

It is produced when dilute acids act on compounds of arsenic with metals, or in certain cases the reaction may be produced by water alone.

It might possibly be used as a non-persistent gas in bombs, or as the heavy dark grey powder of calcium arsenide which would give off the gas over long periods on contact with moisture in the air or on the ground.

When breathed it attacks and destroys the red blood cells and also damages the liver and kidneys from its arsenic content. The symptoms vary from headache, discomfort and breathlessness, in mild cases, to weakness, giddiness and collapse in severe cases. Jaundice may develop later. In high concentrations it can cause death.

The respirator gives protection.

Severe symptoms are usually delayed in their appearance and first aid should consist of rest, warmth and non-alcoholic drinks. Early medical attention is necessary.

(iii) Carbon Monoxide

This gas is formed whenever any material containing carbon burns with an insufficient supply of air and so is found frequently in everyday life as well as wartime. It is therefore very important to understand its dangers.

It is a colourless, odourless, non-irritant gas and so cannot be recognized by the senses.

It is inflammable and burns with a blue flame so often seen flickering over a smouldering fire. In the open it is not dangerous as it is rapidly diluted by mixing with the air but if it is produced in, or obtains entry into, enclosed places, it is a great and very insidious danger as it may not be recognized in time to retreat to safety.

In peacetime, it is most commonly found in dangerous amounts in coal gas, in the exhaust from internal combustion engines, in the after damp of colliery explosions, and in coke stoves and smouldering fires, big or small.

In wartime, not only are the peace time hazards increased by fractured gas mains, large fires, etc., but there is the added risk from the considerable amount of carbon monoxide which is contained in the gases formed when any kind of H.E. explodes and which may enter enclosed spaces being used as shelters or living rooms, from underground, or under-water bursts, or from an explosion within a building or ship.

In the great fire at Hamburg in July 1943, many thousands of people sheltering in cellars were killed by carbon monoxide.

Carbon monoxide produces its poisonous effect, when breathed, by combining with the red colouring matter of the blood and lessening the amount of oxygen it can carry around the body. One of the first indications of the presence of the gas may be loss of power of the limbs preventing retreat to safety, later unconsciousness may follow and perhaps death.

The victim should be promptly removed to fresh air, kept warm and at rest. Oxygen should be given if available and, if breathing threatens to fail, artificial respiration employed.

The ordinary war gas respirator affords NO PROTECTION against carbon monoxide. When working in an enclosed space where this gas is present, a self-contained breathing apparatus or one which draws fresh air from the open by means of a tube should be used.

70. GASES ENCOUNTERED IN FIRE-FIGHTING

Fire-fighters, particularly in enclosed spaces, are liable to risks from the formation of dangerous gases, as well as from deficiency of oxygen.

Carbon dioxide and carbon monoxide will always be present in greater or lesser amounts, depending on the rate of combustion, while other harmful gases, may be given off by the burning materials.

It must also be remembered that certain chemicals contained in fire extinguishers, such as carbon tetrachloride and methyl-bromide, may themselves be dangerous when used in quantity in confined spaces.

The ordinary war gas respirator will *NOT* stop all these gases, neither can it provide oxygen when this is lacking.

TYPE	GENERAL DESCRIPTION	EFFECTS	FIRST AID
NERVE GASES	Persistent or Semi-Persistent colourless liquid. Gives off invisible vapour. No appreciable smell. Liquid rapidly absorbed by eyes, wounds and skin and readily penetrates clothing.	(i) VAPOUR (or fine spray) (*a*) Small doses cause in 5—30 minutes contraction of pupils with dimness of vision and loss of focusing power, running of nose, headache, tightness of chest. (*b*) Larger doses cause in 5 mins.—6 hrs. the same symptoms as above but followed by twitching of limbs, convulsions and death. There may be a delay between the onset of the initial symptoms (*a*) and the twitching, convulsions and death. (ii) LIQUID In eyes, wounds and in contact with skin produces the same symptoms as in (*a*) and (*b*) above.	VAPOUR Put on Respirator. Remove from Gas. Take off outer clothing. Complete rest as soon as first symptoms appear. Turn over to doctor. LIQUID Visible liquid must be immediately dabbed—not wiped—off the skin with a swab of any material handy, treating any wounded areas first. Then remove clothing and scrub the skin with soap and water, again dealing with wounds first. If any symptoms appear transfer to medical supervision immediately. In the event of contaminated food being swallowed, vomiting should be produced at the earliest possible moment either by tickling the throat or giving a large quantity of salt and water to drink.
BLISTER GASES MUSTARD GAS	Very Persistent heavy oily liquid, dark brown to straw colour. Gives off invisible vapour. Smells like garlic, onions, horseradish or mustard. Smell may be faint. Like any oil, readily soaks into clothing and most other materials. It freezes before water.	(i) VAPOUR *Eyes*—irritation and swelling within 24 hours. *Skin*—redness, irritation, blisters, after 12 hours or longer. Damp parts specially affected. *Breathing passages*—loss of voice, brassy cough. (ii) LIQUID *Eyes*—no immediate pain; severe inflammation in 1—2 hrs. *Skin*—redness in 2 hrs, blister 12—24 hrs.	VAPOUR Put on Respirator. Remove from Gas. Change clothing and wash body all over. LIQUID (i) *Eyes*—wash out at once with plenty of water or salt solution if available. (ii) *Skin*—dab off any visible liquid on skin with a dry rag and with fingers rub in anti-gas ointment or apply bleach cream and wash off with water after two minutes. If anti-gas ointment or bleach cream are not available wash part affected with soap and water. (iii) *Clothes*—remove contaminated clothing, apply ointment or paste to affected skin or wash with soap and water.
LEWISITE	Persistent heavy arsenical liquid usually brown in colour. Gives off invisible vapour. Smells strongly of geraniums. Very rapid penetration of skin. Quickly destroyed by water and any alkali.	(i) VAPOUR Immediate and severe irritation to nose and eyes. Damage to eyes and lungs. Reddening of skin and blistering. (Less than by mustard vapour.) (ii) LIQUID *Eyes*—immediate pain and spasm. Grave effect. *Skin*—similar to effects of " Mustard " but blisters develop more rapidly.	As for Mustard Gas.
CHOKING GASES PHOSGENE	Non-Persistent. Almost invisible vapour. May be seen as a white cloud near point of burst. Corrodes metals. Smells of musty hay or decaying vegetation.	Coughing and watering of eyes. Pain in chest. Lung damage develops later—often after a lapse of some hours.	Complete rest and warmth.
TEAR GASES B.B.C.	Very Persistent brown liquid. Gives off invisible vapour with faint smell.	Immediate stinging of eyes and profuse watering. Spasm of the lids. Liquid in the eyes can cause severe damage.	When Respirator is put on or casualty removed to fresh air recovery is usually rapid without treatment. Liquid contaminated clothing should be removed. If liquid gets in eye it must be washed out with water at once.
NOSE GASES D.A. D.M. D.C.	Solid colourless or bright yellow compounds of arsenic. When heated gives off volumes of minute particles generally invisible except near source. Non-Persistent. No smell.	Slight delay in effects but within 5 minutes, sneezing, burning sensation in nose, mouth, throat and chest, later perhaps vomiting in severe cases.	Remove from gas atmosphere. Effects may increase for the first few minutes in fresh air, or when Respirator is put on but will get less as the small amount of gas breathed in before detection works itself off.

APPENDIX B

ADDITIONAL INFORMATION ABOUT RESPIRATORS

1. Modifications of the Civilian Respirator and Special Civilian Types

For people who found even the slight effort of expelling the air past the cheeks too great a strain, a Civilian Respirator was designed in which an outlet valve is mounted on the facepiece between the window and the container. This respirator was issued on production of a medical certificate approved by the local Medical Officer of Health to people who, through age, weak heart, asthma, hay fever, etc., had difficulty in breathing.

For people with very thin faces, pronounced hollows in the cheeks or temples and deep scars on their faces, on whom it is difficult to ensure a gas-tight fit, the facepiece can be fitted with pads of sponge rubber to fill up the hollows. These pads may only be fitted by an Instructor or Warden who has been specially trained and then only while the respirator is on the individual.

2. The Helmet Respirator

This has been designed for people who experience great difficulty in breathing (e.g. sufferers from acute asthma) and for people who breathe through a tube in the throat. It is also suitable for people who, as a result of injury or a surgical operation to the face or head, cannot be fitted with a normal type of respirator.

It consists of a loosely fitted hood of rubberised fabric with a flap at the back and front. The hood rests on the shoulders and the flaps are tied down by a cord which passes under the armpits. Two separate eyepieces are fitted. (*See Fig.* 13.) Air is supplied to the inside of the hood in the same way as in the Baby's Anti-Gas Helmet, the bellows being worked by the wearer. Previously it was only issued on production of a medical certificate as in the case of the Civilian Respirator with outlet valve.

3. The Hospital Respirator

This has been designed for bedridden patients whose condition makes the wearing of an ordinary respirator impossible. It is similar in principle to the Helmet Respirator but has a large window in place of the eyepiece so that the patient can be easily observed. It can only be worn by patients lying down or sitting up so that the skirt and flaps of the hood can be tucked under the bedclothes or other covering.

These respirators were supplied only to hospitals.

4. Vigorous Work in the Civilian Respirator

The Civilian Respirator is not designed for people who will normally have to undertake vigorous work while wearing it but there may be occasions when this is necessary in an emergency and it may be found that there is a tendency for the facepiece to slip forward off the chin. This tendency can be overcome by fitting a tape to support the weight of the container. A piece of wide tape, four feet long, should be passed once round the container immediately above the rubber band and knotted on the opposite side of the container to the eyepiece, leaving

Fig. 13.
Helmet Respirator being worn, showing wearer operating
the bellows.

the ends of equal length. When the respirator has been put on in the
usual way the ends of the tape are passed round to the back of the neck
and tied in a bow. The tape should be drawn just tight enough to
prevent any forward movement of the container, but not tight enough
to cause any displacement of the facepiece. If, as is sometimes the case,
there is also a tendency for the head-harness to slip upwards at the back

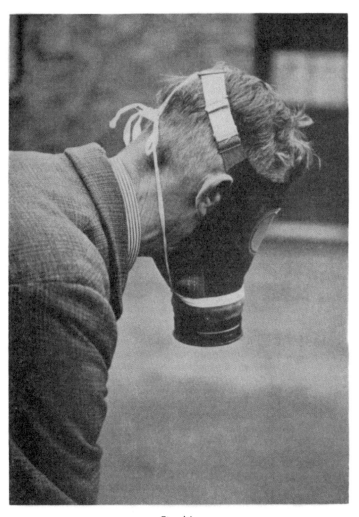

Fig. 14.
Civilian Respirator being worn, showing arrangement of tape to support weight of container and prevent the facepiece from slipping forward.

of the head, this can be overcome by attaching a loop of tape to the bottom slot in the T-buckle and passing the steadying tape of the container through the loop before tying it. (*See Fig.* 14.)

When the respirator is not in use the ends of the tape should be wound round the container and secured so that they will not become entangled with the head-harness while the respirator is being put on.

5. The Respirator Telephone

The speech of anyone wearing a Civilian Duty Respirator is muffled and indistinct and is particularly difficult to understand over a telephone. For telephone operators who must remain at their posts in rooms which cannot be made gas-proof a Respirator Telephone was designed. This is an ordinary Civilian Duty Respirator with a microphone attachment fitted into the protuberance moulded on the left cheek of the facepiece. The microphone is plugged into the switchboard and headphones are worn with the respirator.

6. The Fitting of Respirators

The aim in fitting respirators is to provide each person with the size of respirator which, while making a gas-tight fit on his face, will be as comfortable and as little handicap as possible. The key to a gas-tight fit is the chin—which must fit properly into the facepiece. The correct size is that which gives the wearer the best possible field of vision through the eyepieces or window when the facepiece has been pulled up on the face until it fits snugly under the chin. In a correctly fitted respirator the wearers eyes should be seen approximately at the centre of the eyepieces or window when looked at from the same level. The straps or bands of the head-harness in the Civilian Duty and Service Respirators are adjustable. The top two straps should be pulled up until the facepiece fits snugly under the chin and the others should be tightened just enough to hold the facepiece firmly on the face when the wearer moves his head about. If they are pulled too tight they may prevent the rubber of the facepiece from settling into hollows and thus introduce leaks ; they will certainly cause unnecessary discomfort.

7. The Use of Spectacles with Respirators

If spectacles are worn inside the facepiece of any normal type of respirator the side members are liable to cause leaks through the fitting surface in the region of the temples. In the case of the Civilian Respirator the rubbing of the ends of the frame on the eye panel may damage it.

Spectacles must, not, therefore, be worn with the Civilian Respirator and should only be worn with the Civilian Duty and Service Respirators if the lack of them will seriously handicap the wearer.

Wearers of Civilian Respirators who would be quite helpless without their spectacles can obtain sufficient aid for moving about in safety by wearing their spectacles OUTSIDE the facepiece. A piece of string or elastic should be fastened to the side members of the spectacles and passed over the back of the head to hold the spectacles in place.

8. Test for Gas-tightness and Test of Valves

When respirators are first issued and fitted they will be tested for gas-tightness and if possible their fit will be confirmed in a gas chamber or gas van. The effectiveness of the respirator depends on its gas-tightness and the proper working of the valves. The valves should, therefore, be tested every time the respirator is put on and the test of the valves will also show if the respirator is gas-tight. The wearer of the respirator is the only person who can tell with any certainty whether the valves are working correctly or not.

9. To test the Outlet Valve

In wear this valve should be shut except while breathing out, when it should open to allow the breath to escape freely. To test this, put on the respirator and it will be obvious at once if the outlet valve is not opening properly because resistance to breathing out will be experienced and the breath will escape past the cheeks. Should it be found that the outlet valve is not opening properly hold the facepiece firmly against the face with the palms of the hands and blow out hard. This will often remedy this defect.

It is vitally important that the outlet valve should be tightly shut when the wearer is breathing in. In order to make certain of this and incidentally to test for gas-tightness generally, stop the normal passage of air into the facepiece and attempt to breathe in. Do this by nipping the connecting tube of the Service Respirator or, by holding a piece of smooth cardboard, or the palm of the hand if it is large enough, firmly against the outer end of the container of the Civilian Duty and Civilian Respirators. With the normal entry of air stopped it will be obvious to the wearer if any air comes into the facepiece either through the outlet valve or through any leak past the edges of the facepiece. Should the outlet valve be found to be leaking it may be due to a small piece of grit or dirt on the seating of the valve and this may often be removed by blowing out hard with the facepiece held firmly on to the face. Should it be found that air comes in through a leak at the edge of the facepiece make certain that it is on straight and try again. If the leak is still noticeable the head-harness needs adjusting and this should be done by a specially trained person.

10. To test the Inlet Valve

This valve should open when the wearer breathes in and remain shut at all other times to prevent moist used air going back into the container. To test this put the respirator on and it will be obvious at once if the inlet valve is not opening because the wearer will be unable to draw any air through it. To find out if it is closing properly stop up the normal exit of air from the facepiece and breathe out gently. Do this by holding the sides of the Civilian facepiece on the face with the palms of the hands; by nipping the outlet valve of the Civilian Duty Respirator; or by holding a pad firmly over the outside of the valve holder in the Service facepiece. If air is escaping when the wearer breathes out gently and is not felt passing the cheeks it can only be escaping through a faulty inlet valve or a leak in the connecting tube of the Service Respirator. In the Civilian and Civilian Duty Respirators taking the rubber inlet valve disc off its pin and turning it over before replacing it may sometimes remedy the defect. Nothing can be done about a faulty inlet valve in a Service Respirator and the respirator should be replaced at the first convenient opportunity.

A leaky outlet valve is dangerous in a gas affected atmosphere and the wearer should move out of the gas at once. A leaky inlet valve, on the other hand, is not dangerous because all the air being breathed is still purified in passing through the container. It will, however, cause discomfort and excessive fogging of the eyepieces if the respirator is worn for a long period.

APPENDIX C

RESPIRATOR DRILLS

1. Civilian Respirator

Immediately the presence of gas is noticed or suspected, or the Gas Alarm (Rattle) is heard, proceed as follows :—

(i) STOP BREATHING. Remove headgear and place it between the knees. Remove spectacles.

(ii) Take the respirator out of its carrier and hold it in front of the face with the thumbs under the side straps. (*See Fig.* 15.)

(iii) Thrust the chin well into the bottom of the facepiece, pull the straps over the head with the thumbs and place the T-buckle centrally at the back of the head. (*See Fig.* 16.)

(iv) Feel round the edges of the facepiece to see that no parts of it are folded inwards and make sure that the straps are not twisted. The respirator should now be giving full protection.

(v) Blow out to expel any gas from the facepiece and carry on breathing normally. Replace the headgear.

When the " Gas Clear " signal (handbell) is heard the respirator is taken off by placing a thumb under the T-buckle at the back of the head and pulling it forward over the head so that the respirator is lowered downwards from the face. (*See Fig.* 17.) NO OTHER METHOD OF REMOVING THE RESPIRATOR IS PERMISSIBLE AS IT MAY EVENTUALLY RESULT IN DAMAGE TO IT.

To Adjust a Civilian Respirator on another Person

There may be occasions when it is necessary to put the respirator on another person who is unable to do it for himself, for example, someone who is injured, or a child. It is done from behind and the injured person must either be sitting or lying, if an adult, but a child may be standing provided its head is below shoulder level of the person doing it. The method is as follows :—

(i) Turn the head-harness forward over the front of the face-piece. Hold the respirator in both hands with the fingers outside and the thumbs inside the facepiece on either side of the chin hollow.

(ii) Catch the chin hollow of the facepiece under the chin of the wearer and see that it fits snugly. Then slide the hands up the edge of the facepiece, catching the head-harness on the way, and draw the head-harness over the head into the correct position.

(iii) Adjust the straps of the head-harness to hold the facepiece in position.

2. Civilian Duty and Service Respirators

These respirators will be carried in the " Slung Position " normally, but during periods of alert they should be brought to the " Alert Position."

The Slung Position

Place the sling of the haversack over the head and slip the left arm through it so that the haversack rests on the left hip. The haversack is

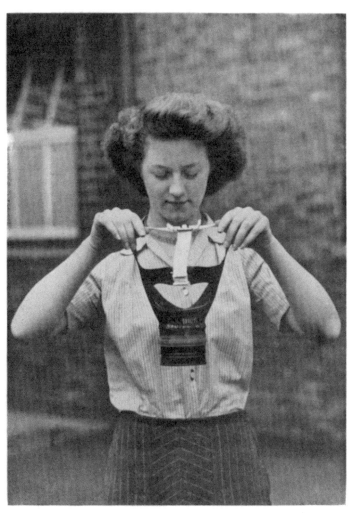

Fig. 15.
Preparing to put on the Civilian Respirator.

kept closed and in the case of the Service Respirator, the press studs of the flap of the respirator compartment must be towards the body.

Alert Position

SERVICE RESPIRATOR

1. Swing the haversack to the front of the body and slip the left arm through the sling.

Fig. 16.
Thrusting the chin into the Civilian Respirator.

2. Undo the press studs of the respirator compartment.

3. Take out the whipcord and thread it through the D ring on the right of the haversack.

The latest type of haversack has no D's. The whipcord is secured to the haversack near the bottom right hand corner and when not in use is carried in a small pocket on the outside of the haversack.

Fig. 17.
Taking off the Civilian Respirator.

4. Lift the haversack well up on the chest and drop the sling down the back.

5. Pass the whipcord through the sling at the back and secure to the D on the left of the haversack with a slip knot, or by taking a turn round the quick release button where this is fitted in place of the D.

6. Fold over the flap of the haversack to cover the respirator.

Swing the haversack to the front of the body.

Open the haversack to the fullest extent (except when raining).

To put on the Respirator from the Alert Position

Immediately the presence of gas is noticed or suspected, or the Gas Alarm is heard, proceed as follows :—

1. STOP BREATHING.

2. Place the chin strap of the helmet under the chin and push the helmet to the back of the neck. Remove the eyeshield.

3. Take hold of the respirator in the right hand with the Service Respirator by the valve holder, but with the Civilian Duty Respirator by the binding securing the container to the facepiece.

4. Pull it out of the haversack and turn it towards the face.

5. Place the thumbs inside the two lower elastics on each side and slide them wide apart.

6. Bring the facepiece up to the face and dig the chin well into it.

7. Pull the harness over the head with the thumbs and see that the pad is centrally placed at the back of the head. (*See Fig.* 18.)

8. Settle the facepiece comfortably on the face and see that the edges are not doubled inwards or the straps of the harness twisted. The respirator should now be giving full protection.

9. Blow out to expel any gas from the facepiece and resume breathing.

10. Bring the helmet forward on to the head and replace the chin strap on the point of the chin.

To put on the Respirator from the Slung Position

It is possible that a surprise gas attack might catch members of the Civil Defence Services carrying their respirators in the Slung position. In these circumstances they must put their respirators on as quickly as possible and, when fully protected, adjust the haversack in the Alert position. The Drill is as follows :—

1. STOP BREATHING.

2. Swing the haversack to the front of the body and, in the case of the Service Respirator, slip the left arm through the sling.

3. Proceed as in putting on the respirator from the Alert position. In putting on the Service Respirator it may be found easier to bend forwards.

4. After putting on the helmet and adjusting the chin strap, bring the haversack to the Alert position.

To take off the Facepiece

When the " Gas Clear " signal is heard, and not before, the facepiece of the Service Respirator or the Civilian Duty Respirator may be removed as follows :—

1. Prepare a fresh eyeshield.

2. Push the helmet to the back of the neck.

3. Insert two fingers of either hand between the chin and the

Fig. 18.
Putting on the Civilian Duty Respirator.

facepiece and remove with an upward and backward movement. (*See Fig.* 19.)

4. With the Service Respirator let the facepiece hang by the connecting tube. With the Civilian Duty Respirator let it hang by one of the straps of the head-harness from the thumb of either hand.

5. Put on the fresh eyeshield and replace the helmet.

Fig. 19.
Taking off the Civilian Duty Respirator.

To Replace in the Haversack

As soon as the facepiece of the Service Respirator or the Civilian Duty Respirator has been taken off it must be replaced in its haversack correctly so that it is ready for instant use when required again.

This is done as follows :—Hold the facepiece in the right hand with the fingers on one eyepiece and the thumb on the other and the valve holder or container lying in the palm of the hand with the inside of

Fig. 20.
Folding the Civilian Duty Respirator.

the facepiece upwards. Drop the pad and straps of the head-harness inside the facepiece. (*See Fig.* 20.) Squeeze the eyepieces together and push the facepiece or respirator into the haversack, forehead part first, with the harness buckles to the wearer's right. (*See Fig.* 21.) Fold over the flap of the Service Respirator haversack.

To adjust a Service or Civilian Duty Respirator on another Person

Should it be necessary to put a respirator on anyone unable to do it himself, it should be done as follows :—

Fig. 21.
Returning the Civilian Duty Respirator to its haversack.

(1) Get behind him.

(2) Take his respirator out of its haversack and hold it in both hands with the thumbs inside the two lower harness straps pointing upwards and the fingers outside the facepiece.

(3) Catch the chin part of the facepiece under the chin and draw the head-harness over the head.

(4) Straighten the facepiece and settle it comfortably on the face.

HOME OFFICE

CIVIL DEFENCE

Manual of Basic Training
VOLUME II

BASIC
FIRE FIGHTING

PAMPHLET No. 2

LONDON: HIS MAJESTY'S STATIONERY OFFICE
1949

SIXPENCE NET

GENERAL PREFACE

The series of Civil Defence handbooks and pamphlets is produced under the authority of the Home Secretary by the Civil Defence Department of the Home Office with the assistance of and in co-operation with the Secretary of State for Scotland and other Ministers concerned.

Measures for safeguarding the civil population against the effects of war which these publications describe, have become an essential part of the defensive organisation of this country. The need for them is not related to any belief that war is imminent. It is just as necessary that preparations for Civil Defence should be made in time of peace as it is that preparations should be made for the Armed Forces.

The publications cover, as far as is possible, measures which can be taken to mitigate the effects of all modern forms of attack. Any scheme of Civil Defence, if it is to be efficient, must be up-to-date and must take account of all the various weapons which might become available. The scale of bombing experienced in Great Britain during the 1939-45 war might be considerably exceeded in any future war, and types of weapons and tactics which were not experienced in this country might conceivably be used against it in the future. It does not follow that any one of the weapons, e.g. the atomic bomb, will necessarily be used, and it is most important that a proper balance is held between what is likely and what is possible.

The use of poison gas in war was forbidden by the Geneva Gas Protocol of 1925, to which this country and all the other countries of the Western Union were parties. At the outbreak of a war, His Majesty's Government would try to secure an undertaking from the enemy not to use poison gas. Nevertheless the risk of poison gas being used remains a possibility and cannot be disregarded any more than can certain further developments in other scientific fields.

The publications are designed to describe not only precautionary schemes which experience in the last war proved to be extremely effective in preventing avoidable injury and loss of life, or widespread dislocation of national industries, but also the training, both technical and tactical, which will be required of the personnel of the Civil Defence Services if they are to be ready effectively to play their part if war should ever break out. The publications aim at giving the best available information on methods of defence against all the various weapons. Information is not complete in respect of some of these weapons and the best methods of countering them, but as results of experimental work and other investigations mature, they will be revised and added to from time to time so that the Civil Defence Services may be kept up-to-date and their training may be on the most modern and experienced lines.

CONTENTS

NOTE

The pagination of this pamphlet is not continuous as it may be necessary to introduce new pages at a later date.

BASIC FIRE-FIGHTING

INTRODUCTION

Perhaps the greatest lesson brought out by the war was that incendiary bombs caused far more loss of life and property than did High Explosive Bombs. As a result of experience, the proportion of incendiary bombs to H.E. bombs in the loads carried by our bombers, was stepped up more and more as the war went on. The present state of German and Japanese cities shows the result.

In this country we escaped comparatively lightly, though much damage was caused none the less. But we were not called upon to experience the results of Atomic Bombing. We were never exposed to the full force of a Saturation Attack.

The magnitude of such a disaster often blinds the uninformed to the continued need for the elementary fire-fighting appliances and technique described in this pamphlet.

Even though no fire-fighting of any kind is possible in the area affected by such a catastrophe, there still remain the outer areas, where the weight of attack " shades off." Here the timely use of even minor appliances in the hands of a well-trained and resolute population is capable of turning the tide, saving untold destruction of life and property.

This pamphlet deals with elementary fire precautions and fire-fighting up to the arrival of the professional fire services. It is designed to put before the ordinary individual the problems which are likely to confront him, and the many steps he can take to help himself and others.

A number of unused paragraphs have been left at the end of each chapter to permit of any additions that may be considered necessary from time to time. This, it is hoped, will avoid the necessity of re-numbering paragraphs.

CHAPTER I

GENERAL

1. HOW FIRE STARTS

Neither liquids nor solids burn, only the vapour given off by them when they are heated and then only when it has been mixed with oxygen and the temperature of this mixture has been raised to a point at which it will *burst into flame*.

Three stages are essential to create a fire.

(i) The heating of the material to the point at which it gives off inflammable vapour.

(ii) The mixing of this vapour with oxygen in the surrounding atmosphere.

(iii) The ignition of the inflammable vapour mixture.

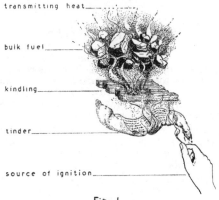

transmitting heat

bulk fuel

kindling

tinder

source of ignition

Fig. I.

2. BUILD-UP OF FIRE

Having got fire, you get more heat.

This additional heat will drive off an increased amount of vapour from the fuel : it will also increase the amount of hot gases arising from the fire and draw in from the surrounding air the extra oxygen needed : further, it will raise the temperature of this mixture until still more fire results.

Having got still more fire it will produce still more heat and so the build-up progresses more and more rapidly.

From the above it will be seen that to continue burning a fire needs:—

FUEL, OXYGEN, HEAT.

3. EXTINCTION OF FIRE

As there are three essentials for the propagation of fire, it follows that if *any one of them* is sufficiently reduced, the fire must go out.

In practice, it is seldom possible to reduce the amount of fuel (by removal of furniture, etc.) or the amount of oxygen (by closing doors and windows) sufficiently to extinguish the fire ; its intensity can however be greatly reduced by the above means. For extinction, the heat is reduced by cooling down with water.

4. COMBUSTIBILITY

The spread of a fire depends on the combustibility of the contents of the place in which the fire has started, and on how those contents are distributed.

By " Combustibility " we mean the facility with which any material will burn. Some are very liable indeed and usually burn fiercely from the beginning. Such materials are " Inflammable." Wood, coal, lino,

4

carpets and rugs, are combustible. Celluloid, petrol, some oils, thin material such as muslin, are inflammable. These are just a few examples.

In the home the combustibility of the various articles is roughly as follows, starting with the most combustible :—

(i) Hanging draperies—such as curtains, tablecloths, coats or dresses, bedclothes, lampshades and other thin materials of that kind.

(ii) Wicker furniture, baskets, and the like.

(iii) Wooden furniture, tables, chairs, wooden bedsteads, cupboards, pictures.

(iv) Wooden fittings, doors, window-frames, fitted cupboards and panelling.

(v) Laid carpets, rugs, lino.

(vi) Rafters, joists, etc.

You have probably noticed that the most combustible things are usually the most portable.

5. FIRE SPREAD IN A BUILDING

In the roof, fire will tend to spread :—

(i) Sideways along the roof space.

(ii) Downwards, owing to the burning material dropping to the floor underneath and setting fire to fresh materials.

On any floor the fire will tend to spread :—

(iii) Upwards at first ; particularly up staircases and lift shafts, both of which act like flues.

(iv) Sideways, along joists ; often under floor boards and out of sight. Also through open doors and windows.

(v) Downwards, when it has burnt a hole in the floor and burning fragments drop through into the room underneath.

6. FIRE SPREAD FROM BUILDING TO BUILDING

If the house on fire is one of a terraced row, there is great danger that the fire will spread along the roof-space to the next house.

The fire may spread to other buildings by direct flame, radiated heat, or burning fragments and sparks. The most likely places it will catch are :—

Wooden Sheds.

Thatched Roofs.

Skylights facing the fire.

Wooden window-frames.

Contents of rooms (through open windows).

CHAPTER II

HOW FIRES ARE CAUSED

12. INCENDIARY AGENTS

So far as property is concerned, war records show that fire from incendiary bombs caused anything from 10 to 100 times as much damage as high explosive, the proportion varying according to the target and the method of attack.

The most effective incendiary was the small magnesium bomb dropped in very large numbers with the idea of " saturating " the target area and so overwhelming the Fire Service. There is little doubt that bombs of this kind will be the main incendiary weapon for a long time to come. Thus, the fire-fighting problem should be much the same in any future war as it was in the last.

The medium and large incendiary bombs have the advantage that they may individually start a fire which will need to be tackled from the beginning by the Fire Service, with its full-sized appliances ; but this advantage is outweighed by the fact that bombers can only carry a comparatively small number of these bombs. Such bombs are only likely to be used against special targets, and not for a " full-scale " fire-raising attack on a built-up area.

13. INCENDIARY BOMB FILLINGS

It can be accepted, then, that unless some new and more efficient filling is discovered, thermite in a bomb with a magnesium wall (as in the German 1 kilo type), is likely to hold its own. For the larger bombs the fillings will probably be a mixture, with petrol or oil as the main ingredient.

Phosphorus, as such, makes an inefficient incendiary, but may be added to incendiary mixtures so as to ignite the filling if the fuse fails and the bomb breaks up on impact, or if the filling is in any way exposed to the air.

Incendiary bombs are not the only cause of fires in an air attack. The blast, and sometimes the earth-shock, caused by High Explosive bombs, often start serious fires by scattering burning coals, etc., from domestic fires on to carpets, woodwork, and other combustible materials.

14. ATOMIC BOMBS

A great additional risk is caused by the fire-raising effects of the Atomic bomb.

"Heat Flash" is a very short-lived wave of intense heat radiated over a considerable distance in all directions at the moment of burst. It will start fires over a very wide area. The combustible content of many buildings is liable to catch fire simultaneously on all floors.

At Hiroshima, buildings, strong enough to stand up against the blast, were completely gutted because they contained inflammable and combustible materials.

Atomic bombs are also likely to start fires on a wide scale in the same way as H.E. bombs.

We must realize that this country, bad though the damage was, got off very lightly compared to Germany and Japan. There is not a single person who has seen the fire damage in either of those countries, who has not been appalled at the sight of what fire can do once it has been allowed to get out of hand.

It is up to us to keep on our toes if we are to prevent the same kind of thing happening here in any future war. The best insurance of all is for the able bodied adult population to be thoroughly trained in elementary fire fighting.

CHAPTER III

FIRE PREVENTION

20. PRACTICAL PRECAUTIONS

Wartime experience of Incendiary and H.E. bomb attack showed the value of taking *beforehand* all practical precautions to reduce the risk of fires starting and spreading.

Everyone knows the immense tasks which faced the Fire Services, and will certainly face them again, probably on an increased scale. We all know, too, how much householders and the officially organized services were able to do, with a little training and knowledge, and how this eased the situation.

Cases will be remembered where incendiary bombs fell on every house in a street and how, by the efforts of the inhabitants, every house was saved. That is the object of elementary fire-fighting, and the simple and practical hints given in this pamphlet.

In other words, in wartime—and in peacetime too—learn first of all how to reduce the risks to a minimum, and secondly, how to overcome them if incendiary attack is experienced.

(i) Clearance of combustible materials

" IT MAY COME IN HANDY SOME TIME " !

How often we have all heard these words ; and how often have they been responsible for the loss by fire of a building which might otherwise have been saved.

Go and look at the contents of your own boxroom or attic. You will find an accumulation of odds and ends most of which are combustible, or inflammable (which is worse). Then imagine an incendiary bomb falling into it.

Even in peacetime such an accumulation of inflammable material in these places is dangerous, but in wartime it is certain to lead to trouble, not only involving your own house but probably your neighbours' as well. Be absolutely ruthless and do not let sentiment play any part. Clear out everything that will burn. If it is necessary to keep certain articles, then store them in some outbuilding away from the main building, if you can.

(ii) Access to your Roof-space

Very often an attic has a ceiling. Perhaps your own has one. Between that ceiling and the roof itself there will be a space.

Sometimes there is no trap-door, or other means of access to the roof space. Then you should have one made.

Lastly, having arranged a means of access, don't forget that you have to use it ; so have a long enough ladder or steps handy.

(iii) Fire-retarding materials

In fire-fighting, particularly in wartime, seconds count. You have now cleared out unnecessary junk from the attic, and by doing that you have won at least half the battle, if not more.

17

There is still the possibility that if an incendiary bomb lodges in some corner, underneath a piece of constructional woodwork, such as a rafter, the heat radiated upwards will start a fire before you can get there and tackle the situation.

You can reduce the risk by coating such timbers with a fire-retarding solution. There are a number on the market ; some are paints, and some are washes. Sodium silicate (waterglass) is an example.

Do bear in mind that *none* of these materials make the woodwork *fireproof*. In other words they will catch fire eventually. What happens is that the outbreak is delayed for a while—usually for long enough to give you a chance to deal with the situation and put the bomb out before it does any mischief.

Fires are often spread as a result of heat radiated from a nearby burning building. This danger may be lessened by ensuring that the windows are kept closed and by treating the curtains with a fire re-tarding mixture.

(iv) Simple Fire-fighting Appliances

It is essential to have some means of tackling fires in the building. In the war, thousands of householders dealt with incendiary bombs and fires in their own buildings without calling the Fire Service or even the Fire Guards. By doing this, they enabled the Fire Service and Fire Guards to concentrate on places where their efforts were essential.

If this was necessary in the last war, how much more necessary will it be in future, when the weight of attack may be far heavier. You must look on what you might call " Self-Help " as part of the normal duty of every citizen. The Germans did and they were successful until their active defences collapsed, so that the full, almost unopposed, weight of the allied attack overwhelmed them.

The most helpful thing you can do is to get a stirrup-pump. Remember too, that no pump is of any use without water ; so you will need an ample supply. Get as many buckets or other containers as you can (buckets are best) and keep them full of water.

Perhaps the biggest fire lesson of the war is that YOU CANNOT HAVE TOO MUCH WATER.

Try to build up a reserve of water from which to refill your buckets. The war-time hint of keeping your bath full of water proved most useful.

Never forget war experience, which showed that hundreds of buildings were lost, though there were plenty of pumps and people to work them, simply BECAUSE THERE WAS NOT ENOUGH WATER.

(v) The Value of Training

You have now done everything to make your building as safe as any building can be in wartime. You have cleared out all combustible material from your attic. You have your stirrup pump, or pumps, your water-buckets and you have ensured a reserve of water.

But there is one essential thing ; and that is to get trained—and thoroughly trained—in the use of your appliances. It is not much use keeping a pistol against robbers unless you know how to use it.

Fire is the worst robber of all. So learn how to use your equipment so that you get the very best out of it.

18

(vi) Industry

The same problems which affect the householder and the same principles which help to solve them, apply to industry. The scale is larger, and the details more complex ; but the same advice holds good :—

(*a*) Never allow combustible and inflammable materials to accumulate. Get rid of all surplus material as quickly as you can, if it is humanly possible to do so.

(*b*) Make use of fire-retardant paints or washes wherever possible.

(*c*) Lay in an ample stock of fire-fighting appliances and see that all your employees are well-trained to play their part in using them. If oil or petrol is stored on the premises foam extinguishers should be installed.

(*d*) Make every effort to ensure an ample reserve of water. Double the amount you think you might need.

(*e*) Be certain that fire-fighters can get to every part of your premises. Unnecessary destruction was caused in the war in warehouses, etc., when fire-fighters found that goods were stacked so closely together in bulk that they could not get near enough to bombs or fires.

By arranging gangways in both directions between such piles of goods, you not only provide " fire-breaks," but enable your fire-fighters to get to the heart of the trouble.

(*f*) Be certain that all employees likely to be engaged on fire-fighting have a thorough knowledge of the layout of the premises.

(*g*) This pamphlet cannot hope to cope with the more complex problems of wartime fires in industry. Advice can be obtained from your local Fire Service.

(vii) Fire Prevention in Peacetime

Thousands of avoidable fires occur in peace-time, and most of them can be prevented by reasonable steps being taken beforehand and above all by being careful. Smouldering cigarette ends, faulty electrical apparatus, unguarded open fires, etc., can all cause fires.

CHAPTER IV

ESCAPE AND RESCUE FROM BURNING BUILDINGS

26. PERSONAL PROTECTION

If you are trapped by fire there are one or two elementary principles to be borne in mind.

A wet cloth, or handkerchief placed over the mouth and nose will give some measure of protection against smoke, by preventing the larger particles from being inhaled (but will give no protection against suffocation from lack of oxygen, excess of carbon dioxide, or poisoning from excess of carbon monoxide).

Quite a small fire can produce a large amount of smoke in which conditions become impossible unless great care is taken. A person lost in a room should make for a wall and then continue round it in the same direction until the door or exit is reached. If it is suspected that another person is lost it is often possible to indicate the whereabouts of the exit by standing close to it and shouting or blowing a whistle.

27. ESCAPE

When moving about in smoke in strange surroundings, it may only be possible to work by touch. This necessarily calls for caution.

The air will be clearest and coolest near the floor and the person entering the room will usually find it advisable to go down on his hands and knees, and crawl (*See Fig.* 2.) When moving forward the free hand should be raised in front lightly clenched, with the back uppermost, to feel for obstructions. If the back of the hand touches a live electric wire the shock will throw the hand clear and will not cause it to clasp the wire, as would occur were the hand open. It will often be possible to detect from this position the glow of a fire which cannot be seen when standing up.

Stairs are a source of danger when escaping from a building which is on fire and should always be treated with caution. Wooden stairs seldom collapse without warning, but may become so weakened by charring that portions of them will give way beneath a person's weight. When using any stairs, always keep close to the wall since the treads will usually bear weight at this point, even though their centres may be weakened. Go down backwards and feel with your foot for each step before putting your full weight on it. If the step is missing one knee will still be resting on the step above and you can catch hold of some part of the stairs with your hands. In searching for the head of a staircase, take care when grasping the handrail, since this may have been weakened and collapse if any weight is applied to it. Metal handrails may be hot enough to burn the hands.

It is often possible to escape by dropping from a window on to the roof of an outbuilding, such as a wash-house or projecting kitchen, and so reaching the ground.

Fig. 2.

When dropping, it is essential to reduce the length of the fall as much as possible. To do this, sit on the window sill, with your legs outside, turn over, grip the sill and lower yourself to the full extent of your arms, then let go and drop. In this way you reduce the distance by about seven feet and are less likely to hurt yourself. (*See Fig.* 3.)

Finally, do not panic. If you are caught on a floor higher than the first one up, you may be able to knot sheets and blankets together, tie one end to some heavy piece of furniture, drop the other out of the window, and climb down, if not all the way to the ground, at any rate until you are able to drop with reasonable safety.

If you live on the third, or higher, floor of a building it is advisable to buy a rope which should be kept in readiness and which will reach to the ground, and be capable of bearing your weight. In peace time it is reasonable to assume that a fire escape will soon arrive, but in time of war it may be delayed and you may have to rely on your own efforts.

If all else fails, shut the door, call for help from the window, and wait to be rescued. A closed door will hold back heat and flame for quite a long time.

28. RESCUE

(i) General

The primary duty of fire-fighters is to save life. Due to fear and excitement, persons trapped often forget the normal means of escape

Fig. 3.

and have a tendency to throw themselves from a window or roof into the street, despite the fact that there may be no immediate danger and that help may be at hand. Where persons are crying out for help they should be reassured and told not to jump. Find out as quickly as possible whether any one is trapped ; this information can often be obtained from neighbours. If it is suspected that anyone is still in the building a thorough and methodical search must be carried out at once.

No hard and fast rule can be laid down as regards rescue, as it depends entirely upon the type of building and equipment available. The general rule is that the search should begin at the top of the building so that the searchers are nearest to fresh air and safety at the end of their search.

(ii) Entry

When trying to enter a building the main door should first be tried. It may not be locked. If entry has to be forced, it should be done by the method which will cause least damage, remembering it is easier to break glass rather than wood. The possibility of entry by the back door should not be overlooked.

(iii) Searching a Building

When possible, it is advisable to work in pairs on entering a smoke-filled room or building. This gives confidence and makes it possible for one to assist the other. People trapped by fire or smoke, particularly children, often take refuge under beds or in cupboards where they hide

27

to escape the smoke and flames. Searching though swift, should be thorough, every room should be investigated and no possible hiding place, however unlikely, overlooked.

(iv) Searching a Room

Searching a smoke-filled room is not an easy task and is unlikely to be successful unless carried out on a definite plan. Once inside the room a complete circuit should be made, keeping close to the wall, feeling under and on the beds, and opening and feeling inside cupboards, wardrobes and other articles of furniture. Finally, the room should be crossed diagonally to make sure no one is lying in its centre. (*See Fig.* 4.)

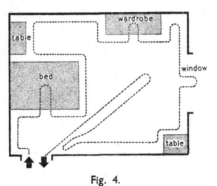

Fig. 4.

Always remember that floors immediately above the fire, may have been weakened sufficiently to become dangerous and care should be exercised when it is necessary to search the centre of the room. Whether or not the windows should be opened to obtain fresh air during the search depends on circumstances. Only when it is known that the fire is in a distant part of the building and is being tackled, or if the atmosphere is cool, is it safe to open the windows.

When opening a door behind which fire may be found, the possibility of a back draught of flame caused by the intake of air should not be overlooked. The most obvious warning of danger is the presence of heat. The metal shank connecting the two door knobs is a good conductor of heat and if this or the door knob prove to be very hot then the door must be opened with care. A room should not be entered, except for rescue purposes, without a stirrup pump for the immediate application of water to the fire. (*See Fig.* 5.)

If the door opens towards you then the foot should be placed against the bottom of the door, and the handle turned gently. (*See Fig.* 6.)

There may be a considerable pressure in the room due to the expansion of the heated gases. It is desirable to crouch in such a way that any heated gases or flames which are released pass over the head.

(v) Moving an Insensible Person

It is not an easy matter to lift an insensible person, and carrying involves the maximum danger in smoke, both from suffocation and

28

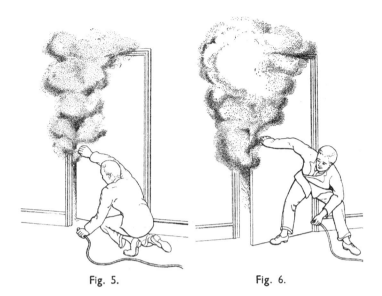

falling. To move an insensible person, turn him on his back on the floor, tie his wrists together, kneel across him and place your head through the loop formed by his arms; then you can crawl on hands and knees, dragging him with you although he may be far heavier than yourself. To move an insensible person downstairs, lay him on his back, head downwards on the stairs, place your hands under his armpits, so that his head rests on the crook of your arm and ease him gently downstairs.

CHAPTER V

FIRE-FIGHTING EQUIPMENT—ITS USE AND CARE

34. GENERAL

(i) The Householder

War experience proved that in well-trained and resolute hands, the simplest appliances and equipment were capable of dealing with the incendiary bomb menace.

If you are a householder, or the occupant of any but large business premises, you should have :—

Buckets of water .

Buckets of sand or earth

Stirrup hand pumps (say one to every three or four people).

(ii) Business and Industry

Large business and industrial concerns normally have a variety of appliances and their own trained firemen. These arrangements are usually adequate in peacetime ; but in time of war more is needed.

The ideal should be that every employee is trained in the use of the smaller appliances and that enough appliances are available to bring the maximum possible strength to the attack of the fire menace.

This means that besides Self-propelled Pumps and the lighter power-driven units of the " Trailer " and " Wheel-barrow " types, a plentiful stock of stirrup pumps, buckets and an ample reserve supply of water should be available.

35. APPLIANCES FOR HOUSEHOLDERS AND SMALL BUSINESS PREMISES

(i) Water Buckets

Get as many of these as you possibly can. You cannot have too many. The ordinary bucket holds a little short of two gallons, and you will find that this is the most convenient size.

You must have at least two always in use at the pump and enough extra to ensure a continuous supply from the nearest source of reserve water.

Even in the absence of a pump, a non-stop chain of buckets, in capable hands, can quench a fire in its early stages, though this will not be enough if the fire has gained a hold.

Keep every bucket full of *clean* water. Impress on everyone that they are not there as receptacles for match-sticks, cigarette ends and rubbish of that sort.

Do not keep all the buckets massed in one place. It might be that when the time comes the fire would prevent you from getting at any of them. Space them out in such a way that no matter where the fire may be, you can always lay your hands on a sufficient number.

Inspect your buckets at regular intervals, not only to make sure that they are clear of rubbish, but also because they will need " topping-up " every now and then.

(ii) Sand Buckets

Keep a few buckets full of dry sand or earth. Builders' sand is better than sea-sand, and earth, if used, must be free of grass roots and other combustible material of that kind.

If anything goes wrong with your pump or your water supply, then a couple of buckets full of sand or earth will partially smother a magnesium bomb and, by cooling it down, will delay its tendency to burn through the floor.

In addition sand or earth is very useful for smothering burning oil, as you will learn in the next chapter.

(iii) Stirrup Hand Pumps

The stirrup-pump is by far the best piece of elementary fire-fighting equipment. It is easy to use, easy to keep in good order and, what is more, makes more effective use of limited water supplies than anything else.

It can be used by two people, or in an emergency, even by one. The normal stirrup pump team should be four, but if the man-power situation will not permit, then three should be used.

No. 1. Tackles the bomb and the fires with the hose.

No. 2. Works the pump.

No. 3. Brings up further water supplies.

No. 4. (If available) assists No. 3 to bring up water. In the event of a long carry being necessary, No. 4 will bring up supplies to a pre-arranged point leaving No. 3 to take them forward from there.

Nos. 2, 3 and 4 change over at intervals, but every member of the team must be trained to do any of the three jobs in case of need.

The drill for a team of four is given in Appendix " A," and for a team of three in Appendix " B."

The pump (*See Fig. 7.*) is very simply made, and there are only three moving parts :—

(*a*) The plunger tube, to the bottom of which is fitted the piston.

(*b*) The metal ball which forms the non-return valve in the piston.

(*c*) The metal ball which forms the foot valve in the base of the barrel.

In the bottom of the pump is a strainer, which can be unscrewed and taken out if necessary.

To use : put the barrel of the pump into a bucket of water so that the metal stirrup rests on the ground outside the bucket.

No. 2 holds the pump firmly in position by putting his foot on the stirrup.

Training and practice will show you the best pumping rate to maintain a steady stream of water, and you will find that short quick strokes give the best results.

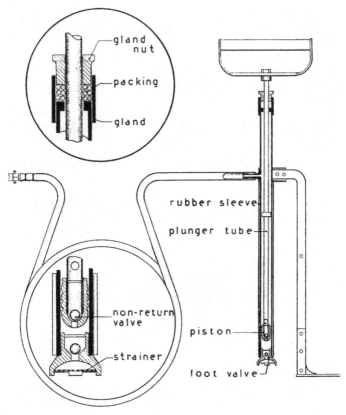

Fig. 7.

Provided you test the pump at least once a fortnight—better still, once a week—it will go on giving you good service more or less indefinitely, but if anything should go wrong, it is probably due to one of the following :—

    (i) Rusted ball valves.

    (ii) Ball valves stuck on the seating through lack of use.

    (iii) Choked strainer cover.

    (iv) Choked hose nozzle.

The most common defect of the earlier models is rusted ball valves, due to the use of steel balls which are liable to rust fairly quickly if the pump is not regularly used.

To put this right, remove the strainer at one end and the pump handle at the other, and pull the plunger out of the lower end of the pump barrel. Then you can remove the rust with a pocket knife. Later models were fitted with phosphor-bronze balls which do not rust.

When you withdraw the plunger, do not interfere with the packing-gland. If the gland does leak, you can usually put it right by tightening the gland nut. If this fails, pick out the packing altogether, and re-pack with a length of oiled string.

Do not over-tighten the gland-nut, or you will find the pump hard to work.

If the ball valves stick to the seating, you can usually free them by pushing a pin, or a piece of wire, up through the filter. If this fails, unscrew the strainer altogether and lever up the ball with a thin piece of stick. If this does no good you will have to dismantle the pump.

You can clear a choked nozzle by unscrewing it and removing the dirt from the hole.

Some nozzles are dual purpose, and deliver a spray or jet at will. Others only deliver a jet. With this type, the spray can be achieved by placing the thumb or finger partially over the hole.

Spray should be used on an oil fire to cut off the oxygen supply. You must not use the jet, its only effect would be to scatter the burning oil.

Regular use of the pump makes you familiar with the best method of handling it and shows up any faults in the pump itself. Use it for washing windows and cars, for watering gardens and for laying dust.

If you want your pump to last do NOT use it for spraying strong disinfectant or insecticide.

Keep it where you can get at it easily.

Look after it and keep it in order, from a fire fighting point of view it is your best friend.

Again and again during the war, this little pump triumphantly justified the claims which were made for it.

Provided that the fires have not spread to any great extent beyond the room in which they started, they can be attacked with every prospect of success.

Even when a whole room is blazing and flames are shooting out through the window, it does not follow that the fire is out of control. The effect of 15—20 gallons of water from two stirrup pumps on such a fire has to be seen to be believed. There were cases where it was extinguished within ten minutes.

You will find other instances of the pump's capabilities in Chapter VIII.

(iv) Domestic Water Supplies

Cases did occur where householders, to save the expense of buying pumps and buckets, fixed lengths of hose to taps.

This is unsound, and is *not* recommended. Domestic water supplies usually come from a gravity tank in the attic or roof-space. It is true that you might get quite a good head of water on the lower floors of a tall building ; but on the upper floors, and particularly in the attic or roof space (two places where incendiary bombs are the most likely to land) you will get little or no head of water.

Besides this, the town water supply may fail, in which case, having emptied your gravity tank, you will be without water.

(v) Chemical Extinguishers

At first sight a chemical extinguisher may seem to be the ideal light portable apparatus for use in wartime. When you go into the matter you find they have a number of serious disadvantages. Chemical extinguishers are designed to cope with a fire in its early stages, before the flames have really got a hold. They were *not* designed for a situation such as is caused by an incendiary bomb.

These are the disadvantages :—

(i) The average time during which they give a jet of water is only two minutes. After that they are empty and useless until they are re-filled. This takes time and is usually a job for the agent of the firm and not for you.

(ii) They are rather heavy and bulky and very awkward to get up through a narrow trap-door into a roof-space. Women would find them too heavy.

(iii) Some makes are dangerous to use in a confined space as they are liable to give off poisonous vapours.

(iv) They are difficult to use from behind cover.

(v) They are expensive. You can buy two or three stirrup pumps for the price of one extinguisher.

In view of all the above, it is obvious that your money is much better spent in buying a stirrup pump.

Naturally, in large premises, where a number of extinguishers are already installed, use them by all means, *provided always* that you have the man-power to spare, and are not wasting personnel better employed using stirrup pumps.

CHAPTER VI

HOW TO ATTACK A FIRE

41. RECONNAISSANCE

From what has been said previously it is obvious that in tackling a fire the following must be borne in mind :—

Generally the fire will be extinguished by cooling with water, therefore the closer one can get to the heart of it the more effective will be the jet, and the maximum the effect of its impact. At the same time, so far as it is possible the supply of oxygen must be kept to a minimum ; and so, as many doors, windows and other openings must be closed as is consistent with a safe line of retreat. Any combustible material in the vicinity of the fire should be removed as opportunity offers. Moreover there may be more than one fire-source.

A thorough, though rapid reconnaissance is a vital preliminary to attack ; *time so spent is never wasted.*

In making this reconnaissance, it must be remembered that part of the approach, and the attack on the fire, will have to be made in the prone position, as near the floor there will normally be more cool air, better visibility and less heat and smoke than at a higher level.

Unless the fire is quickly brought under control it will spread, therefore it is vital to attack the heart of the fire rather than the more spectacular-looking flames ; none the less all combustible material near the fire is itself a potential fire and unless cooled from time to time, may burst into flame.

In the event of there being more than one stirrup pump available the additional ones may be used either to reinforce the first, or to attack the fire from more than one direction and at the same time prevent the fire spreading.

When the fire is out, all debris must be cooled with water and a final reconnaissance made to ensure there are no hot spots which might flare up after the fire-fighters have left.

The first reconnaissance may show that the fires are too large for the capacity of the appliances available, if so, additional help should be summoned and the available appliances used to hold the fires pending the arrival of reinforcement. Particularly may this be so in the case of an atomic bomb where fires may be started simultaneously in all parts of a building. In this extreme case the fire fighters should concentrate on saving life.

No matter how large the area of fire, there will always be a perimeter where the attack has been less concentrated and here fires can, and MUST, be fought to prevent a bad situation from becoming worse.

Except for the extreme case mentioned above, the object at all times should be to extinguish the fires no matter what complications there may be. Such things as phosphorus, oil, incendiary bombs with explosive charges and so on are additional dangers, the presence of which must never be allowed to interfere with the fire fighting, though they may call for alterations of technique.

42. FIRES CAUSED BY INCENDIARY BOMBS

(i) Magnesium

When tackling a fire caused by a magnesium I.B., no departure is needed from the principles of fire-fighting already outlined. The I.B. will normally be the heart of the fire and should be attacked as such. (*See Fig.* 8.)

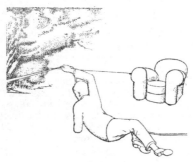

Fig. 8.

A jet of water directed at the I.B. will cause considerable spluttering of the magnesium away from the fire-fighter and may start other fires in the vicinity.

Should the bomb have been burning for some time before the situation is tackled, it may have reached the stage when spluttering has stopped and the bomb reduced to a molten puddle of magnesium. In this case the fires started by the bomb will probably have a good hold and must be attacked with water at once. The only danger from the molten bomb will be in burning through the floor boards.

Incendiary bombs may be fitted with explosive attachments, therefore when fighting a fire caused by incendiary bombs, full advantage should be taken of any available cover against splinters. (*See Fig.* 9.)

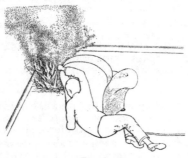

Fig. 9.

If none is available, the risk must be accepted and the fire tackled regardless of possible injury.

(ii) Phosphorus

These fires can be readily controlled by water, preferably in the form of spray, but it must be remembered that phosphorus will re-ignite if allowed to become dry. Cases were known in the war of phosphorus re-igniting after a lapse of ten days. It is necessary to keep wet all inflammable surfaces which are contaminated by phosphorus until such time as it can be removed by scraping or some other means. Remember that phosphorus on the skin or clothes will re-ignite unless kept damp and can cause serious burns.

(iii) Oil

Oil fires should not be attacked with water in bulk, such as a jet. The burning oil may float on the surface of the water and so cause the fire to spread. They should be smothered with earth or sand to exclude oxygen, or may be blanketed with a fine spray of water. The latter method has the additional advantage of cooling.

CHAPTER VII

FIRE-FIGHTING HINTS

The principal points in fire-fighting are briefly summarised below in the form of " DO's " and " DON'TS."

DO

    (i) Break a panel near the lock if it is necessary to force a door.

    (ii) Turn off gas at the main on entering. This will prevent an explosion.

    (iii) Leave electricity " on " but if it is already " off " find out the reason before putting it on again.

    (iv) Start at the top and work downwards when searching a house.

    (v) Exclude oxygen by keeping doors and windows closed when possible.

    (vi) Crawl, don't walk, when in thick smoke.

    (vii) Keep near walls, where floor and stairs are strongest.

    (viii) Attack fires at closest possible range.

    (ix) Attack the heart of a fire.

    (x) Attack oil fires with sand, earth or foam.

    (xi) Before leaving be sure that all fires are out.

    (xii) When leaving turn off electricity at main.

    (xiii) Remember that phosphorus will re-ignite when dry.

    (xiv) Keep all fire-fighting appliances in order.

    (xv) Keep ample supplies of water, YOU CANNOT HAVE TOO MUCH.

DON'T

    (i) Go alone in a smoke-filled building except to save life.

    (ii) Enter a burning building or room, except to save life, without fire-fighting appliances.

    (iii) Play water on electric wiring.

GENERAL

    (i) When in smoke, and looking for a window from which to escape, remember that fire may be reflected from a mirror and make it resemble a window.

    (ii) Make a note of the position of the nearest :—

        (*a*) Fire Station.

        (*b*) Emergency water supplies, e.g., ponds, rivers, etc.

CHAPTER VIII

ELEMENTARY FIRE-FIGHTING EXPERIENCES IN WAR-TIME

During the war, reports on many incidents were received at the Home Office and Scottish Home Department. Some were on the work of Wardens and Police, some related to the Fire Service and some covered the work of the Fire Guard. This chapter contains a selection of war-time experiences in elementary fire-fighting.

All are taken from official reports and each proves that training and constant practice are required to make an efficient fire-fighter. Read them carefully, some apply to fire-fighters who trained and some to those who did not.

A trained man is a valuable help, an untrained one is a liability, not only does he fail to assist others but he has to receive assistance.

Which are YOU going to be?

48. HOLDING A FIRE IN CHECK

A fire broke out in a small factory but was held in check by Wardens and Fire Guards until the arrival of the N.F.S. who, with their major appliances, soon extinguished the blaze. Had this fire gained a hold it would have spread, owing to the direction of the strong wind at the time, and gutted the main shopping centre.

49. DISCIPLINE AND TRAINING

(i) Reports from certain residential areas make it clear that many Fire Guards took shelter with their families and made little attempt to deal with the bombs, many houses being burnt out. This cause of failure lies in the lack of leadership and discipline.

Reports on business premises in the same town state that the parties were at their posts ready to go into action at once. The teams were composed of men working in the same employment who knew one another and were accustomed to working together. They had been properly trained and their equipment was ready to hand. They did excellent work.

The general inference to be drawn is that everything depends on discipline, leadership and training. Very little reliance can be placed on the unco-ordinated efforts of individuals acting without competent leaders or positive orders.

(ii) A small number of incendiary bombs fell on and round a church where there were three Fire Guards on duty. One I.B. penetrated the roof and lodged in the rafters. A Fire Guard got on to the roof (no easy task) and with an axe hacked away at the rafters to dislodge the I.B. which with the burning rafters fell into the nave, as intended, where they were soon dealt with. These Fire Guards had been thoroughly trained.

(iii) Two young nurses, two maids and a middle aged cook comprised a Fire Guard " squad " on duty at a hospital. A number of I.B.'s fell on the roof of the building and in the grounds. Those in the grounds were left to burn out whilst the others were promptly and efficiently tackled with a stirrup pump and the fires extinguished. It was a case showing that good work can be done by trained women Fire Guards.

50. LACK OF WATER

(i) A hospital was lost owing to reliance being placed on the electrically-operated pumps. The electricity supply failed early in the raid. Well trained stirrup pump teams, and an adequate static water supply might have saved the building.

(ii) The Fire Guards in a factory used the bulk of their static water supply on a neighbouring fire, trying to stop it spreading to their own premises. When their own building caught fire, there was not sufficient water to deal with it as the mains had gone. Thus the negligence of the first factory in not making provision for adequate static water supplies resulted in the destruction of both factories.

51. SPREAD OF FIRE

(i) Incendiary bombs fell on the fire-resisting flat roof of a modern steel framed building and were at once dealt with by the Fire Guards. The chief danger to the building lay in the spread of fire from other buildings around, all of which were on fire.

One window faced an alley, 9 ft. wide, across which there was a four storey building of old and combustible construction, which was gutted. A $4\frac{1}{2}''$ brick wall had been built inside the wooden window frame. This frame was entirely burnt away but the interior of the room was unmarked by fire. Had the window not been bricked up there is little doubt that it would have constituted a serious hazard to the building.

(ii) A 50 Kg. phosphorus bomb burst in a terrace house. Four stirrup pump teams went into action and although the back rooms of the house were gutted, the fire was cut off and, not only was spread prevented to the neighbouring premises, but the front rooms were saved.

(iii) Four incendiary bombs penetrated an upper room of a three storey building where a large stock of camouflage netting was stored. This netting, owing to the proofing process, was highly inflammable and almost immediately a fierce fire was raging. Two Fire Guards tackled the fire with a stirrup pump whilst a third man carried water. At a later stage a number of naval ratings arrived and offered assistance.

By relays of water in buckets and by the use of stirrup pumps the fire was fought for nearly an hour, and spread of fire prevented. When the N.F.S. arrived, lengths of hose were run out and the fire was soon under control. This fire was confined entirely to two rooms on the upper floor.

52. PHOSPHORUS

The need for the quick removal of phosphorus splashes from walls, timber and the like, is most important, as it is not only liable to cause further outbreaks of fire but also physical injury to people, particularly children, coming into contact with it unwittingly. In one raid, this clearance was not done for three days and as a result two people received burns.

53. MAKING SURE THE FIRE IS OUT

A small incendiary bomb went through the roof of an unoccupied house and lodged between the rafters and the top ceiling. To gain entry the door had to be forced and the rapidly spreading fire was tackled with stirrup pumps and buckets of water. The fire was apparently extinguished but broke out again some time after the raid. This time the whole of the property was gutted. It is important to make sure that a fire really is out before it is left.

54. THE VALUE OF LEADERSHIP AND TEAM WORK

A modern departmental store of fire-resisting construction, with a fire-resisting roof without roof lights, was entirely surrounded by fire. On two sides the danger was great, as the burning buildings were not more than 10 feet away.

The chief Fire Guard said he had always realised that the windows constituted the chief danger to the building, and had formed the habit of laying out 60 ft. lengths of $\frac{1}{2}''$ hose fed from a large roof tank, together with stirrup pumps and buckets. On alerts, one man was present on each floor and could summon help by means of whistle signals.

When the attack began, the men pulled down the blackout curtains on the exposed windows and removed combustible material from their neighbourhood. They succeeded in preventing more than slight damage by running from window to window and hosing the steel window frames. In two or three places the fire had entered and taken hold of wooden fittings, but energetic action prevented spread.

After the raid the building stood intact, surrounded by an area of complete devastation.

55. STATIC WATER SUPPLIES

Most residents in a heavily raided town had water containers full and readily available, but, even with all this reserve, it became necessary in some areas to draw on the mains. Despite the fact that they were mostly undamaged, the demands of the N.F.S. had so lowered the pressure that in some areas it was impossible to obtain more than a trickle from the taps. It is impossible to store too much water.

56. THE VALUE OF TRAINING

Between two and three thousand incendiary bombs were dropped on a residential area about one-third of a mile long and one hundred yards wide. In some streets there was not a house that was not penetrated by a bomb. A large proportion of the houses had three to five bombs in them, and a church had as many as twenty. There were 127 fires but the Fire Guard was well trained and well led. The N.F.S. received seventeen calls but in only two cases did they have to unroll their hose, and even in these cases an extra stirrup pump might have been sufficient. Not a single house was burnt down though there was heavy damage and many rooms were gutted.

57. WATER AGAIN

A Fire Guard Post for a business premises block was inspected during the early evening and the buckets of water which should have been available on the first floor were discovered in an inner room. The occupier, who kept a hairdressing saloon, explained that his customers might be upset if fire buckets were kept in the saloon or in the passage and that it was his practice to fill the buckets at night. Two more empty buckets were found on the stairs between the first and second floors. Two new bins full of paper and rubbish (which might have been filled with water) were found on the top floor.

There is no prize for knowing what happened when the building was hit by incendiaries that night.

APPENDIX A

STIRRUP PUMP DRILL FOR A TEAM OF FOUR

Drill

The duty party consists of 4 persons who should be numbered 1 to 4, No. 1 is in charge of the Team.

When Moving to Attack a Fire

No. 1 carries out a reconnaissance.

No. 2 carries the pump.

No. 3 carries two filled buckets

No. 4 carries two filled buckets.

On the Order from No. 1

" *Get to work* " No. 1 goes forward with the nozzle.

Nos. 3 and 4 place the buckets where ordered by No. 1 and No. 3 assists No. 1 in running out the hose. He then returns to No. 2 and assisted by No. 4 maintains the water supply. He also keeps in touch with No. 1.

Nos. 2, 3 and 4 exchange duties when required.

No. 2 places the pump in the bucket and pumps a few strokes to fill the hose.

"*Water on*" No. 2 pumps.

"*Water off*" No. 2 stops pumping.

"*Knock off and make up*" Hose is cleared by pumping and gear is made up, the hose being coiled and secured.

CLASSIFIED DETAIL OF DUTIES

No. 1	No. 2	No. 3	No. 4
In charge of team. Makes reconnaissance. Selects position for pump. Goes forward with nozzle to deal with incendiary bomb and resulting fire. Gives order " Water on " and " Water off " as required.	Operates pump. Is relieved by Nos. 3 and 4 when desired.	Lifts hose forward to No. 1. Keeps in touch with No. 1. With No. 4 maintains the water supply and when required relieves No. 2	Assists No. 3 to maintain the water supply. In the case of a long carry brings water supplies to a prearranged point from which No. 3 takes them forward to the pump. Relieves No. 2 when required.

APPENDIX B

STIRRUP PUMP DRILL FOR A TEAM OF THREE

Drill

The duty party consists of 3 persons, who should be numbered 1 to 3. No. 1 is in charge of the team.

When Moving to Attack a Fire

No. 1 carries out reconnaissance.

No. 2 carries the pump.

No. 3 carries two filled buckets.

On the Order from No. 1

" *Get to work* " No. 1 goes forward with nozzle.

No. 3 places the buckets where ordered by No. 1 and assists him in running out the hose. He then returns to No. 2 and maintains the water supply, and relieves No. 2 at the pump when required. He also keeps in touch with No. 1.

No. 2 places the pump in the bucket and pumps a few strokes to fill hose.

"*Water on*" No. 2 pumps.

"*Water off*" No. 2 stops pumping.

"*Knock off and make up*" Hose is cleared by pumping and gear is made up, the hose being coiled and secured.

NOTES

(i) No. 2 maintains water supply when No. 3 is pumping.

(ii) Where man-power allows, a fourth person can be used to maintain the water supply.

If only two persons are available, No. 1 carries the pump, and No. 2 carries 2 filled water containers. Where only one person is available, he should take the pump and one bucket of water, and would have to operate the nozzle from the pumping position.

CLASSIFIED DETAIL OF DUTIES

No. 1	No. 2	No. 3
Is in charge of team. Makes reconnaissance. Selects position for pump. Goes forward with nozzle to deal with incendiary bomb and resulting fire. Gives orders " Water on" or " Water off " as required.	Operates pump. No. 3 relieves him when desired.	Lifts hose forward to No. 1 ; maintains water supply and relieves No. 2 as necessary ; keeps in touch with No. 1.

HOME OFFICE

CIVIL DEFENCE

Manual of Basic Training
VOLUME II

BASIC
FIRST AID

PAMPHLET No. 3

(*Reprinted* 1951 *incorporating Amendments No.* 1)

LONDON: HIS MAJESTY'S STATIONERY OFFICE
1949

PRICE 1s. 3d. NET

GENERAL PREFACE

The series of Civil Defence handbooks and pamphlets is produced under the authority of the Home Secretary by the Civil Defence Department of the Home Office with the assistance of and in co-operation with the Secretary of State for Scotland and other Ministers concerned.

Measures for safeguarding the civil population against the effects of war which these publications describe, have become an essential part of the defensive organisation of this country. The need for them is not related to any belief that war is imminent. It is just as necessary that preparations for Civil Defence should be made in time of peace as it is that preparations should be made for the Armed Forces.

The publications cover, as far as is possible, measures which can be taken to mitigate the effects of all modern forms of attack. Any scheme of Civil Defence, if it is to be efficient, must be up-to-date and must take account of all the various weapons which might become available. The scale of bombing experienced in Great Britain during the 1939-45 war might be considerably exceeded in any future war, and types ot weapons and tactics which were not experienced in this country might conceivably be used against it in the future. It does not follow that any one of the weapons, e.g. the atomic bomb, will necessarily be used, and it is most important that a proper balance is held between what is likely and what is possible.

The use of poison gas in war was forbidden by the Geneva Gas Protocol of 1925, to which this country and all the other countries of the Western Union were parties. At the outbreak of a war, His Majesty's Government would try to secure an undertaking from the enemy not to use poison gas. Nevertheless the risk of poison gas being used remains a possibility and cannot be disregarded any more than can certain further developments in other scientific fields.

The publications are designed to describe not only precautionary schemes which experience in the last war proved to be extremely effective in preventing avoidable injury and loss of life, or widespread dislocation of national industries, but also the training, both technical and tactical, which will be required of the personnel of the Civil Defence Corps if they are to be ready effectively to play their part if war should ever break out. The publications aim at giving the best available information on methods of defence against all the various weapons. Information is not complete in respect of some of these weapons and the best methods of countering them, but as results of experimental work and other investigations mature, they will be revised and added to from time to time so that the Civil Defence Corps may be kept up-to-date and training may be on the most modern and experienced lines.

Binders for the series of Civil Defence publications are available from H.M. Stationery Office, price 1s. 6d. net (by post 1s. 8d.).

CONTENTS

NOTE

The pagination of this pamphlet is not continuous as it may be necessary to introduce new pages at a later date.

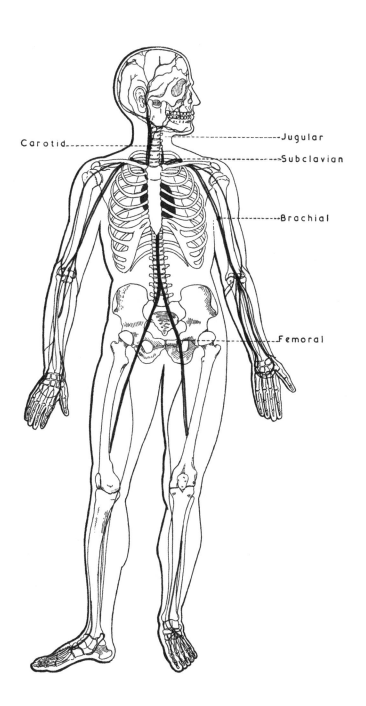

Carotid - Jugular

- - - Subclavian

- - - - - - - - - Brachial

- - - - - - - - - - - - - Femoral

CHAPTER I

POINTS TO REMEMBER

1. (*a*) **Symptoms**—are abnormal sensations felt by a patient and complained about.

(*b*) **Signs**—are abnormal conditions found in a patient on examination.

2. The Pulse

Every time the heart beats it pumps blood into elastic walled tubes called arteries which carry the blood to every part of the body. The blood travels along as a wave distending each portion of the tubes as it reaches it with a jerk or jolt which can be felt, or even seen, in certain arteries which lie upon bones and are near the surface. This is called the " pulse." As the normal heart beats 72 times every minute the pulse does the same. This is known as the " *Pulse rate.*"

The easiest method of feeling the pulse is to place the tips of the fingers on the front of the forearm of a person just above the bend of the wrist and on the thumb side. The number of beats of the pulse per minute is timed by the second hand of a watch.

3. Pressure points to stop bleeding from Arteries

Imagine the various blood tubes (arteries) to be like hosepipes. If you step upon a hosepipe when water is flowing through it and compress it against a hard substance like stone or brick you will stop the flow of water so long as you keep your foot upon the pipe. In the same way if you compress an artery with your fingers against a hard substance, in this case a bone, you will stop blood from flowing through it.

The places where you can compress arteries against bones are known as *Pressure points.* You must remember these places and know exactly where to find them.

A few of the most important as described below is all you need to know.

(*i*) *In the Neck*

Severe bleeding in the neck will be coming from an artery called the Carotid, and you must compress this artery to stop the bleeding.

T O D O T H I S. Lay the patient down and kneel by his injured side facing his head. If the wound is on the left side grasp the nape of his neck with the fingers of your right hand at the back and your thumb in front below the wound about $1\frac{1}{2}$ inches above where the collar bone meets the breast bone, on a line running between this point and the angle of the jaw, as shown in Fig. 1. When you feel the artery beating press it backwards against the spine with your thumb, taking care not to press upon the windpipe, and to *use only enough force to stop the bleeding.* There is a carotid artery on each side of the neck, but *on no account must you compress both arteries at the same time, otherwise you will kill your patient.* If the wound is on the right side of the neck you must of course use your left hand instead of your right.

(*ii*) *Injury to Jugular Vein*

The Jugular vein bringing blood back to the heart which runs alongside the Carotid artery is also usually wounded at the same time and

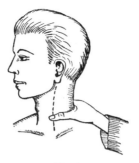

Fig. 1
Compression of Carotid Artery.

bleeds profusely. Pressure upon the artery alone will not stop this. To do so spread out the fingers and thumb of your free hand beneath the patient's chin, with the fingers behind the neck, and press your thumb *above the wound* (i.e., nearer to the head) on the same line and in the same way as you are doing for the artery with the other thumb.

(iii) In the Upper Limb

Severe bleeding from the shoulder or armpit can be stopped by compressing an artery (subclavian) which lies below the middle of the collar bone.

TO DO THIS. Lay the patient down and kneel at the side of the injured shoulder facing his head. Quickly but gently uncover the upper part of his chest. If the injury is on the left side draw the patient's head towards you with your left hand to relax the neck muscles. Place your right palm on his shoulder with the fingers behind and press downwards and backwards with your thumb upon the artery which lies in the hollow above the middle of the collar bone, *remembering not to use too much force.* If you are on the right spot the bleeding will stop. Both thumbs may be used, as this is less tiring, in which case, without moving the right hand place the palm and fingers of your left hand on the patient's chest and press the thumb on top of the other. Do not let your hands and arms obstruct the application of a dressing (*See Fig.* 2).

N.B.—With a wound on the right side your hands will of course be reversed.

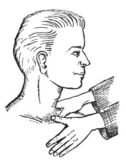

Fig. 2
Compression of Subclavian Artery.

4

(iv) *In the Arm and Hand*

If blood is coming from a wound in the arm below the shoulder and cannot be stopped by ordinary means you must do this by compressing an artery (brachial) in the upper arm.

TO DO THIS. Make the patient sit or lie down and place yourself at the side of or behind him. If the left arm is bleeding, grasp his left wrist with your left hand and bend the elbow. Pass the fingers of your right hand round the under side of the middle of the upper arm so that the fingers are on the inside and the thumb on the outside. Feel for the artery beating in the groove below the biceps muscle (the line of the artery roughly corresponds to the inner seam of a coat sleeve above the elbow), and press it outwards, i.e. towards you, against the bone. *Gentle pressure is sufficient.*

N.B.—If the injury is on the right side reverse your hands. (*See Fig.* 3.)

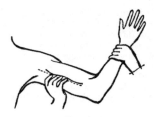

Fig. 3
Compression of Brachial Artery.

(v) *In the Groin*

Bleeding from a large artery (femoral) in the thigh is *extremely dangerous* as blood spurts out with great force. Unless you can compress this artery within a short time of the injury the casualty will die from loss of blood.

TO DO THIS. Lay the patient down flat and kneel by his injured side facing either his feet or his head. Raise the thigh and bend the

Fig. 4
Compression of Femoral Artery.

knee so that the foot remains upon the ground. The crease in the clothing at the top of the thigh indicates the *line of the groin*.

Encircle the upper end of the thigh with the palms and fingers of your two hands so that the thumbs are on the front of the thigh and the fingers at the back. With one thumb feel for the beating of the artery in the centre of the line of the groin. When you feel it place the other thumb on top of the first and press the artery downwards with both thumbs against the hip bone upon which it lies, *using only just enough pressure to stop the bleeding (See Fig. 4)*.

4. Respiration

Respiration means breathing. The normal healthy person breathes 15 times every minute. To find out how many times a person is breathing lay him down and place your hand lightly upon his chest or belly. See how many times your hand rises and falls in one minute and time this with the second hand of your watch. Each time your hand rises and falls constitutes one breath. The number of times a person breathes per minute is called the " *Respiration rate*."

CHAPTER II

FIRST AID AND THE HANDLING OF CASUALTIES

11. General Principles

At any time during or after enemy air raids you may be called upon to give first aid to an injured person, or one who is only frightened and suffering from shock, though uninjured. It is up to you to do what you can on the spot to deal with immediate danger to his life, and to prevent any injury or condition from becoming worse.

Do not try to do more than is absolutely necessary ; the longer you take over superfluous things the longer is the delay before your patient is safely in a hospital. At an incident you may find a number of casualties requiring your attention. Do not at once start to work on the first casualty you see, who may be only slightly injured, but make a rapid survey of the situation, find out all you can from onlookers as to how the incident happened ; enquire about the presence of other casualties whom you cannot see, and note any possible sources of danger, such as crumbling buildings, fires, broken gas and water mains and the like. Decide which of the casualties need your help most urgently and attend to them first, doing your work in a methodical manner which will give you self-confidence and inspire the others. A casualty may be bleeding profusely from a wound ; the bleeding must be stopped at once and the wound dressed. A bone or bones may be broken ; these must be attended to. Pain must be relieved. Shock must be minimised as far as possible. Burns must be treated. A man may be wholly or partly buried in debris and when extricated be found to have stopped breathing. Unless you can quickly remove the cause of his stoppage of breathing and give him artificial respiration he will die from suffocation. Unconscious casualties are frequently met with, and you can do a great deal for them if you apply your knowledge and use your common sense. Always remember that *common sense and initiative play a very important part in first aid.*

When your first aid treatment is completed you must decide what to do with the casualty. All cases which you consider serious, or seem in a bad way, must be sent on a stretcher in an ambulance to hospital ; the quicker they reach there after being made safe to travel the better chance they will have of ultimate recovery.

Do not rely entirely upon your own opinion if you have any doubt as to whether you are doing right or not, but consult a doctor, if one is easily available at an incident, or a fellow worker whose knowledge and experience are superior to yours, as soon as you can.

A condition known as shock is present to some extent in every casualty, even affecting the uninjured or only slightly injured. Its consideration is of the greatest importance in carrying out first aid measures, as these are designed to protect casualties from the effects of shock and to minimise it as far as possible.

Never forget that a casualty is a *human being* who has had a terrifying experience and suffered a great shock. It is your duty as a person

11

rendering first aid to do all in your power to gain the confidence of an injured person by firm but gentle handling, and to relieve his anxiety by sympathy and convincing reassurance.

To sum up

In dealing with casualties at an incident your chief aims must be :—

(i) To preserve life by correct and prompt action.

(ii) To protect from further shock.

(iii) To prevent an injury from becoming worse by careful handling and by reassurance.

(iv) To arrange for early removal to shelter and skilled care.

(v) *Above all* you must realise that *speed can be combined with gentleness and care.*

CHAPTER III

SHOCK

14. Definition of Shock

SHOCK is the chief cause of death among air raid casualties when the victims are not killed outright.

In its simplest everyday form shock is seen when a person is suddenly startled by the receipt of bad news, seeing a horrible sight, by a sudden blow or fall however caused, and the like. The shock may be sufficient to cause him to faint even though there is no obvious injury, or indeed, any injury at all. People usually recover rapidly from this kind of shock with appropriate treatment, although cases do occur when it causes death by itself, especially in elderly people, young children, and people with weak hearts.

A far more serious type of shock is usually met with in air raid casualties and is a true " killer." It occurs with *every* injured person to a more or less extent, and the danger to his life depends largely upon the severity of his injury. Severe wounds causing loss of much blood ; injuries, whether bones are broken or not, caused by crushing ; severe burns, breaking of the bones of the thigh or back are examples of injuries which produce intense shock, and may prove fatal. It is therefore of extreme importance for you to study and remember the symptoms and signs of shock so that you will be able to recognise and treat it properly.

15. Symptoms and Signs of Shock

A person may feel giddy, cold and sick, and actually vomit. He may lose consciousness, wholly or partly, and fall down. His *skin* becomes pale, cold and clammy, and beads of perspiration may stand out on his forehead. If he becomes worse the colour of the skin changes to blueish grey, and later, in severe cases, to a leaden colour, most noticeable in the lips and lobes of the ears.

HIS PULSE beats faster than normal, i.e. more than 72 times per minute, and is weaker and more difficult to feel. In severe cases of shock the *pulse* is the most important thing for a first aider to note. If it is beating say 100 times to the minute and does not get less but, on the contrary, tends to increase this is a danger sign. If it increases rapidly (up to say 150-180 times a minute) and becomes harder to feel the patient is in a bad way and is probably bleeding internally.

BREATHING is usually quiet, shallow and often hardly noticeable, generally quicker than normal, i.e. more than 15 times to the minute. In bad cases of shock in which there is internal bleeding a condition known as " air hunger " occurs. (This is described later under " bleeding.")

THE EYES may have a glassy stare and the pupils are larger than normal ; the larger the pupils the more serious the condition.

A SHOCKED PERSON may be alert and apprehensive, even excitable if he is conscious, but as his condition gets worse he becomes

17

confused and may be unable to reply to even the simplest questions, gradually or quickly relapsing into complete unconsciousness.

All the above symptoms and signs will be more pronounced if bleeding is coming from a wound outside or inside the body, and also if at the time of his injury the casualty was tired, cold, hungry and afraid.

16. Treatment of Shock

Lay the patient down gently with his head low and turned to one side, unless he has an injury to his head or chest, in which case raise his head and shoulders and support them. *Loosen* clothing round his neck and waist. In most simple fainting attacks this and keeping the patient warm is all that is needed and he soon recovers. If he is conscious and only feels faint it is generally sufficient to sit him up and get him to bend forward with his head between his knees until he feels better. Support him if necessary and give him plenty of air.

Stop any bleeding from an External Wound

Relieve pain by placing the patient in the position most comfortable to him and support any injured part. *Keep him warm* by blankets or clothing and by covered hot water bottles at his feet and sides of chest. (*N.B.*—Hot water bottles must not be too warm, and must be protected so that they do not burn the patient.)

Always remember that a shocked casualty must never be overwarmed to the extent of sweating as this increases shock.

The foot of the stretcher upon which the casualty is lying may be raised about 9 inches off the ground and supported on such things as a roll of blanket, sandbags or bricks.

Give hot, sweet tea, coffee or cocoa if the patient is conscious and can swallow. A teaspoonful of sal volatile in the equivalent of a wine glassful of water is also useful. *On no account* give anything to drink if there is a wound in the abdomen or chest, or you suspect internal bleeding. *Do not give any alcohol.*

Remember what you have learnt about *handling, reassuring* and *cheering up* the casualty. Relieve his anxiety about the fate of relatives and friends who were with him at the time of his injury. Do not leave him alone while you are waiting for him to be taken to hospital, but get someone to stay with him and put him in a sheltered place if possible, even if it is only behind a piece of masonry. Do not let bystanders worry him.

Any bad case of shock, or one in which you have any doubt, *must be sent to hospital on a stretcher in an ambulance as soon as possible* after you have attended to him. If a doctor is available at an incident get him to see the patient but lose no time in doing so ; *every second of delay in getting the patient to hospital is bad for him.*

CHAPTER IV

BANDAGES, SLINGS AND DRESSINGS

20. The Triangular Bandage and its uses

This bandage is made by taking a piece of calico or linen, usually 40 inches square and cutting it into two pieces from one corner to another, thus making two triangles, each of which is one bandage.

The longest edge is called " the lower border " or " base," the pointed end opposite to it " the point," and the two corners " the ends."

Triangular bandages are used in the following ways :—

(*a*) As a " whole-cloth," i.e. fully spread out.

(*b*) As a " broad-fold," by bringing the point to the middle of the lower border and then folding over again in the same way.

(*c*) As a "narrow-fold," by folding a broad-fold once, long edge to long edge (*See Figs.* 5, 6, 7 and 8).

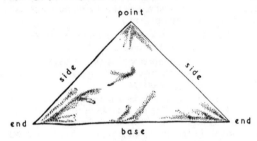

Fig. 5
Whole-Cloth Triangular Bandage.

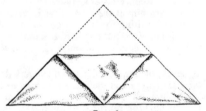

Fig. 6
Once Folded Bandage.

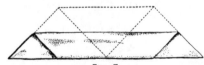

Fig. 7
Broad-Fold Bandage.

23

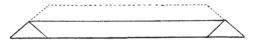

Fig. 8
Narrow-Fold Bandage.

TRIANGULAR BANDAGES are used to keep dressings or splints in position, to afford support to an injured part as a sling, to bind a broken lower limb to its fellow or a broken upper limb to the trunk. They are also used to make pressure to arrest bleeding, and are useful in preventing swelling from such injuries as a badly sprained ankle.

N.B.—When applying bandages and slings it is to be remembered that they must always be tied with a "*reef-knot*," never with a "*granny*".

To tie a reef-knot take one end of a bandage in each hand, pass the end in the right hand over that in the left and tie a single knot. Pass the end in the left hand over that in the right and complete the knot. The rule for tying a reef-knot is "*right over left, left over right.*"

To fasten a splint to a limb broad or narrow-fold bandages can be used. Place the centre of the bandage over the splint, pass the ends round the limb, cross them on the inside and tie off on the outside over the splint.

A few examples of how a triangular bandage is used as a bandage are given below. Further information can be obtained from the diagrams.

The top of the head

Lay the centre of an unfolded (whole-cloth) bandage on the dressing on top of the head so that the point faces the back of the head and its lower border lies along the forehead, just above the eyebrows. Make a short fold in the lower border and pass the two ends round the back of the head above the ears. Cross the ends over the point of the bandage,

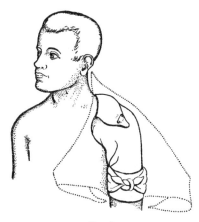

Fig. 9
Application of Shoulder Bandage.

24

bring them to the front again and tie off in the middle of the forehead. Place a hand on the head to steady the dressing and pull the point down until the bandage is taut on top of the head. Bring the point up over the ends and pin on top of the head.

The Shoulder

Lay the centre of an unfolded bandage on the top of the shoulder over the dressing with the point upwards and the lower border across the middle of the upper arm. Fold in the lower border, carry the ends round the arm, cross them, bring them to the front again and tie off.

Support the arm in a small arm sling, draw the point of the bandage under the sling at the neck, fold it over and pin it to the bandage on the shoulder (*See Fig. 9*).

The Hip

Pass a narrow-fold bandage round the waist and tie it. Take an unfolded triangular bandage and place it with its centre over the dressing on a hip, point upwards, and its lower border lying across the thigh. Pass the ends round the thigh, cross them, bring them to the front and tie off on the outer side of the thigh.

Draw the point up under the bandage at the waist, turn it down and pin it to the portion on the hip (*See Fig. 10*).

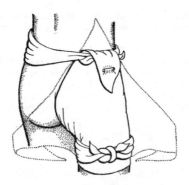

Fig. 10

Application of Bandage to Hip.

Triangular bandages used as slings

Examples of the application of slings are given below (*See Figs. 11, 12, 13, 14 and 15*). Two types most commonly used are described.

The Large Arm Sling

With the point of a whole-cloth bandage in one hand and one end in the other, face the patient and lay the bandage against his body with one end over the shoulder on the sound side and the point towards his injured side. Pass the upper end round behind his neck and allow the free end to hang over the collar bone on the injured side for about three inches. Gently bend the elbow of the injured arm and place the forearm

25

and hand on the centre of the bandage with the hand a little higher than the elbow. Support the arm with one hand while you gather up the free lower end and tie it to the end hanging over the collar bone. Bring the point round over the elbow and fix it to the front of the bandage with one or more safety pins.

The Collar and Cuff Sling

This is made by placing a " *clove hitch* " over the hand and round the wrist and fastening the free ends round the neck.

TO MAKE A CLOVE HITCH take a narrow-fold bandage and make one loop towards the centre with the free end in your right hand *in front*. Now make another similar loop with the free end in your left hand *behind* and place the two loops together with the second in front of the first. Slip the loop thus formed over the hand on to the wrist and pull the two free ends tight for tying. A clove hitch knot does not tighten when both ends are pulled, otherwise it might constrict blood vessels in the wrist.

Improvised Slings

Slings can be improvised by pinning the sleeve on the injured side to the coat ; by turning up the lower edge of the coat and pinning it ; by putting the hand inside the coat or waistcoat and buttoning it, or by using scarves, ties, strips of clothing or belts.

Fig. 11

Application of Large Arm Sling (First Stage).

26

Fig. 12
Application of Large Arm
Sling—Completed.

Fig. 13
Application of Small Arm Sling.

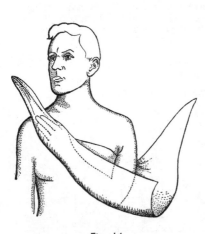

Fig. 14
Application of St. John Sling (First Stage).

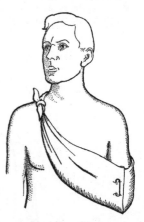

Fig. 15
Application of St. John
Sling—Completed.

21. The Rubber Bandage

This consists of a length of elastic about four feet long and two and a half inches wide with two tapes sewn at one end for tying (*See Fig.* 16). This can be used to stop bleeding by winding it round a limb with even pressure immediately above the dressing (i.e. between the heart and the wound), and with each turn over the previous one. The tapes are tied securely round the limb over the bandage, taking care that this does not slip while the knots are being tied. A rubber bandage *must never be hidden by a dressing and it must be loosened at frequent intervals, of not more than fifteen minutes,* to see if the bleeding has stopped.

This is of *extreme importance* and failure to do it may result in the patient losing his limb from gangrene.

A rubber bandage must be applied *over* a dressing to cover the stump of a limb which has been torn off, in order to stop bleeding. It should be applied firmly as near to the edge of the stump as possible without a danger of its falling off. *When used for this purpose it must not be loosened at intervals*, but left in position.

Fig. 16

Rubber Bandage.

22. Dressings

A dressing usually consists of layers of lint or gauze, on top of which is a thick pad of cotton wool and a bandage which keeps the dressing in position.

Sterilised Pad Dressings.

Certain types of made up pad dressings consisting of the above, previously sterilised and wrapped ready for use in packets are used for casualties at incidents. (*See Figs.* 17, 18, 19, 20 *and* 21.)

They are :—

    (i) *Large and Medium first aid dressings.*

    (ii) *Mine dressings.*

    (iii) *Shell dressings.*

The first field dressing carried by every soldier is an example of this form of dressing.

If none of these are available a clean, freshly folded pocket handkerchief, a clean triangular bandage used as a pad (with their inner surfaces next to the wound), or a clean piece of paper or an envelope opened up with its inner clean surface next to the wound may be used as purely temporary substitutes.

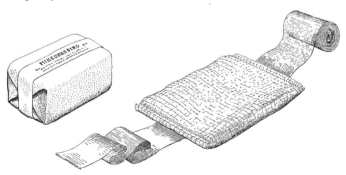

Fig. 17

Made up Pad Dressing—Mine Dressing.

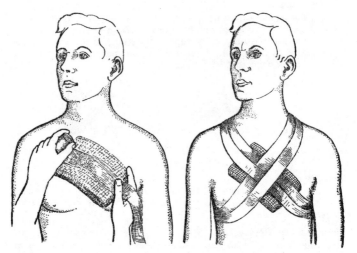

Fig. 18
Application of Pad Dressing to Chest.

Fig. 19
Application of Pad Dressing
to Chest—Completed.

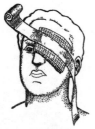

Fig. 20
Application of Pad Dressing
to Eye Injury.

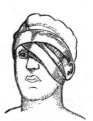

Fig. 21
Application of Pad Dressing
to Eye Injury—Completed.

CHAPTER V

BLEEDING (HAEMORRHAGE)

26. Two Types of Bleeding

(i) *External Bleeding*

Bleeding may be either slight or severe, and this you should be able to recognise at once if it is coming from a wound. When you see blood escaping this is *external bleeding*.

Blood may either spurt out or flow in a small or large stream. In any case your job is to stop it as soon as possible, and it stands to reason that if blood is spurting out or flowing in a large stream, the sooner you stop it the better, otherwise your casualty will die from loss of blood.

(ii) *Internal Bleeding*

There is another kind of bleeding, which is not coming from a wound which you can see, but which, for all that, can be equally or even more dangerous. This is when bleeding occurs inside the belly, the chest, or the skull and is called *internal bleeding*.

This form of bleeding can be classified under two headings :—

> *Visible* (which you can see).
>
> *Concealed* (which you cannot see).

Examples of *visible internal bleeding* are :—

> (*a*) An injury to the belly which may cause blood to be passed in the motions or vomited.
>
> (*b*) An injury to the chest which may cause a person to cough up blood.
>
> (*c*) An injury to the skull which may cause bleeding from the nose or ears.

CONCEALED INTERNAL BLEEDING may occur in any of the above parts without any external wound or any signs of bleeding, and you will only be able to suspect that it is taking place from certain symptoms and signs which it produces in a person. Even though your attention may be taken up with bleeding from an external wound, you must never lose sight of the possibility of *concealed internal bleeding* occurring at the same time, especially if your patient seems worse than his external wound warrants, as this may be comparatively trivial.

Remember that of these two types *concealed internal bleeding* is the more dangerous, and many lives are lost through failure to recognise it in time.

27. Symptoms and Signs of Bleeding

All the symptoms and signs of shock may be present in a person suffering from loss of blood, and their severity largely depends upon the amount of blood lost.

Two or three symptoms and signs however are prominent when a great deal of blood has been lost. They are :—

AIR HUNGER. In this condition the patient feels that he cannot get enough air and is being suffocated. He becomes intensely distressed and may struggle violently, tearing at his clothing and throat in the effort to obtain more air. Air hunger should always make you suspect bleeding—probably internal.

THIRST is often very marked and bitterly complained of.

BUZZING IN THE EARS and dimness of vision occur later and constitute a very grave sign, often heralding the approach of complete unconsciousness and death.

28. Treatment of External Bleeding

Lay the patient down flat unless his head or a limb are bleeding, in which case raise the part and prop it up. Blood will then not be able to flow so easily as it has to be pumped uphill from the heart. *Do not raise a limb with a broken bone.*

Your immediate object is to stop the bleeding as soon as possible by putting pressure on the bleeding spot. To do this :—

Expose the bleeding point by opening or cutting off clothing, but do not needlessly expose the patient or remove or destroy more clothing than is necessary.

Remove any pieces of glass, metal, stone or other debris lying near the wound, but *do not* attempt to touch any embedded in the wound.

If there are no such pieces and you are certain that no bone is broken, press with your fingers or thumb directly on the bleeding point and keep them there while a dressing is being made ready. If a clean handkerchief or a dressing is immediately available place this on the wound before you apply pressure, but speed in stopping the bleeding is the great necessity and no time should be wasted.

Take one of the first aid dressings in sealed packets called " mine dressings " or " shell dressings." Get someone to open up a packet, hold the bandage on each side of the pad, put the pad directly on the bleeding point in place of your fingers, and bandage it firmly so that the pad is pressed tightly on the wound. Press your fingers again on the dressing until the bleeding seems to have stopped. If blood comes through and soaks the dressing, do not take it off but put another on top and bandage even more firmly.

If there are substances sticking in the wound and it is in a limb, you cannot press your fingers upon it, but you can stop the bleeding by winding a *rubber bandage* round and round the limb above the wound (i.e. between the wound and the heart) and tying it firmly with the tapes (remembering what you have been told about loosening it at intervals). You must not put a pad dressing on to a wound which has pieces of glass or other substances sticking into it, as this will drive the pieces further into the wound, so take several sterilised pad dressings and build up a soft mound round the wound with them to take off the pressure, after which you can apply another sterilised pad dressing on the wound and bandage lightly with impunity. This is known as a *built up dressing* and can also be used in bleeding from other than a limb (*See Fig.* 22).

In severe cases where blood is spurting from a wound, or where blood is dripping through a dressing already applied, put on a second or even third dressing and bandage firmly. If bleeding continues use pressure with your fingers or thumb on the correct *pressure point* for that part.

Release your pressure gradually to see if the bleeding has stopped, *but take care to use only enough pressure to stop it.*

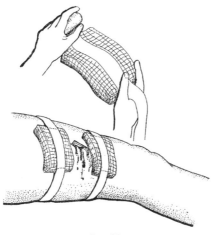

Fig. 22
Application of " Built-up " Dressing.

Get the patient to hospital as a stretcher case in an ambulance as soon as possible, and, if you suspect that he may still be bleeding or likely to, accompany him to keep up pressure on the pressure point until the hospital is reached. Write an H on a label or piece of paper and tie it to him.

29.　Treatment of Internal Bleeding

As soon as you decide that a casualty is bleeding internally, you must take all measures to protect him from further shock and send him as a stretcher case in an ambulance to hospital as soon as possible. Do not put hot water bottles near any part from which you think blood may be coming, or give him anything to drink, even if he is very thirsty.

Use the utmost care in handling and moving him and write an X on a label or piece of paper which you should affix to him.

CHAPTER VI

WOUNDS

33. Types of Wounds

Many kinds of wounds are met with among air raid casualties, ranging from minor cuts and bruises to limbs torn off or large gaping wounds in other parts of the body. The following are examples :—

(i) LACERATED wounds are caused by pieces of jagged metal from bombs, by flying debris, or when a person is blown by blast against some unyielding sharp object. These wounds are usually large and may do serious damage to the trunk and internal organs ; limbs are frequently torn off. Owing to the intense shock which such wounds produce there may be little bleeding either external or internal at first, but it will come on as the casualty recovers from his shock.

(ii) PUNCTURED wounds are caused by small fragments of bombs which penetrate the skin and may damage internal organs. They may also be caused by pieces of glass, brick, stone, metal or wood. The wounds they make on the skin may appear trivial but internal bleeding often occurs with severe shock.

(iii) PENETRATING AND PERFORATING. Penetrating wounds are caused by massive bomb splinters and are more often found in persons near to the explosion of a bomb with no intervening structure as a protection. They may also be caused by broken glass, flying rubble or by machine gun or rifle bullets.

In a *penetrating* wound the missile is retained in the body ; in a *perforating* wound it passes right through the body, leaving an entrance and an exit wound.

(iv) CONTUSED WOUNDS are caused by blunt articles such as falling beams and may be associated with abrasions with little damage to the skin but extensive damage by crushing and bruising to the underlying muscles and internal organs. Such a wound is also caused when people are flung against a hard substance by blast.

(v) WOUNDS OF THE EYE are common and most frequently caused by flying fragments of broken glass or by pieces of debris, stones or bricks. Fire Service personnel are frequent sufferers from this form of injury.

(vi) BURNS AND CRUSHING INJURY which will be dealt with later.

(vii) COMPLICATIONS. A majority of wounds are accompanied by *bleeding ;* some are associated with *broken bones ;* all injuries in which the skin is broken are liable to poisoning by germs, and all casualties whatever their injury may be will suffer from some degree of *shock* which may be slight or severe.

Remembering these facts should provide you with a clue for the correct first aid treatment of wounds, and enable you to put into practice what you have learnt.

34. First Aid Treatment of Wounds

As in cases of bleeding get the casualty to lie or sit down.

Stop Bleeding.

Protect from further shock.

Treat broken bones if present.

Cover the wound as quickly as possible with a clean dry dressing.

Never attempt to cleanse a wound at an incident. In exceptional cases where there is extensive damage and severe shock a dressing may be applied through tears in the clothing to avoid further uncovering of the wound. This will help to keep germs out of the wound and will ease pain.

Be careful not to waste time in putting dressings on multiple unimportant wounds which are not a danger to life in themselves but the shock from them is—you will be delaying the removal of the patient to hospital by so doing.

DRESSINGS AND BANDAGES.

    (*a*) First aid dressings, large and medium.

    (*b*) Mine dressings.

    (*c*) Shell dressings.

    (*d*) Triangular bandages.

Apply one of these as described for the treatment of external bleeding. If a limb is injured support it with one of the triangular bandages used as a sling after applying the dressing. Do not stint the dressings. If you are dealing with a large wound apply a large dressing (e.g. shell dressing) or several of them. The casualty will be grateful for the protection and warmth and they will ease the pain.

35. Treatment of Special Wounds

A few hints are necessary for the first aid treatment of special wounds which may be encountered, such as :—

(i) Wound of the Belly (Abdomen)

The most common injury in air raids is a penetrating wound of the belly wall by pieces of metal, fragments of glass, stones or rubble which have entered it from the front. In cases where a person has been lying or crouching down when hit the missile may enter the belly through the buttock or back and first aiders may miss this wound if they suspect an internal injury to the belly and only look for a wound in front. If the belly wall is opened up the intestines will protrude and this greatly adds to the severe shock from which the casualty is suffering. Any wound of the belly must be regarded as extremely serious as it may prove fatal within a short time.

The chief dangers are :—

Internal bleeding.

Shock.

Blood poisoning caused at the time of the injury by germs which may cause death at a later date.

First Aid Treatment

Lay the patient down on his back on a folded blanket or articles of clothing with his knees drawn up and a rolled up blanket or coat beneath them. Support his head and shoulders on pillows, folded blankets or greatcoats piled upon one another. This prevents more intestines from coming out if any have already done so. Put a protected hot water bottle (*N.B.*—not too hot) at his feet and between his thighs— *do not place one near the wound.* Wrap him in blankets leaving a space for the wound to be dressed.

Dress the external wound. If intestines are protruding *do not* attempt to touch them or push them in again but cover them at once with a large first aid dressing (preferably shell) and bandage firmly but not too tightly in position. A second dressing may be applied on top of the first and the two kept together by a broad-fold triangular bandage over both and the previous bandages. *Now* cover the abdomen with a blanket (*See Fig.* 23).

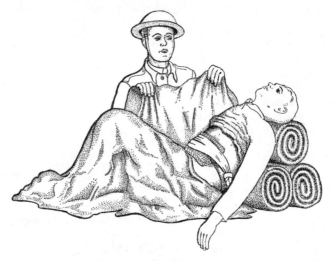

Fig. 23
Treatment of Wound of Belly.

If no intestines are protruding treat the patient as above whether the wound is horizontal or vertical.

Do not give anything by the mouth.

Get the patient to hospital lying on a stretcher in an ambulance as soon as you possibly can, but do not move him unnecessarily until he is ready to be placed in the ambulance. Move him with the utmost care and gentleness, as every movement increases his shock. *Call a doctor* to see the casualty if one is available. *Tie on a label and mark it with an X.*

(ii) Wounds of the Chest

Penetrating wounds of the chest by pieces of metal, glass, stones or rubble may prove rapidly fatal from severe injury to a vital organ, such as the heart or lungs, or from internal bleeding.

An example of a serious injury to the chest is when air enters it from without, through a wound, and causes the lung on that side to collapse. This may produce what is known as a " *sucking wound* " as when the patient breathes in and out air is sucked into and blown out of the chest with a whistling sound. Breathing becomes increasingly difficult as the lung is pressed upon by the air and tends to collapse further, and the patient's life is in danger.

Ribs may be broken with or without any external wound, and their jagged sharp broken ends may do a great deal of damage to the contents of the chest especially the lungs, causing very profuse bleeding, either external or internal.

The chief dangers are :—

    (1) *Bleeding.*

    (2) *Shock.*

First Aid Treatment

Lay the patient down on his back on a folded blanket inclined towards the injured side, with his shoulders slightly raised, and place a second folded blanket lengthwise at his back as a support. Loosen any tight clothing round his neck and waist. Put a protected hot water bottle between his feet and thighs *but not near his chest.* Wrap him in blankets.

Place the arm on the injured side in a large arm sling or support it on a bundle of clothing.

Dress any external wound. If air is being sucked in and blown out of the chest put a large pad dressing over the wound and bandage it lightly round the chest.

Do not give anything to drink.

Get the patient to hospital on a stretcher in an ambulance as quickly as possible and tie a label on him with an X marked upon it.

HANDLE THE PATIENT WITH THE UTMOST CARE.

(iii) Wounds of the Eyes

These may be caused by particles of dust, stones or wood blown into the eyes, or more serious injuries may be due to fragments of metal from bombs or by splinters of glass which have penetrated the eyeball. The pain these injuries produce, whatever they are, is intense and shock is often very marked.

First Aid Treatment

Do not attempt to examine the eyes at an incident or to remove any particles which may have got into them. Your hands will be dirty and you will only do more harm than good by trying to open the eyes to see what the damage is.

Never attempt to wash out the eyes but cover one or both eyes if affected with a dressing and bandage lightly but securely in position. (*N.B.*—The only exception is in the case of contamination of the eyes by mustard gas when they should be washed out thoroughly with water as soon as possible.)

Protect the casualty from further shock and send him to hospital as a stretcher case as soon as you can. There he will receive expert treatment by an eye specialist.

CHAPTER VII

FRACTURES

SEE DIAGRAM OF SKELETON

41. Cause of Fractures

A fracture is a broken bone. Those fractures with which you are principally concerned are caused by :—

(i) DIRECT VIOLENCE

When a missile such as a bomb splinter, a piece of brick or falling debris strikes a bone and breaks it at the point where it is struck this is known as a " fracture by direct violence."

(ii) INDIRECT VIOLENCE

A bone may be broken at some distance from the place where violence is actually applied. For example if a man falls heavily on an outstretched hand he may break the collar bone on that side without injuring the hand ; a person jumping from a height and landing on his feet with his legs held stiffly may break his back. This is known as a " fracture by indirect violence."

42. Types of Fractures which you must be able to recognise are :—

(i) A CLOSED OR SIMPLE FRACTURE.

This results from an injury which breaks a bone without causing any external wound at the site of the break.

(ii) AN OPEN OR COMPOUND FRACTURE.

With this type there is a wound of the skin at the site of the fracture, and this allows communication between the outside air and the broken bone, hence the term " open."

(iii) A COMPLICATED FRACTURE.

When the sharp jagged ends of a broken bone damage an internal organ such as the brain or lungs, or tear some important blood vessel or nerve, this is known as a " complicated fracture."

A " closed " fracture may be made " complicated " or " open " by rough handling.

43. The Symptoms and Signs of a Fracture are :—

SHOCK—Always present in some degree with any fracture. May be severe.

PAIN AND TENDERNESS at the site of the fracture, quickly followed by bruising and swelling.

BLEEDING if there is an open fracture.

LOSS OF POWER in the affected part. Generally speaking if a limb is broken it cannot be moved, and never without pain.

IRREGULARITY on the surface of the bone e.g. on the collarbone or the bone of an arm. In an open fracture the ends of the broken bone may be sticking out of the wound.

DEFORMITY AND UNNATURAL MOVEMENT. You may find a person's leg which has been broken crumpled up underneath him with the foot turned round the wrong way. The bones of the leg may be bent in a place where there is no joint e.g. between the knee and the foot if both bones of the leg are broken.

CREPITUS. This is a grating sensation which may sometimes be felt and even heard and is caused by the ends of the broken bone rubbing one against the other when moved. *On no account* must a first aider ever try to obtain this sensation by rubbing the ends of the bone together. By doing so he may make the break worse, and in any case will cause much pain and increase shock.

44. First Aid Treatment of Fractures

When all the above symptoms and signs are present in a person who has perhaps injured a limb you will find it fairly easy to spot the injury as a fracture. In many cases, however, the only information you will be able to obtain will be from the casualty himself (who may say he heard a bone snap), or from bystanders who witnessed the injury ; symptoms and signs may be few. Severe pain and swelling with inability to move a limb following an injury should always make you suspicious of a fracture. If you are in any doubt as to whether there is a fracture or not you must treat it as if there is one.

Lay the patient down. This will lessen shock. If you suspect a fracture of the skull raise his head and shoulders a little and support them.

Stop bleeding if the fracture is open, and apply a dressing. In all open fractures there is some bleeding, but it can generally be stopped by putting on a dressing and bandaging lightly. If bleeding continues you will have to use indirect pressure, especially if the bleeding is from an artery.

Place the casualty in the position most comfortable to him and protect him from further shock, with the means at your disposal.

Immobilise the fracture. By this is meant to fix the damaged part so that any movement by the patient or by you cannot cause the broken bone to move, as this will increase the deformity, cause great pain, and make his shock worse. *Only when you have secured the fracture* should you consider moving the patient, and not before.

Remember that it is not your job to try to "set" a fracture, so if it is a limb which is broken try if possible to fix it in the position in which you found it, using the utmost care and gentleness and moving it as little as you can. If the limb is distorted call for a doctor or someone more experienced in first aid than you are. *Do not try to straighten the limb yourself* or to push back any pieces of bone sticking out of an open fracture.

45 How to Immobilise a Fracture

The instructions below relate entirely to fractures in the upper and lower limbs ; fractures in other parts are described separately.

The two methods adopted for immobilisation are :—

By using unyielding substances such as wood, metal and the like as splints.

By using the trunk as a splint in the case of fractures of the upper limbs, and the opposite limb (if uninjured) in the case of fractures of the lower limbs. This method is known as " body splinting."

(i) PREPARED SPLINTS are made from pieces of wood or metal cut to the desired shape and length so that they can be bound to a broken limb to prevent it from moving. As they are hard substances *they must always be padded* with cotton wool, lint or anything soft such as articles of clothing before they are placed next to a limb. Each splint must be sufficiently long to keep not only a broken bone from moving *but also the joints above and below the fracture.* Thus, if a bone in the forearm is broken the splint must reach above the elbow and extend below the wrist. Splints are fastened to a broken limb by triangular bandages, straps with buckles, or, as improvisation, ties, pocket handkerchiefs and the like can be used. Splints can be applied next to a limb or over the clothing covering it. The *knots in bandages or buckles of straps must always be fastened on top of the splint* never on a limb.

(ii) IMPROVISED SPLINTS. As prepared splints may not be available when you need them you will have to improvise substitutes for them. Such things as walking sticks, folded umbrellas, pieces of wood from debris, tightly rolled up newspapers with a stick in the middle, maps and the like make excellent splints, provided they are firm enough and sufficiently long and wide to fulfil the purpose.

N.B.—Never forget to pad splints, and do not tie bandages too tightly so that they stop the circulation in a limb.

(iii) BODY SPLINTING. It is not only often extremely difficult to obtain any material for splints or to apply them under the conditions which exist during air raids especially by night, and moreover, searching for splints or their substitutes and applying them will only delay the despatch of a casualty to hospital and increase his shock by the handling which the application of the splints necessarily entails. If therefore you find a casualty with a broken collar bone, or broken bones in an arm or hand secure the affected limb to the body with triangular bandages, with a final one as a sling, thus using the body as a splint. Put padding between the limb and the body before securing.

In the case of the lower limbs if a thigh bone or the bones of one leg are broken put pieces of padding material between the knees and the ankles and first of all tie the feet together with a triangular bandage. Next fasten narrow fold triangular bandages over pieces of padding above and below the fracture, whether of a thigh bone or bones of the leg. Pass a broad-fold triangular bandage round both thighs and below both knees tying the knots over padding on the sound limb. If a long wooden prepared splint or substitute is readily available this may be used for a fractured thigh in addition, provided that its application does not increase the delay. It should reach up as far as the armpit and be secured to the chest by a broad-fold bandage passed round it over the splint and extended below the feet.

46. Special Fractures

There are some fractures which cannot be treated by splints, but require special recognition and treatment. Examples are given below.

(i) Fracture of the Skull

The skull is a rounded closed bony box which contains the brain. It consists of a domed top, flat curved bones with their convex surfaces outwards forming the forehead, sides and back of the head, and a flat bottom. This part of the skull is called the " *cranium* " to distinguish it from the face, its top portion is called the " *vault* " and its bottom the

53

" *base.*"   Upon this " base " the under part of the brain rests, the remainder filling up the bony cavity but not quite touching the bones. The brain itself which is roughly the same shape as the box, is whitish-grey in colour, weighs about three pounds in a normal adult and, on account of its shape and wrinkled surface is often likened to a gigantic walnut.   It is made up of an enormous number of nerve cells, nerve fibres and blood vessels, so it can easily be imagined how serious any damage to it can be.

The parts of the skull most likely to be fractured are :—

    (*a*) The vault.

    (*b*) The base.

(*a*) FRACTURE OF THE VAULT

Due to *direct violence* e.g. a blow or fall upon the head, and may be " *open* " or " *closed.*"

The skull cap may be crushed or splintered and pieces of the bone driven inwards on to the brain forming a " *depressed fracture.*"   *Bleeding* which accompanies the fracture may be unable to escape outwards so pours into the skull and presses upon the brain, causing what is known as " *compression of the brain.*"   With every fracture of the skull there is bound to be some bleeding but this does not always press upon the brain.   In most cases of injury there is a shaking up or stunning of the brain, which produces " *concussion of the brain.*"   This varies in intensity, according to the severity of the injury, from a headache and dazed state which passes off, to complete unconsciousness.

(*b*) FRACTURE OF THE BASE OF THE SKULL

Generally due to *indirect violence* as for instance, by a blow upon the jaw, or when a person falls from a height and lands upon his feet or buttocks.   In such cases the " *base* " or shelf within the skull, upon which the brain rests, is cracked or broken and, as in a fracture of the vault, bleeding occurs and may press upon the brain.

It will be seen from the above that the main dangers of a fractured skull are its effects upon the brain and nervous system.   Of these effects *concussion* by itself is the least severe, and may pass off without serious consequences.   If, however, blood is pressing upon the brain, and continues to do so, a casualty will become rapidly worse and his life will be in great danger from *compression.*

It is therefore of the utmost importance for you as a first aider to be able to know what to look for so that you can find out if a skull is broken, and if so, whether it is causing pressure upon the brain by pieces of bone or bleeding, or not.

In any case you must regard every fracture of the skull as serious and *bear in mind* that even if signs of compression of the brain do not come on at once they may do so later.

In consequence, get a doctor to see the casualty as soon as you can so that he can be removed to hospital with the least delay.

Symptoms and Signs

The following *symptoms* and *signs* presented by a casualty suffering from *concussion* or *compression* of the brain should help you to arrive at a decision.

(c) CONCUSSION OF THE BRAIN

Headache and giddiness, perhaps vomiting. May only last a few seconds or minutes then pass off or, if the blow is severe, unconsciousness may come on at once and last for several hours.

All signs of *shock* are present (e.g. face pale and cold, pulse feeble and quick, breathing quiet and shallow).

The *pupils of the eyes* are as a rule equal in size and become small when a light is shone into them regaining their normal size when it is removed. The same effect is produced in daylight by simply covering the eyes with a hand for a moment and then removing it.

You must remember, however, that it is often extremely difficult to examine the eyes of a casualty at an incident, and moreover you can do damage to them by opening them with dirty fingers and allowing dust and grit to get into them. Never attempt to do this yourself, especially in the case of an unconscious casualty. It is far better to carry out necessary first aid and send him to hospital as soon as possible whether you suspect him to be suffering from *concussion* or *compression*.

If you lift the arms or legs of the casualty off the ground you will not get any feeling of limpness in them as will occur if they are paralyzed ; moreover, the casualty will not complain of numbness or loss of sensation in them. An unconscious casualty will frequently vomit when he regains consciousness. This is a fairly constant sign. A confused mental condition may persist for a time after he is quite conscious, and he may remember nothing of what has happened to him.

(d) COMPRESSION OF THE BRAIN

Signs of compression may follow directly upon those of concussion, or after an appreciable interval. Sometimes a casualty may seem to have recovered from concussion but later symptoms and signs of compression appear. This may be due to bleeding inside the skull, lessening or stopping on account of shock and then restarting as the patient recovers from this.

Severe headache and restlessness. Twitching of muscles of body or of one or other limb on one side only. As bleeding continues twitchings cease and limbs become limp and placid. Unconsciousness may soon develop.

Face is flushed and hot.

Breathing is slow and snoring. The cheeks are puffed in and out with every respiration.

Pulse is slow but forcible.

Both pupils of the eyes are larger than normal and one is *larger* than the other. They do not become smaller in the presence of light.

If one or other or both limbs on one side are raised they will feel *lifeless* and *limp* compared with those of the other side. If the patient is conscious he will say that they are numb and he cannot feel you touching them.

(e) SYMPTOMS OF FRACTURE OF THE BASE OF THE SKULL

Symptoms and signs are usually those of concussion or compression, often there are only signs of concussion with a bruise on the head to account for them.

Loss of consciousness does not always occur.

Bleeding from the *nose* and *ears,* sometimes the *mouth,* or into *one eye* making it blood-shot.

N.B.—If in addition to a head injury you find these signs you must always suspect a *fracture of the base of the skull.*

(*f*) FIRST AID TREATMENT OF FRACTURED SKULL

Lay the patient down with his head on a pillow, rolled up blanket or clothing. Apply a mine dressing over any *wound* and bandage lightly. If you suspect a depressed fracture put a *built-up sterilised pad dressing* round the wound before putting a dressing on top, and bandage lightly. If blood is coming from the ear, nose or mouth, put a light dressing over the *ear only* to prevent germs getting in. Turn the patient's head towards the side from which blood is escaping and *make no attempt to plug the ear or to stop the bleeding. Protect from further shock.* Give nothing to drink, even if the patient recovers consciousness, in case he may vomit. *Get a doctor as quickly as you can.*

The casualty must be sent to hospital on a stretcher in an ambulance at the earliest opportunity. If unconscious his head must be turned to one side and supported in that position by sandbags to prevent movement.

(ii) Fracture of the Lower Jaw

This may be caused by a blow on the jaw from a flying missile, such as a brick, and there may be little or no external wound, or a portion of the jaw may be carried away by a piece of H.E. bomb, leaving a gaping wound with profuse bleeding.

(*a*) FIRST AID TREATMENT

Warn the casualty not to try to speak and apply a clean dry dressing (e.g. shell) to any external wound.

With the patient leaning forward support the lower jaw with the palm of one hand, gently pressing the teeth of the lower jaw against those of the upper ; then apply a bandage to maintain this position. The best form of bandage which is simple and easy to apply is the " *barrel bandage.*" This should be used when there is a danger of the tongue slipping backwards into the throat and blocking the windpipe. To apply this bandage, without relaxing support of the jaw, place the centre of a narrow fold triangular bandage under the jaw and well back over the dressing. Carry the ends of the bandage upwards in front of the ears and loosely tie the first loop of a reef knot on top of the head. While an assistant supports the jaw, hold the loose ends in your hands and with your fingers open out the knot on the head to form two loops, one passing forwards and the other backwards. Guide the forward loop on to the forehead just above the eyebrows, and carry the backward loop to the back of the head just above the nape of the neck. Gather up the free ends of the bandage and adjust them so that each cross-over is just in front of an ear. Then tie them on top of the head. (*See Fig.* 24.)

(*b*) TRANSPORT

If the patient is fit to travel to hospital as a sitting case he should sit with his head held forward and downward with his open hand supporting the chin.

If he is a stretcher case he must be placed face downward with a small pad under his chest so that his head hangs forward and his tongue cannot fall backwards into his throat. A second small pad placed under his

Fig. 24
Application of Barrel Bandage.

forehead is useful as a support. A bowl is placed beneath his face to catch blood or vomit, and of course he must be watched by the ambulance attendant during the journey to hospital.

(iii) Fracture of Collar Bone

Generally a closed fracture but may be open as a result of being struck by a fragment of bomb or debris.

57

Severe pain, swelling and tenderness at the site of injury, with irregularity along the surface of the bone, especially marked in a thin person.

Deformity of the shoulder, the rounded portion being flatter than the sound side.

Some loss of power in the limb. The patient cannot raise the arm above the shoulder and, as the pain is increased when the arm hangs down, supports the arm at the elbow with the opposite hand, and bends his head towards the injured side to ease the strain on the muscles of the neck. A characteristic attitude.

(b) FIRST AID TREATMENT

Dress any external wound after removing sufficient clothing to expose it. Place a pad about the size of a man's fist in the armpit ; put the arm close to the side with the forearm across the chest, the open hand pointing towards the opposite shoulder. Apply a sling and bandages as shown in Fig. 25. *Feel the pulse* at the wrist on the injured side to make sure that the pad in the armpit is not stopping circulation.

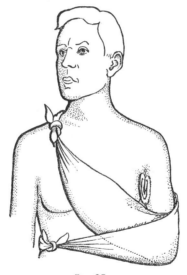

Fig. 25

Treatment of Broken Collar Bone.

If both collar bones are broken

(1) Three triangular bandages are necessary. A narrow-fold bandage is passed over each collar bone and through the armpits over a pad placed in each and tied with a reef knot to form rings round the shoulders, leaving the ends of the bandages free. Tie these ends together over a large pad of dressing in the middle of the back so as to brace back the shoulders and correct any deformity of the broken bones.

(2) Cross the patient's arms on his chest and apply a broad-fold bandage over the arms and round the body to act as a double sling. Tie the knot of the bandage below the wrists. (*See Fig.* 26.)

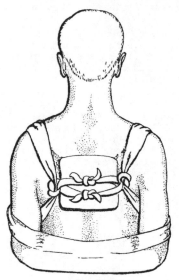

Fig. 26
Treatment of Both Collar Bones Broken

(iv) Fractured Ribs

May be broken by *direct violence*, such as a blow on the chest from a bomb fragment, debris or a fall, or by *indirect violence* when pressure is applied to the back and front of the chest and the ribs bend outwards and break at a point away from the site of the pressure.

(*a*) SYMPTOMS AND SIGNS

These depend upon whether the broken ends of the ribs are driven into the lung by *direct violence* or not, as in the case of *indirect violence*.

The chief are :—

Severe pain in the chest at the site of fracture, made worse by breathing deeply or coughing. Tenderness is present at once, swelling and bruising may appear later.

If a lung is damaged bright red blood mixed with froth is coughed up and difficulty in breathing occurs.

An open wound over the fractured area which allows air to be sucked into and blown out of the lung with a whistling sound, *is a very serious condition.*

Shock is always present to some degree with broken ribs, but is very marked when a lung is damaged.

(*b*) FIRST AID TREATMENT

For a closed fracture with no lung injury, place the centre of a broad-fold bandage just below the site of the fracture and tie it on the opposite

59   C 2

side of the chest. As the patient breathes out the knot should be firmly tied. A second similar bandage is then placed with its centre just over the fracture, so as to overlap the first bandage by half its width.

Support the arm on the injured side in a large arm sling, place the patient with his body inclined towards the injured side, supported by a folded blanket at his back.

If a lung is injured dress any external wound. If air is going into and coming out of the lung through the wound place a large pad dressing over the wound and bandage lightly. Do not apply bandages as for a closed fracture, but support the arm in a large arm sling.

Protect from · further shock and send the patient to hospital as a stretcher case as soon as possible. Call a doctor if available at the incident to see the patient.

(v) Fracture of the Spine

This fracture commonly known as a " broken back " is especially serious on account of damage which may be done to the spinal cord contained within the bony framework of the backbone. This is likely to happen if, in addition to a fracture, one or more bones of the spine are dislocated and press upon, or even sever the spinal cord.

This fracture is caused as in other fractures by :—

D I R E C T   V I O L E N C E such as a blow on the spine from falling beams or debris, especially if a person is stooping at the time ; by the impact of a fragment of bomb, or by falling against a hard object such as a wall, railing or ladder, or by :—

I N D I R E C T   V I O L E N C E as when a person jumps from a height or from a moving vehicle and lands on his feet with the legs held rigid.

(*a*) S Y M P T O M S   A N D   S I G N S

Pain and tenderness at the site of injury aggravated by any movement.

Shock always present but very marked when the spinal cord is damaged.

A wound may be present, or swelling and bruising over the injured area.

A casualty may be either *conscious* or *unconscious*. Where the spinal cord is uninjured a casualty is generally conscious, and may even be able to walk. With severe damage to the spinal cord in most cases he will be unconscious.

Paralysis and *loss of sensation* in the limbs shows that the spinal cord is injured ; either the arms or the legs only or both may be affected.

All first aiders must remember that a broken back need not necessarily cause paralysis, only when the spinal cord is damaged does this occur. They must therefore not assume that a back is not broken because there is no paralysis.

(*b*) F I R S T   A I D   T R E A T M E N T

If you suspect that a casualty has a fractured spine, call a doctor at once if one is available at the incident and, pending his arrival, warn the patient not to move and, without moving him, keep him warm with blankets or clothing and hot water bottles. (*N.B.*—As the patient may have lost the feeling in his limbs special care must be taken to prevent the bottles from burning them.)

If no doctor is available summon expert assistance before you attempt to do anything further.

With this assistance put pads between the ankles, knees and thighs and tie a figure 8 narrow fold bandage around the ankles and feet, fastening the knot under the soles. Tie broad-fold bandages around both knees and thighs over the pads placed between them.

(c) REMOVAL FROM THE INCIDENT

Special attention must be devoted to this since any error may have grave consequences.

In moving or lifting the patient his spine *MUST NOT* be bent or twisted in any way. He must be carried lying *ON HIS BACK* wherever the injury to the spine may be. If he is found in some other position, he must be very carefully turned over *IN ONE PIECE* by two or more helpers, four if possible.

A stretcher with a blanket folded lengthwise upon it is brought close to the patient. A Civil Defence stretcher is the best type to use as its bed portion is rigid and flat. If a wood and canvas stretcher has to be used, it should if possible be made rigid and flat by placing transverse boards on its bed portion. If a stretcher is not available a door, shutter or plank of suitable length are excellent substitutes. (*N.B.*—See that neither the blanket nor the patient's clothes are wrinkled when he is laid upon the stretcher.)

The lifting and placing of the patient upon the stretcher should be done in one of the following ways according to the material and the number of helpers available—*taking particular care* to see that the whole length of the patient's head, back and legs are *kept straight* in one line.

By Blanket lift

(*a*) Five helpers are required, especially where the spine is dislocated, but if not available not less than four can just manage. A blanket is placed lengthwise on the ground in line with the patient and rolled up for half its width.

One helper supports and very gently pulls on the feet and legs while another does the same to the head, as the other helpers carefully turn the patient on to his side. The rolled up portion of the blanket is then placed close to the patient and he is gently replaced on his back upon the unrolled portion of the blanket. The rolled portion is then unrolled so that he lies in the centre of the blanket. The two edges of the blanket are then rolled up against the patient's body and grasped by a helper at each side, one hand under the buttocks and small of the back and the other under the shoulder blades. Without releasing the traction on the head and feet all four helpers lift the patient carefully and evenly while the fifth helper slides a stretcher beneath him. If no one is available for this the helpers should move with short smooth side paces until they reach the stretcher and gently lower the patient on to it, having previously placed upon the stretcher pads made of clothing rolled up, or folded triangular bandages, large enough but not too large to preserve the normal curves of the spine. These pads should be placed so as to be under the neck and small of the back when the casualty is laid upon the stretcher. (*See Fig.* 27.)

To prevent any movement of the casualty while being carried on the stretcher or loaded into the ambulance, triangular bandages should be passed over his chest, hips, below his knees, and tied to the stretcher poles on each side. Sandbags or rolls of clothing should be placed on each side of the head to keep it steady.

(*b*) If a blanket is not forthcoming, the patient's coat may be opened out and rolled firmly up against the sides of his body. The helpers on each side grasp the rolled up coat and the clothing round his thighs while other helpers support and maintain traction on his head and legs.

Fig. 27
Stretcher Pads for Spinal Injuries.

By Webbing Bands.

This method is particularly useful when casualties are found lying on uneven surfaces or in enclosed spaces where it is difficult for rescuers to work. A reference to Figures 28, 29, 30, 31 and 32 will show how these webbing bands are used for placing under a casualty and for lifting him.

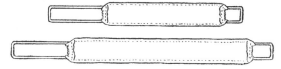

Fig. 28
Webbing Bands.

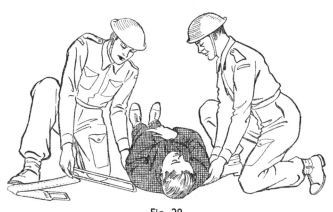

Fig. 29
Placing under Casualty.

Fig. 30

Lifting Casualty.

Fig. 31

Webbing Bands as applied near wall.   Placing Band under Casualty.

Fig. 32

Bands correctly placed for lifting.

CHAPTER VIII

SUFFOCATION (ASPHYXIA)

51. Definition and causes of Suffocation

Suffocation is a condition in which normal breathing is interfered with or stopped.

There are many causes of suffocation, and these are classified under separate headings with examples of the types which you are likely to meet among air raid casualties.

Inability to breathe because the air passages are obstructed.

By mechanical means.

Examples are blocking of the nose and mouth by dust and dirt (e.g. from damaged buildings) ; a dislodged dental plate stuck in the throat of an injured person, especially one who is unconscious ; inhaling blood into the lungs from a broken jaw, or food or liquid which has been vomited into the mouth and then sucked down into the lungs. Drowning is a classical example of this form of suffocation, but you are not likely to meet many cases of this.

By pressure on the air passages.

Examples are pressure on the chest by fallen masonry, and beams or when persons are buried under debris ; crushing of the chest when people are jammed tightly together in a crowd. An instance of this occurred during the last war when a large number of people died as the result of a panic at a London tube station used as a shelter.

Paralysis and spasm of the mechanism of breathing.

Cases of this are most likely to be met with in persons who are in contact with a " live " electric wire in a damaged building or on a road.

Spasm of the breathing muscles with stoppage of breathing occurs during an epileptic fit, or in young children with convulsions. You may meet cases of these conditions brought on by fear and excitement during air raids.

Breathing certain poisonous gases.

C A R B O N M O N O X I D E, a very poisonous gas, is present in gas escaping from broken mains, damaged gas ovens and the like ; the fumes from a H.E. bomb in a closed space ; during tunnelling operations by Rescue personnel, and may cause serious interference with breathing and frequently death from suffocation.

Certain gases used in industrial concerns, two examples of which are ammonia and chlorine.

In chemical warfare phosgene and other lung irritant gases.

52. General symptoms and signs of Suffocation

These depend on whether the suffocation is partial or complete ; the former may pass on to the latter.

A person finds difficulty in breathing and becomes restless. Breathing becomes jerky and a struggle takes place to remove any obstruction and obtain air. A man tears at his throat and clothing.

Coughing and spluttering. Where the throat is partially blocked there is a whistling sound as the air passes through the narrowed opening.

The face becomes livid ; the veins in the neck stand out like cords and are filled with blood ; the lips and finger nails turn blue ; the eyes protrude and are staring and blood-shot.

Unconsciousness follows slowly or quickly and may pass on to :—

(ii) COMPLETE SUFFOCATION

The first stage of restlessness and fighting for breath may last up to five minutes, according to the degree of obstruction. Complete unconsciousness follows and breathing entirely stops. Within a short time the heart stops beating.

53. First Aid for Suffocation

THE FIRST STEP is to remove the casualty from the source of danger, for example :—

A gas or smoke filled room, a live electric wire, or the source of danger from the casualty, such as debris or pieces of furniture lying upon him.

You have already learnt how to get a person out of a burning room and how to protect yourself and him while doing it. Remember, you will not be protected if you put on your respirator when entering a room filled with coal gas, as the respirator gives no protection, and is in fact a danger because it masks the smell of the gas and its filter gets clogged up with smoke particles. If you do put on a respirator its filter must be covered by such things as a pocket handkerchief, towel, or an old sock. The Breathing Apparatus used by the Rescue and Fire Services is invaluable in gas-filled rooms or in tunnelling operations. In many cases it is sufficient for a rescuer to take a deep breath and hold it.

Contact with a live wire. Do not attempt to drag a person away from contact with a live wire without first protecting (insulating) yourself, otherwise you will receive a shock which may be fatal. If the current cannot immediately be switched off, you must first if possible try to find something which is a non-conductor of electricity to stand on. Rubber is ideal but is seldom available. Other things are a thick piece of wood or glass, bricks, a piece of linoleum, a mackintosh folded several times or a thick layer of straw. *Whatever is used it must be dry* ; anything moist conducts electricity. Try to pull the person off the wire with a dry wooden walking stick with a crooked handle covered with several pieces of dry newspaper, or another folded mackintosh. (*N.B.—Never use an umbrella* as its metal ribs are conductors, and it may have a metal stick). Other things to protect your hands are rubber gloves, a rubber tobacco pouch, dry hot water bottle, a thick roll of dry newspapers or a dry coat. It may be possible for you to free the casualty by throwing a dry coat held by the sleeves over his head, or using a loop of dry thick rope.

THE SECOND STEP is rapidly to make certain that the nose and mouth are not obstructed in any way, and to clear them if they are.

THE THIRD STEP is to loosen all tight clothing and commence artificial respiration at once (this means the restoration of normal breathing by artificial means) if the casualty has stopped breathing. At the same time the body temperature and the circulation must be maintained by blankets and hot water bottles while artificial respiration is in progress. Try and get the casualty to a safe place if you can, and discourage onlookers who may impede you and prevent your patient from having all the air he needs.

54. How to carry out Artificial Respiration

(i) BY SCHAEFER'S METHOD

This can be done by one person only, using his hands. It is simple and easy to apply, consequently it should be used at an incident as it is of the utmost importance to " get cracking " at the earliest possible moment; every second's delay makes recovery less likely. (*See Fig.* 33.)

Instructions.

(*a*) Lay the patient down flat on his face *with his head turned to one side* and his arms laid forward above his head. This position helps the flow of anything from his mouth, and is particularly useful in cases of drowning ; moreover, his tongue cannot fall back into his throat and block it up if he is unconscious, as it would otherwise do were he lying on his back.

(*b*) Kneel beside or astride the patient's thighs facing his head and place the palms of your hands on the small of the back on each side of the spine, the wrists nearly touching, the thumbs close to one another and the fingers fitting into the soft part on either side between the ribs and the hip bones.

(*c*) Keeping the arms straight bend your body slowly forward from the knees and hips until your shoulders are directly above your hands and your weight is pressing on the patient's back. This presses his belly against the ground and compresses the contents of the belly against the diaphragm and lungs driving air out of them. As you swing forwards count slowly—one—two or—twenty-one—twenty-two to obtain the correct timing in seconds. (*N.B.—Do not press too hard.* Remember that the muscles of an unconscious person cannot resist, so too heavy pressure may rupture the liver or break ribs.)

(*d*) Without moving your hands swing your body slowly backwards to its original position, thus relaxing pressure upon the back. The contents of the belly now fall back into their normal position the diaphragm descends and air is sucked into the lungs. While you are doing this count slowly—one—two—three or twenty-one—twenty-two—twenty-three.

Repeat this forward and backward movement twelve times a minute (two seconds for pressure, three seconds for relaxation). When natural breathing re-appears regulate your movements to correspond with it. Wrap the patient in blankets and apply hot water bottles. *Rubbing the legs and arms* towards the heart restores the circulation *but this should not be done until breathing recommences.*

CAUTION 1. This method must not be employed when there is an injury involving possibly a broken back or injury to abdomen. In such a case the following should be used, omitting Schaefer's method and putting the casualty straight on to a stretcher for rocking.

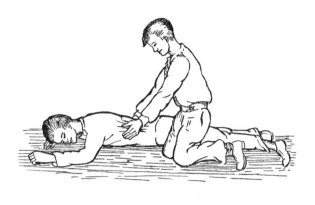

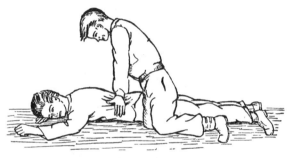

Fig. 33
Schaefer's Method of Artificial Respiration.

(ii) EVE'S ROCKING METHOD OF RESUSCITATION

This is an effective supplementary method which can be used after artificial respiration has been started by Schaefer's method. Its principle is that by rocking a person, with a "see-saw" motion, the weight of the belly contents moves the diaphragm up and down, alternately driving out and sucking in air as in Schaefer's method. One person can carry out the rocking, but two are required for the preliminary stages. (*See Fig.* 34.)

The materials required are a plane (stretcher, door or broad plank) to which the casualty can be fastened, a fulcrum on which the plane can be rocked, and nails, chocks or other means to prevent the centre of the plane from slipping on the fulcrum during rocking. No time must be lost in changing over from one method to another. The stretcher and fulcrum (a trestle is best) are brought alongside the casualty (already being treated by Schaefer's method) and he is rolled on to the stretcher face downwards, with his head turned to one side, and Schaefer's method is continued while wrists and ankles are bound to the stretcher

The stretcher is then lifted on to the fulcrum and rocking through an angle of 45° (half a right angle) commenced at the timed rate of nine rocks per minute (four seconds head down, three seconds feet down). *Warmth is essential* to restore the circulation while this is being done, and blankets and hot water bottles must be used for this purpose.

If a trestle (2′ 8″ high is best) cannot be obtained, a rope slung from a beam, a broken wall, a builder's two-wheel cart or two chairs back to back can be used as improvisations. A reference to the diagram will make the above clear.

Fig. 34
Eve's " Rocking " Method of Resuscitation.

CAUTION 2.

Artificial respiration by any method *must never* be performed on persons poisoned by phosgene or other lung irritant gas, or on people injured by blast.

CHAPTER IX

BURNS AND SCALDS

59. Causes of Burns and Scalds

Both burns and scalds are caused by heat, the one by flame or dry heat, the other by hot fluids or steam ; the effects are very similar.

A BURN IS CAUSED BY :—

Dry heat, such as fire ; hot or molten metal ; the flash of a bursting bomb or ignited petrol. Unprotected hot water bottles are often a cause of burns, especially when used with unconscious patients.

A live electric wire ; a live rail ; by lightning.

Strong acids, such as sulphuric, and strong alkalis such as quick lime.

A SCALD IS CAUSED BY :—

Wet heat, such as boiling water and steam.

Hot oil or tar.

Boiling cooking fat and the like.

For the purposes of first aid, burns are classified as (i) superficial and (ii) deep.

(i) SUPERFICIAL BURNS may cause only a reddening of the skin, or patches of skin may be destroyed and blisters form.

(ii) DEEP BURNS destroy the skin and superficial tissues beneath it. In bad cases muscles, nerves, blood vessels and even bones may be destroyed, and whole areas charred.

60. Effects of Burns

The chief dangers from burns of any part of the body are :—

SHOCK. This comes first because it is the most important and one of the chief causes of death after burns especially among children and persons who are badly burned. There is far more shock with a superficial burn which covers a large area than a deep burn involving a smaller area, and a burn of the chest or abdomen is more dangerous than one which chars part of a limb.

BLOOD POISONING which comes on later as a result of germs getting into the wound. *Remember these two important factors when you are dealing with a burn.*

61. First Aid for Burned Casualties

It stands to reason that if you find a person suffering from burns in a burning building, lying beneath smouldering or burning debris, or in a room full of coal gas escaping from a damaged gas main, you must remove him as soon as possible from the source of danger, or the source of danger from him.

Before entering a burning room to get a casualty out you must protect yourself by covering your nose and mouth with a wet handkerchief or opened up triangular bandage, and take similar material to cover the casualty's face. When you enter the room crouch low to reach the victim, and if his clothing is on fire pull him to the ground and smother the flames by wrapping him in a blanket, greatcoat or mackintosh, wet if possible. When the fire on the burning clothes is extinguished get him out to a place of safety as soon as you can and carry out first aid treatment as under :—

Do not remove more clothing than is absolutely necessary, in particular do not attempt to pull off clothing which is sticking to a burn ; pain and shock are thereby greatly increased and by exposing the burn to air.

Protect him from further shock by proper measures.

Blisters should on no account be pricked but left intact.

Do not attempt to cleanse the wound or apply any kind of oils or greasy substances.

Cover the burn with a large clean *dry* first aid or shell dressing, several if necessary, as soon as you can, and bandage firmly. Handle the part as little as possible.

Pain is relieved by immobilising the part. A sling may be sufficient for a slight burn of an upper limb, but in all cases of severe burns of upper or lower limbs, especially if delay may occur before the casualty can reach a hospital, the application of a splint over the dressing may be considered.

Give plenty of fluids to drink.

All cases of severe burns must be sent to hospital as stretcher cases at the earliest opportunity and treated as priority cases for despatch from an incident. Cases of burns usually travel well if they are sent to hospital without delay and without undue handling.

62. Flash and Radiation Burns from Atomic Bombs

When an atomic bomb bursts all kinds of radiations, as they are called, are discharged instantaneously and range from what we know as infra-red rays to those described as X-rays.

The radiations or rays which burn are emitted in a fraction of a second and affect the exposed skin of persons within a mile and a half of the bomb burst.

The period of the burning action is so short that almost anything in the way of clothes, or any other intervening substances however flimsy, affords protection ; white materials are more efficient than black of the same thickness.

Unless there is long enough warning for taking cover there is as yet no satisfactory means of preventing flash burns of exposed parts, e.g., face and hands.

People exposed within a few hundred yards of the bomb burst may have their skin dark brown or blackened, and whether or not otherwise injured, die very quickly. Those at a greater distance suffer burns which are " superficial " rather than " deep " and vary from something comparable to severe sunburn to severe blistering with loss of the surface cuticle. *They are extremely painful.*

First Aid Treatment

Burns caused by an atomic bomb in no way differ from those already well known and described above. The treatment is the same as for ordinary burns.

CHAPTER X

CRUSHING INJURY

67. The Cause of the Injury

At an air raid incident you may have to extricate a man who has been pinned down by a beam across his legs in a partially demolished house.

This man when freed may appear little the worse for his experience and complain only of numbness and stiffness in the leg which was under the beam. He will be taken to hospital and with rest and appropriate treatment may completely recover. Again, he may not and within a few hours develops " shock." With proper treatment he may also recover from this as most cases do. The odd one, however, after recovering from his shock is found to be gradually passing less and less urine, and unless this condition responds to treatment he will die within 6—8 days.

This very serious condition is the result of the cutting off of the blood supply to the muscles of a limb which is crushed, and in consequence the muscles die. Certain substances are produced in the dead muscles which poison the kidneys and prevent them from functioning properly. This damage to the kidneys occurs when the urine is acid, as it normally is. It is done soon after the limb has been freed, but does not become evident until after several hours, by which time the patient should be in hospital. It is easier to prevent damage to the kidney than to cure it ; prevention is therefore of the utmost importance and no time should be lost in taking steps towards this end.

You must try to make the urine of the casualty *alkaline* and this is obviously done by giving him alkaline liquids to drink. This should be done for *all persons* who have been trapped by debris for an hour or more whether only a limb or other part is affected, as they may later develop this serious condition, however well they may appear at the time of their release.

68. First Aid Treatment

With the above in mind.

If there is a doctor at the incident notify him as soon as a trapped casualty is located. If no doctor is immediately available report the presence of the casualty to the Officer in Charge of the incident or to a responsible member of the Rescue Service.

Pending the arrival of a doctor, carry out the following treatment if *only a limb or limbs are involved.*

Give plenty of liquid, up to four pints, if there are no signs of injury to the belly. This should be given before the pressure on the limb is relieved, *but on no account should it delay extrication.* Try to obtain some baking soda (Bicarbonate of soda), *NOT WASHING SODA,* dissolve about two teaspoonful to a pint of cold water and get the patient to drink as much of this as he can. Follow this with drinks of hot sweet tea or coffee. Other alkalis (magnesia powder, alkali powder for indigestion and the like), or even plain water can be given if baking soda is not available.

If the casualty is conscious and in a position difficult to reach it may be necessary to use a rubber feeding tube and cup. Unless liquids can be given without harm to the casualty, as by sucking some into his lungs, you must await the arrival of the doctor who will direct this operation.

When the casualty is extricated protect him from further shock and send him to hospital on a stretcher in an ambulance as soon as possible.

N.B.—The limb which has been crushed must not have hot water bottles placed near it, and *should remain uncovered.*

CHAPTER XI

INSENSIBILITY

71. Insensible Or Unconscious Casualties

Unconscious casualties found during or after air raid incidents are often a big problem to those who have to deal with them as they cannot get any information from the victims as to what has happened to them or what they feel.

You have already read in the preceding pages of many injuries which can cause a person to become unconscious. What follows now is a summary of the chief causes of unconsciousness which you are likely to meet with, how to recognise the various causes, and how to render the most efficient first aid for an unconscious person.

It is comparatively easy for you to recognise the cause and know how to treat it if you find a person lying unconscious with an obvious serious injury, but the difficulty arises when you find an unconscious person with no visible injury to account for the unconsciousness. It is then that you will have to rely upon what you have learnt, and make a careful but rapid examination to discover from the signs which are present what is the matter with the casualty before you can hope to render the correct first aid.

Remember that a prolonged examination is *unnecessary* and indeed *inadvisable,* as if a person is injured seriously enough to make him unconscious the quicker he is sent off to hospital the better. You may however be able to do something to help him, and even save his life, by prompt and correct action on the spot.

Many air raids occur at night and you will find it extremely difficult on many occasions to make up your mind as to the reason why a casualty is unconscious as owing to the darkness, and the noise caused by exploding bombs, falling debris and the like, and from the fact that the casualty's face and clothing are probably covered by dust and dirt you may fail to recognise his presence, mistaking him at first for a heap of clothing or rubbish.

First of all you must realise that unconsciousness as found in air raid casualties is most frequently the result of some injury, but it may also be caused without any apparent injury, and by certain diseases which would perhaps not have come to light had it not been for air raids. Unconsciousness is therefore divided into two groups in the most convenient form for you to remember.

(i) Unconsciousness with Visible Injury

> (a) Open fractures of the skull or any part of the face, with concussion or compression of the brain.
>
> (b) Severe open wounds with bleeding in any part of the body.
>
> (c) Open fractures in any part of the body.

(d) Multiple injuries caused by fragments of bombs which may or may not be associated with much bleeding.

(e) Suffocation following an injury to the jaw which has allowed the tongue to block the air passages ; and from electric shock with burns.

(f) Burns and scalds.

(g) Severe contusions on any part of the body.

(ii) Unconsciousness without Visible Injury

(a) Closed fractures of the skull with compression of the brain.

(b) Internal bleeding in chest or abdomen.

(c) Shock which may cause only a fainting attack or be very serious and sometimes fatal.

(d) Suffocation from pressure on chest, swallowing dentures, blocking of nose and throat by dust or dirt, and by an electric shock without burns.

(e) Certain conditions such as Apoplexy (caused by the bursting of a blood vessel in the brain and producing compression) and diabetic coma are sometimes precipitated during air raids in persons suffering from disease of the blood vessels in the brain and from diabetes. (Diabetic patients can often be identified as such by a special card they carry and a fibre disc worn round the neck or wrist, notifying that they are suffering from diabetes.) Epileptics sometimes have epileptic fits as a result of air raids.

N.B.—Shock is of course the predominant feature in all the foregoing.

The following points will be found useful to a first aider who finds an unconscious person.

72. Approach to Patient

On reaching the patient notice the following in regard to his appearance and surroundings.

(i) In what position is he lying ? Natural or unnatural.

(ii) Is he breathing or not ? Does his breathing appear normal or abnormal ?

(iii) Is his face pale, flushed, or blue ? If you cannot see the colour of the patient's face owing to darkness, or because it is covered with dirt, some idea of his condition may be obtained by placing your hand on his forehead. If his face is pale the skin may feel cold and clammy ; if it is flushed or blue the skin may feel hot.

(iv) Is there a wound or any signs of blood about ?

In short, try to picture to yourself in what way he differs from a normal person whom you might find asleep. The information obtained from your own observations and from relatives or bystanders who may be able to tell you what happened before the patient became unconscious, how long he has been unconscious, whether the onset was sudden or gradual will be of value to you and also to the doctor when he arrives. Your immediate treatment may save the patient's life.

73. General First Aid Treatment

Send for a doctor at once.

Pending his arrival—when the patient's face is pale keep him lying flat with his head turned to one side. If his face is flushed or blue raise and support his head and shoulders.

Control any serious bleeding.

Loosen all tight clothing and let him have plenty of air.

Deal with any broken bones.

Keep him warm with blankets and protected hot water bottles.

Do not attempt to give anything by the mouth.

Get the casualty to hospital as soon as possible if no doctor is available.

CHAPTER XII

TRANSPORT OF CASUALTIES

79. Blanketing a Stretcher

Before a casualty is laid upon a stretcher you must cover it with a blanket folded lengthwise, or an overcoat, so that he does not lie directly upon the canvas or metal bed-portion. This adds to his comfort and reduces shock. *Remember* that it is more important to put blankets under him than over him. With two layers of blanket underneath and one on top a casualty is better off than with one layer underneath and two on top.

Two blankets only are required to blanket a stretcher properly. The way to do it is as shown in Figures 35, 36 and 37.

> (i) Lay one open blanket (A) lengthwise across a stretcher with one side close to the head end, and one end of the blanket having a slightly longer overlap of the stretcher than the other.

> (ii) Fold a second blanket (B) in three folds lengthwise and lay it on top of the first blanket (A) along the stretcher with its upper edge about 15 inches below the upper edge of the

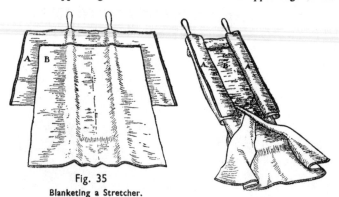

Fig. 35
Blanketing a Stretcher.

Fig. 36
Blanketing a Stretcher.

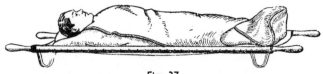

Fig. 37
Blanketing a Stretcher.

first blanket (A). There will be now four thicknesses of blanket upon which the casualty will lie.

(iii) Open out the two ends at the foot of blanket (B) for about 2 feet to form two flaps.

(iv) Roll up or pleat in concertina fashion the overhanging ends of blanket (A) and place them on the edges of the stretcher so that they will not drag on the ground when the stretcher is brought close to the patient.

(v) When the patient is laid upon the stretcher wrap the two flaps of blanket (B) round his feet and tuck the ends between them.

Open out the rolled up folds of blanket (A) and wrap first the short then the long end round the patient tucking it well in at one side.

Your casualty will now be warmly blanketed.

TO SECURE BLANKETS AS A PACK ON A STRETCHER

(1) Lay blankets (A) and (B) on the stretcher as described in (i) and (ii) above.

(2) Fold in the two edges of blanket (A) taking the folds to the sides of the stretcher twice, then once again on to the stretcher.

(3) Place the foot-end of blanket (B) on the stretcher, then fold it over and over with blanket (A) to form a flat pack, in the centre of which a hot-water bottle is placed. Secure the pack thus formed to the stretcher with a strap passed round it and the stretcher.

80. Lifting, Loading and Carrying a Stretcher

LOADING INTO AMBULANCE. The placing of an injured person upon a stretcher, carrying him from an incident and loading the stretcher into an ambulance is in accordance with methods which experience has shown to be the most comfortable for the patient. You should therefore know how to do this properly so that by disturbing him as little as possible you will lessen his discomfort and prevent further shock. Elaborate drill in carrying out the above is not necessary for you, as any form of drill must of necessity be modified to meet difficult situations. You should, however, be capable of efficiently performing the simple exercises depicted below which aim at providing and maintaining concerted action and good team work among those dealing with casualties.

(i) *Lifting a stretcher*

Four men of approximately the same height are allotted as bearers to carry each stretcher. For convenience they are numbered 1, 2, 3 and 4, each four men constituting a stretcher squad. The No. 1 bearer of each squad is the leader and gives all orders.

The position which these bearers take up in relation to a stretcher are :—

(*a*) No. 1 on the right of the stretcher with his toes in line with the front end of the right pole.

(*b*) No. 2 on the left of the stretcher in Line with No. 1.

100

(*c*) No. 3 on the right of the stretcher behind No. 1 and his heels in line with the rear end of the right pole.

(*d*) No. 4 on the left of the stretcher in line with No. 3.

These positions are permanent.

On the command "LIFT STRETCHER—COLLECT WOUNDED" all four bearers stoop together and lift the stretcher from the ground with the hand nearest to the stretcher. They then double by the shortest route to the patient and halting three paces from and in line with his head ; place the stretcher on the ground and stand up to await further orders.

(ii) *Loading a stretcher*

On the command " *load stretcher* " No. 1 bearer goes to the *right* of the patient at his hips, Nos. 2, 3 and 4 to the *left* of the patient at his knees, hips and shoulders respectively. All bearers now turn inwards together, kneel on one knee and pass their hands, palms upwards, beneath the body of the patient, No. 2 bearer supporting the legs, Nos. 1 and 3 by joining hands the thighs and hips and No. 4 the shoulders and head. At a given signal the patient is lifted gently off the ground on to the knees of 2, 3 and 4 bearers, No. 1 disengages and brings the stretcher which he places in front of the bearers ready for the patient to be lowered on to it. He then takes up his former position and again links hands with No. 3. On the command " *lower* " the patient is lowered gently on to the centre of the stretcher, the bearers disengage, rise and resume their permanent positions at the poles of the stretcher.

(iii) *Loading a stretcher with only two bearers*

The stretcher is again placed in line with the patient as before. After giving first aid the two bearers stand astride the patient facing the stretcher. The patient's arms are folded across his chest if he is unconscious but, if not, he may be able to help by grasping the leading bearer round the neck with one or both hands as he bends down, the bearers both bend together, lift the patient by the shoulders and thighs and shuffle forwards straddling the stretcher as they reach it.

(iv) *Lifting and carrying the loaded stretcher*

On the command " *lift stretcher* " all bearers stoop together, grasp the stretcher poles and lift the stretcher holding it at the full length of their arms.

At a given signal they step off together with the inner foot (i.e. that nearest the stretcher) so as to be out of step to prevent the stretcher from swinging.

As a rule it does not matter whether a casualty is carried head first or feet first, but when going uphill it is more comfortable for him to be carried head first, unless there is some reason to the contrary.

When an obstacle such as a wall, fence, or wreckage is encountered the front handles of the stretcher should be rested upon a firm part of the obstacle and the stretcher held level by the rear bearers while those in front cross to the other side and again grasp the front handles. All bearers then lift together moving the stretcher forward until the rear handles can be rested upon the obstacle and the stretcher kept level by the bearers in front. The rear bearers then cross the obstacle and the carriage of the stretcher is resumed.

(v) *Loading a stretcher into an ambulance*

    (1) The stretcher is brought to the ambulance by the four bearers and lowered to the ground one pace from and in line with the vehicle, the patient's head to the front.

    (2) No. 1 bearer gives the command " *load*."

    (3) All bearers turn inwards, lift the stretcher together and, taking a side pace to the ambulance, raise the stretcher gently to the level of the berth to be loaded, Nos. 1 and 2 bearers placing the front runners of the stretcher upon the tracks in the ambulance. The ambulance attendant enters the ambulance to guide the stretcher and secure it, while Nos. 1 and 2 bearers assist Nos. 3 and 4 to slide it into place.

81. Methods of Carrying casualties when stretchers cannot be used

Examples of various methods in which you can carry a patient when stretchers are not available or cannot be used are fully described in the Basic Rescue Pamphlet.

    (i) Two-handed and four-handed seats (By two persons).

    (ii) Fore and aft method (By two persons).

    (iii) The fireman's lift (By one person).

CHAPTER XIII

REMOVAL OF CASUALTIES AND DISPOSAL OF THE DEAD

87. Labelling of Casualties

It is not necessary for all casualties to be labelled, nor invariably for particulars of their names and addresses to be taken, but certain types of casualty, as mentioned below, as well as all unconscious casualties and all dead bodies should be labelled before being removed from the incident.

Tie-on casualty labels, with a symbol written on them, should be used ; failing this a piece of paper attached to a button or pinned to the clothing will serve.   If possible, the forehead of the casualty should also be marked with indelible pencil with the same symbol.

The symbols used for marking casualties and their interpretation are as follows :—

88. Symbols Used.

Symbol on label and/or forehead.	*Interpretation.*
X	Requires priority of removal from the incident and of examination when reaching hospital. This is used mainly, but not exclusively, for wounds of the chest and abdomen, for internal haemorrhage, and for *all* unconscious casualties.
T	A tourniquet has been applied. The time of application of the tourniquet and subsequent releases should also be indicated on the label.
H	Severe haemorrhage has occurred.
M	Morphine has been given. The time of administration and dose should be written on the label.
C	Contaminated or suspected of having been contaminated by PERSISTENT GAS.
XX	Poisoned by Nerve Gas or Non-Persistent Gases or suspected of having been so poisoned.
P	Burnt by Phosphorus.
R	Radioactivity.

Standard Casualty Label
Front Side

Strike out if { UNCONSCIOUS CASUALTY   SYMBOL ON
not needed { DEAD BODY   OTHER SIDE
ADDRESS WHERE FOUND..

....

POSITION IN BUILDING..

TIME AND DATE WHEN FOUND..

APPARENT CAUSE OF DEATH OR INJURY..................................

NAME AND ADDRESS, OR OTHER AID
TO IDENTIFICATION

Leader
SIGNED ....or Deputy.................................Party.

Reverse Side

DATE............................... TIME................................

CRUSH INJURY	SYMBOL

LIMB COMPRESSED FOR.....................
(period if known)

LIMB RELEASED at............................
(time)

BAKING SODA, etc., given.............tea-
                                    spoonfuls

TOTAL FLUID GIVEN

BEFORE RELEASE.........................pints

SYMBOL column:
If MORPHINE has been given,
Time ....

Dose ....
IF TOURNIQUET has been applied
Time Applied.......................

„ Released................

Leader
SIGNED ....or Deputy ....Party.

Diagnosis of Death

In the absence of a doctor the Rescue Party Leader should take the responsibility of diagnosing death in clear cases, but where there exists any doubt as to whether life is extinct the advice of a doctor should be obtained on the spot.

If no doctor is immediately available, to avoid delay the casualty should be sent direct to a hospital and not to a First Aid Post.

Collection of Bodies

When dead bodies are recovered they should be deposited in the nearest convenient building and some suitable covering placed over them, pending removal; they should not be left on the highway or in an open space. The public and all persons not directly concerned should be kept away whilst bodies are being recovered.

Labelling of Bodies

In addition to the details on the casualty label the following information should be given where possible.

1. If the body is contaminated by Blister Gas, or is suspected of being contaminated, the label should be clearly marked with a " C ".

2. For those suspected to have died from the effects of poisoning by Nerve Gas or Non-Persistent Gases, the label should be clearly marked " XX ".

3. For those suspected to have died from Radioactive Effects the label should be clearly marked " R ".

Removal of Bodies

Recovered bodies should be removed to the mortuary as soon as possible, after labelling.

HOME OFFICE

CIVIL DEFENCE

Manual of Basic Training

VOLUME II

BASIC RESCUE

PAMPHLET No. 4

LONDON: HIS MAJESTY'S STATIONERY OFFICE
1949

PRICE 1s 6d NET

"First aid in the truest sense"

S.O. Code No. 34-324-2-03*

GENERAL PREFACE

The series of Civil Defence handbooks and pamphlets is produced under the authority of the Home Secretary by the Civil Defence Department of the Home Office with the assistance of and in co-operation with the Secretary of State for Scotland and other Ministers concerned.

Measures for safeguarding the civil population against the effects of war which these publications describe, have become an essential part of the defensive organisation of this country. The need for them is not related to any belief that war is imminent. It is just as necessary that preparations for Civil Defence should be made in time of peace as it is that preparations should be made for the Armed Forces.

The publications cover, as far as is possible, measures which can be taken to mitigate the effects of all modern forms of attack. Any scheme of Civil Defence, if it is to be efficient, must be up-to-date and must take account of all the various weapons which might become available. The scale of bombing experienced in Great Britain during the 1939-45 war might be considerably exceeded in any future war, and types of weapons and tactics which were not experienced in this country might conceivably be used against it in the future. It does not follow that any one of the weapons, e.g., the atomic bomb, will necessarily be used, and it is most important that a proper balance is held between what is likely and what is possible.

The use of poison gas in war was forbidden by the Geneva Gas Protocol of 1925, to which this country and all the other countries of the Western Union were parties. At the outbreak of a war, His Majesty's Government would try to secure an undertaking from the enemy not to use poison gas. Nevertheless the risk of poison gas being used remains a possibility and cannot be disregarded any more than can certain further developments in other scientific fields.

The publications are designed to describe not only precautionary schemes which experience in the last war proved to be extremely effective in preventing avoidable injury and loss of life, or widespread dislocation of national industries, but also the training, both technical and tactical, which will be required of the personnel of the Civil Defence Corps if they are to be ready effectively to play their part if war should ever break out. The publications aim at giving the best available information on methods of defence against all the various weapons. Information is not complete in respect of some of these weapons and the best methods of countering them, but as results of experimental work and other investigations mature, they will be revised and added to from time to time so that the Civil Defence Corps may be kept up-to-date and the training may be on the most modern and experienced lines.

CONTENTS

NOTE

The pagination of this pamphlet is not continuous as it may be necessary to introduce new pages at a later date.

INTRODUCTION

Areas of devastation following Allied bombing raids.

BASIC RESCUE

INTRODUCTION

Rescue work under modern bombing conditions is a highly skilled operation, requiring considerable study and training. A comprehensive manual on the subject is being prepared.

This pamphlet is not intended for the experts but aims at providing the basic information and training essential to all who may be called on to start rescue work before the arrival of, or in the absence of, the regular Rescue Section. After you have read it however, and especially if you attend the basic rescue classes in your area, you will be able to do much to help your fellow citizens should the need arise.

The pamphlet tells you in simple language what to do from the time you arrive until you have effected a rescue, or are able to hand over to a fully trained rescue party.

Technical detail has been reduced to a minimum and as far as possible the subject is dealt with from a practical point of view.

Instruction in first aid does not form part of this pamphlet though brief references to it are made in some chapters. Rescue and first aid cannot, however, be separated and the first essential for rescue training, is a knowledge of first aid as set out in the pamphlet entitled " Basic First Aid."

In view of the fact that stretcher bearing may be a heavy commitment in any future war the chapter of the " Basic First Aid " pamphlet dealing with blanketing a stretcher, and loading, lifting and carrying a stretcher, is repeated as an appendix to this publication.

You have heard of the saturation attacks on Germany, the atomic bombs on Japan and of the widespread destruction created by these types of raids. In the event of another war we must expect large areas of damage.

We are all inclined to be overwhelmed by the idea of a vast area of devastation but if we stop and think we realise that from a rescue point of view this large area will be broken up into a number of smaller incidents.

Any difficult rescue work such as tunnelling will need the services of skilled rescue parties but experience has proved that the first people to arrive after the fall of a bomb wish to do everything they can to help. They should be encouraged to do so since by timely and proper action lives may be saved and suffering reduced. In rescue work however, a little training and knowledge is imperative. It is one of the exceptions where a little knowledge is essential and not dangerous. Getting a casualty out of the debris is one thing, saving his life is quite another.

Lives may be endangered by well meaning persons without any knowledge of rescue work even though they may be acting in what seems to them to be a perfectly natural and common sense way. The more people who understand the basic principles set out in this pamphlet the better for the casualty. Even if you cannot accomplish a difficult rescue, at least you will not make the task of the rescue parties harder, nor further endanger the lives of persons who may be trapped under the debris.

All rescue operations are a matter of team work, and the pamphlet is based on the work of a team of eight, including the leader, though this does not mean that any lesser number cannot successfully carry out the work. As you read through the pamphlet you will realise that in rescue work there can be only one leader in a team and that his orders must be obeyed. The life of a casualty, and possibly your own, may depend on the prompt response to an order. Rescue work demands common sense rather than brawn.

Finally there is an old saying which reads "An ounce of practice is worth a ton of theory." This is particularly true of rescue work and the more practical exercises you attend the more you will learn.

Note : A number of unused paragraphs have been left at the end of each chapter to permit of any additions that may be necessary from time to time. This, it is hoped, will avoid the necessity of renumbering paragraphs.

Photographs (Figs. 1, 5, 6, 7, 10 and 11) reproduced by kind permission of Mr. S. M. Evans, M.B.E., A.R.I.B.A.

CHAPTER I

TYPES OF BUILDINGS

1. Main Categories

Buildings can be divided into two main classes, the unframed building in which the floors and roof are supported by the walls, and the framed building in which the steel or reinforced concrete frame takes all the main loads. In this latter type of building the walls can be, and indeed often are, added after all the floors and roof are in position.

In the suburbs the majority of buildings are of the unframed type though in many cases modern blocks of flats of the framed type are to be seen. In the central area of any city there are examples of both types but the number of steel framed buildings is steadily increasing.

2. Unframed Buildings

As the majority of buildings are in this class, let us see how they are built. (*See Figs. 1 and 2*). It is not intended to give you highly technical instruction, but to prepare a background so that you can follow the chapters on the rescue of trapped casualties.

The outer walls are built up on foundations consisting of a concrete bed, though in some districts stone or brick foundations are used. At a suitable point a damp proof course, consisting of a layer of felt or slate, is laid to stop damp rising up the walls. With brick walls it is laid immediately above ground level and below the level of the wooden floors, but where floors are of solid concrete it is laid immediately above the ground floor level.

The outer walls vary in thickness according to the weight they have to carry. In ordinary dwelling houses they are usually solid walls, 9″ in thickness, though in some cases cavity walls are built. These normally consist of two 4½″ brick walls with a 2″ space between. The two walls are joined together with wall ties, which are pieces of wire or metal strip twisted in the centre to prevent water travelling from the outer to the inner wall. In three storey houses the lower storey may have 13½″ brick walls. If you look at any brick wall you will find that it has been built so that the corners of the bricks do not form continuous vertical lines. This is due to the bonding or overlapping of the bricks, the object being to strengthen the wall.

Party walls, usually 9″ in thickness divide two adjoining properties while partition walls which divide the various rooms are normally 4½″ brick, though timber partitions covered with lath and plaster or wall boarding are often used on upper floors. Breeze block partitions may be used on either ground or upper floors.

Chimney stacks are built from the foundations to well above the roof line and incidentally give added strength to the walls. In semi-detached and terraced houses they are normally built in the party walls, one stack between two houses.

At ground level a thin layer of concrete, called the site concrete, is laid over the whole site to prevent damp rising and the growth of vegetation.

On the site concrete are built the sleeper walls which carry the ground floors. The wooden floors are laid on timber joists which in turn rest on wall plates (pieces of timber about 3″ × 4″). Ground floor joists are usually 4″ × 2″ as they have the support given by the sleeper walls, whereas upper floor joists which have to span wider openings are of stouter timber, usually 7″ × 2″ or 9″ × 2″. The joists are set on their narrow edges and in general run across the shortest way of a room. In some cases parts of the ground floor e.g. sculleries, kitchens, etc. have solid concrete floors. They may however be finished with wood flooring, tiles, or one of the many composition floorings.

In the majority of brick buildings roofs are pitched, that is, they form an inverted V. The rafters, mainly of 4″ × 2″ timber, are fixed at one end to the wall plate and at the other to a piece of timber forming the ridge and known as the ridge board.

Battens are nailed across the rafters to carry the slates or tiles. In the better type of house the rafters are covered with boarding on which are laid the slates or tiles, to give better insulation against the elements.

In most dwelling houses wooden staircases are used. Usually the whole flight is built in the workshop and fixed in the house as a unit, normally against the party wall.

3. Framed Buildings

These are buildings in which a steel or reinforced concrete skeleton frame is built first. The floors and roof can be added before any walls are built. The walls can, if desired, be built after all this other work has been completed and this point should be remembered when you read about the effect of blast on framed buildings.

As with unframed buildings a concrete foundation is laid. This may however be a single block of concrete for each stanchion, which in a steel framed building will consist of a vertical column of steel. At suitable heights rolled steel joists are connected to form the floor and wall supports. (See Fig. 3). In most cases stanchions and joists are encased in concrete or brickwork after the service pipes have been clipped in position. The casing serves the double purpose of hiding the pipes and assisting in fire prevention.

In a reinforced concrete building the stanchion consists of a column of concrete reinforced with steel rods. The floors and walls are supported by reinforced concrete beams connected to the stanchions. (See Fig. 4).

Framed buildings usually have floors made from reinforced concrete, hollow tiles or varying kinds of slabs, some hollow, which are laid between the supports. These may have a boarded, wood-block or composition floor laid on top of the main floor.

Roofs may be flat or pitched. In the majority of cases the whole, or part, of the roof is flat consisting of a reinforced concrete slab tied to the top of the steel or concrete frame. If a pitched roof is used it will be on the lines of that used in unframed buildings but with steel trusses supporting the timber rafters.

The external openings between floors are filled in with brickwork, hollow blocks etc. set in cement mortar, the window frames often being built in as the work proceeds.

6

Fig. 1

Unframed building showing how walls support the floors (Note collapsed concrete roof).

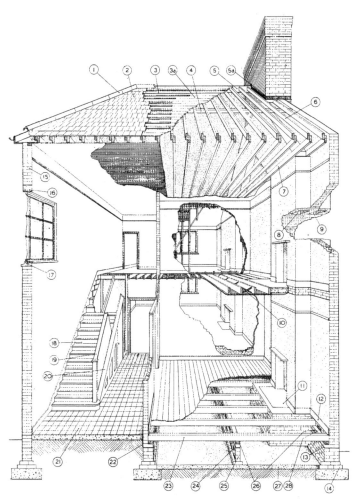

Fig. 2

Constructional details of an ordinary dwelling house.

(1) Ridge Tile.
(2) Tiles.
(3) Tile Batten.
(3a) Close Boarding.
(4) Purlin.
(5) Ridge Board.
(5a) Flashing.
(6) Common Rafter.
(7) Ceiling Joists.
(8) Flue from Room.
(9) Flue from Adjoining House.
(10) Herring Bone Strutting.
(11) Concrete Hearth.
(12) Skirting.
(13) Damp-proof Course.

(14) Footing Course.
(15) 9'' Solid Wall.
(16) Reinforced Concrete Lintel.
(17) Sill.
(18) Staircase.
(19) Handrail.
(20) String.
(21) Solid Floor.
(22) Vertical Damp Course.
(23) Floor Joists.
(24) Honeycomb Walling.
(25) Sleeper Wall.
(26) Wall Plates.
(27) Site Concrete.
(28) Air Brick.

Fig. 3

View of the interior of a steel framed building under construction, showing the vertical steel columns or stanchions, with the brackets to which the horizontal joists are bolted. At bottom centre can be seen the " footing " which transmits the load from the column to the concrete foundations. Note the commencement of laying a pre-cast concrete beam floor.

Fig. 4
A reinforced concrete framed building, complete with monolithic roof before construction of the panel walls.

Fig. 5
Effects of bomb damage on unframed buildings.

Fig. 6
Note how voids have been formed by the collapse of floors.

Fig. 7
Effects of bomb damage on a framed building.

CHAPTER II

TYPES OF BOMB DAMAGE

4. Causes of Damage

Air raid damage can be caused in various ways such as :—

    (i) Impact of the bomb on the building
    (ii) Blast, caused by the explosion
    (iii) Fragmentation
    (iv) Earth Shock

Let us consider how this will affect (*a*) an unframed building and (*b*) a framed building.

5. Effect on unframed buildings (*See Figs.* 5 *and* 6)

Any bomb which strikes a building even though it fails to explode, will cause damage by the force of its impact. It will break down the adhesion between roof and walls, internal partitions and main walls, and walls and foundations. The damage caused by a heavy unexploded bomb may be great enough to lead an untrained person to believe that a small bomb has exploded. There are, however, signs which tell the experienced that a large unexploded bomb is buried in the vicinity.

When a bomb explodes, the rapidly expanding gases transmit a considerable shock to the surrounding air and produce a pressure pulse which is immediately followed by a suction wave. The effect of the pressure pulse is to blow the walls inwards, the debris piling on the floors.

The floors of a dwelling house are not constructed to carry tons of wreckage and so in due course, they may bend, or break across at the centre of the joists, crashing down to form the roof of two voids, the bulk of the debris falling to the lowest point. The over-loading of the ground floor may well lead to similar collapse into the basement.

The suction wave is, however, the cause of most damage to buildings, external walls being sucked outwards, the bulk of the debris falling into the garden or street. The floors and roof, with some of the internal walls, are deprived of support and collapse in a heap, separated only by the furniture and such portions of the walls as remain. There may be voids formed by the furniture supporting the collapsed floors. It is possible to crawl through them in comparative safety provided that such supports are not disturbed.

6. Effect on framed buildings

Steel framed and reinforced concrete buildings react differently to the effects of H.E. bombs, though in both cases the skeleton framework is rigidly knitted together. The panels (walls) between the steel uprights may be blown in or sucked out just as in unframed buildings, but the roof and floors may stay in position because most of the supporting stanchions will remain, though some, which catch the full force of the blast, can be ripped away. In some cases the floors and roof may be torn out in addition to the walls yet the stanchions remain more or less intact (*See Fig.* 7). Twisting and distortion of a steel frame may be due to blast but is usually caused by fire.

Reinforced concrete buildings distort but do not collapse to the same extent as the reinforcement binds the whole together. In consequence, when anyone is trapped under reinforced concrete wreckage, the work of cutting a way in is considerable. As the concrete is held together by steel rods it is very difficult to lift one piece from off the next. This type of rescue demands the experience and equipment of the fully trained Rescue Section.

Blocks of flats, modern cinemas and theatres, hotels, and city offices embody these two types of construction. Every incident will have its individual problems and no two are alike.

CHAPTER III
PRELIMINARY RECONNAISSANCE

10. Sequence of operations

You often hear the term " Reconnaissance " used in rescue work ; it means " making a *systematic* search ". Whilst it is impossible to lay down hard and fast rules to cover every emergency it is possible to give a general sequence of operations. For convenience reconnaissance is divided into stages as set out below :—

Stage 1

Deal with surface casualties, giving priority to those in immediate danger. At the same time the team leader makes a quick but thorough examination of the site.

Obtain and record all possible information on the supposed whereabouts of casualties.

Stage 2

Search slightly damaged buildings for casualties. Maintain contact with those who can be seen or heard or whose whereabouts can be definitely ascertained.

Stage 3

Explore all places where persons could be trapped and remain alive.

Stage 4

Explore places where persons may be buried, but where their chance of remaining alive is remote or non-existent.

Stage 5

Carefully strip the site of debris until all bodies or parts of bodies are accounted for.

Not all the stages set down are within the scope of a team trained in basic rescue. You will, however, be able to deal with the first three stages and be able to give valuable assistance in the last two stages to a fully trained rescue party.

11. Reconnaissance (Stage 1)

While the surface casualties are being attended to the leader makes a reconnaissance of the area in which the team is to work so that he can obtain a clear picture of the nature and extent of the damage. Once this is obtained he can organise the work of his team and rescue will proceed on sound lines. He will have to collect information from wardens and neighbours, make a general survey of the site, note such factors as fractured gas mains, flooding, dangerous walls and other parts of the structure and formulate a plan of action.

Whether an incident is small or large it conforms to the same general outline. Working inwards from the perimeter you come to the surface casualties, those caught in the open or blown there by the effects of the explosion (*See Fig.* 8). Next comes the slightly damaged property, where windows have been smashed, doors blown off their hinges and tiles dislodged, but where the walls still stand. These houses must be searched as there may be casualties within. Finally in the central area you reach the seriously damaged buildings in which you may expect to find the trapped and the more seriously injured.

Fig. 8
Surface casualties caused by the effects of an explosion.

12. Surface Casualties (Stage 1)

The majority of these casualties will be found on the edge of the incident. They require first aid and removal to a place where warmth and shelter are available. Before they are removed you must, if they are conscious, obtain their names and addresses and any information they can give about the incident. If the casualty is unconscious a label must be tied to his clothing giving the time and place where found. All unconscious persons must be treated as stretcher cases. A responsible officer should try to find out who they are before they are sent, in an ambulance, to hospital.

If however, you find casualties trapped or injured in the presence of fire, coal gas, damaged walls, or in basements which are liable to flooding from damaged water mains you are confronted with an EMERGENCY RESCUE (*See Chapter IV*).

13. General Principles of Casualty Handling

It is better to do too little than to attempt too much and do the wrong thing. Your aim should be to prevent further shock and injury by :—

Re-assuring the patient and *keeping calm yourself*.
Stopping bleeding with pad and bandage.
Keeping the casualty warm.
Relieving pain.
Moving the casualty as little as possible.
Allowing fresh air to reach the casualty.
Not unnecessarily cutting or removing clothing.

18

14. Recording Information

It is very important that the team leader should have a record of all casualties sent to a hospital or other centre after receiving first aid treatment.

This deals with the people who have received treatment, but it does not solve the question of those missing, believed trapped.

Information about those presumed to be in a building may be obtained from various sources. The warden will know a great deal about the local inhabitants and if present will collect this information, leaving you free to deal with the actual rescue operations. Neighbours are a valuable source of information and at an early stage in the proceedings they should be asked what they know about the incident. All this information should be cross-checked wherever it is possible to do so. Hundreds of hours were wasted in the last war in searching for persons supposedly trapped, when they were safe in hospital or away from home when the incidents occurred. In some cases injured people had been taken away in cars by well intentioned but untrained members of the public. It has been said that time spent on reconnaissance is seldom wasted and it is equally true to say that time spent on recording the movements of casualties is time saved.

15. Searching Slightly Damaged Buildings (Stage 2)

Although the buildings on the fringe of an incident are only slightly damaged they must be thoroughly searched and you may expect to find casualties, conscious and unconscious, suffering from shock and severe cuts and bleeding caused by flying glass. Some may be lightly trapped through the sudden movement of heavy furniture as in Figure 9 and others may be choked by dust from fallen ceilings.

Fig. 9

Interior of slightly damaged building.

19

There is always a risk of fire owing to hot coals etc. from open fires having been scattered by the blast. In houses where gas is used there is the danger of coal gas poisoning and explosion owing to—

(i) lights, stoves etc. having been blown out by blast.

(ii) house mains having been fractured by earth shock.

It is for this reason that rescuers must not smoke or use naked lights when searching a building.

16. Searching Damaged Buildings (Stages 3 and 4)

Nearer to the centre of an incident the buildings will be more heavily damaged and all of them must be searched even though no definite information is available that any persons are trapped in them (*See Fig.* 10).

Too much stress cannot be laid on the need for searching all likely places for casualties who may still be alive and of effecting their release *before* any attempt is made to rescue victims who have little chance of survival. This does not mean that every nook and cranny must be searched for possible casualties, it means that *likely* places must be fully explored.

Typical places include :—

(i) Air raid shelters, inside and outside the buildings.

(ii) Points near fireplaces and chimney breasts.

(iii) Spaces and cupboards under staircases.

(iv) Basements.

(v) Voids under floors that have partially collapsed.

(vi) Rooms not entirely demolished but from which exit is barred by debris.

You may find casualties who have received severe crush injuries from fallen masonry, brickwork, beams, party walls, heavy furniture etc. These persons will be suffering from shock and may be suffocated by the dust falling from the debris, in which case the breathing passages must be cleared. (*See* Chapter VIII in Basic First Aid Pamphlet.) Persons suffering from crush injuries need special treatment *before* release. Full details of the treatment are given in Chapter X of The Basic First Aid Pamphlet.

Always observe the following safety precautions when searching damaged premises :—

(*a*) Wear a steel helmet if one is available.

(*b*) Do not enter dangerous places without informing some member of your team. If possible take a companion to help in case of accident.

(*c*) Do not smoke or strike matches in case coal gas is present and always be on the alert for the smell of escaping coal gas.

(*d*) Avoid touching loose electric wires.

(*e*) Walk as close as possible to the wall when on damaged upper floors or stairs.

(*f*) Disturb debris as little as possible to avoid collapse.

17. Recognition of Dangerous Structures

When entering a badly damaged building you must take care to avoid becoming a casualty. You must look for, and be able to recognise, dangerous structures.

Fig. 10

All likely places, including Anderson shelters, must be searched for casualties.

Fig. 11
Dangerous structures.

Danger from partly collapsed walls, unsafe staircases, damaged beams, etc., may confront those who enter a building immediately after it has been damaged (*See Fig.* 11).

You may at times have to take a certain amount of risk to complete a rescue operation. Unavoidable risks should be reduced to a minimum. Remember, too, that foolish risks mean extra casualties and the possible loss of one or more members of your team.

18. Calling and Listening for Trapped Persons (Stages 3 and 4)

In cases where a rescuer is confronted with a heap of rubble, bricks etc. a calling and listening period should be introduced. This has in the past saved many lives and is carried out in the following manner.

The leader places his men at suitable vantage points around the area in which persons may be trapped. He then demands complete silence and each member of the team in rotation calls " Is anyone there—Can you hear me ?" The other members of the team listen intently for any reply. If none is heard it is a good plan to tap on a wall, or on any gas or water pipe, beam, etc., running into the debris, all of which are good conducters of sound, and again listen for an answer. Once communication of this kind has been established with a trapped person, it should as far as possible be continually maintained because :—

(i) It keeps up his morale, it helps him to withstand whatever pain and discomfort he may be suffering and may even keep him alive.

(ii) It helps the rescuer to work in the right direction, often a difficult matter particularly in the dark.

(iii) The victim, if conscious, may be able to give you warning of any movement in the debris likely to cause him further injury.

19. Marking Buildings after Search

The objects of marking are to :—

(i) Save time and labour by indicating that the building has been thoroughly searched for trapped casualties.

(ii) Indicate the service responsible for the search *e.g.* Wardens, Rescue, Fire, etc.

(iii) Indicate that the building contains some particular danger.

The following standard markings must be used :—

A capital letter " S " chalked near the entrance will denote that the building has been searched. This will be underlined and underneath will be chalked the initial letter of the service responsible for the search, thus :—

$\frac{S}{W}$ = Searched by Wardens Section

$\frac{S}{F}$ = Searched by Fire Service

$\frac{S}{R}$ = Searched by Rescue Section

Where searchers find dangerous conditions e.g. leaning walls, damaged staircases, holes in floors, escaping coal gas etc. they should chalk the letter " D " after the standard marking. Thus the symbol—

$\frac{S}{W}$D

means that the building has been searched by Wardens and that you should look out for dangerous conditions somewhere in the building.

Dangerous buildings should be marked in a prominent position on all sides where entry is likely to be made.

A piece of board, or some improvised barricade, even string tied across an opening, will assist in warning anyone trying to enter the building.

20. Damage to Public Utility Services

Searchers in damaged buildings should turn off gas, water and electricity services at the main.

They should make themselves familiar with the " local " positions of stop taps and mains.

Where casualties are in danger from damaged services and the main stop taps or switches are not accessible the following temporary measures may be used.

   (i)   *Gas*
      If the pipe is made of lead, hammer the ends flat. A piece of clay or something similar will temporarily stop a leak.

   (ii) *Water*
      A wooden plug should be driven into the end of the open pipe. If the pipe is split, a piece of clay bound with sacking or old cloth will help to stop the flow.

  (iii) *Electric Cables*
      If the fuses cannot be found and taken out, any dry non-conductive material such as a broom handle, dry piece of wood, rubber hose, etc., may be used to remove live wires from the casualty or the casualty from live wires.

CHAPTER IV
METHODS OF RESCUE (Part I)

25. Emergency Methods

When casualties are in danger of receiving further injuries by fire, coal gas, flooding or from dangerous structures such as leaning walls, it is necessary to remove the cause of danger from the casualty or the casualty from the danger. If it is vital to remove the casualty to safety he must be moved regardless of his injuries. Only when the casualty is in imminent danger of death by remaining where he is does removal take priority over the stoppage of bleeding. There are several methods by which he can be moved, among them being the pick-a-back, human crutch, fireman's lift, fireman's crawl, fore and aft method, two and four handed seats. These are described and illustrated below.

Emergency methods should only be used when time will not permit of the use of more orthodox methods.

26. Methods Suitable for one Rescuer

(i) *Pick-a-back*

Carry the casualty in the ordinary pick-a-back position. This is the best way if he is conscious and able to hold on.

(ii) *Human Crutch*

Where the casualty can help himself the rescuer stands at his injured side and places the casualty's arm round his shoulder grasping the wrist with his hand. At the same time he passes his other hand round the casualty's waist gripping his clothing at the hip, and thus assists him by acting as a crutch. (*See Fig. 12*).

Fig. 12
Human Crutch.

C 2

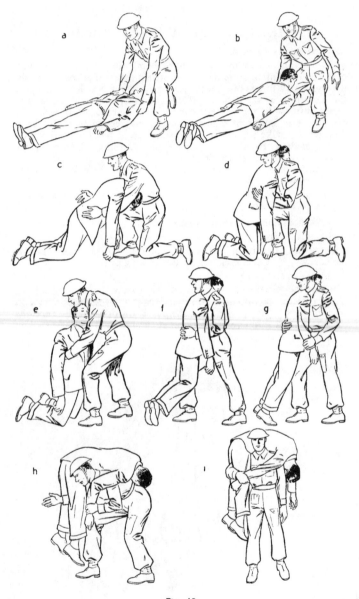

Fig. 13
Fireman's lift.

(iii) *Fireman's Lift*

This is one way of carrying a helpless or unconscious patient and allows the bearer a free hand. It is easier for the bearer than pick-a-back, but not so comfortable for the patient. Various stages of the lift are shown in Figure 13.

If the casualty is lying on his back kneel on one knee (usually the right) at his head, place your right hand upon his right shoulder, and with your left hand beneath his left shoulder turn him over gently on to his face so that his forehead and face are supported on your right forearm. (*See Figs.* 13*a* & *b*).

Place your hands beneath the casualty's shoulders and lift him up to a kneeling position, supporting him against your body with his head on your right shoulder. (*See Figs.* 13*c* & *d*).

With your hands in the casualty's armpits stand up and lift him on to his feet, pressing his body close to yours ; shift your hands from his armpits and clasp them together round his waist. (*See Figs.* 13*e* & *f.*)

Keep your right arm round the casualty's waist and grasp his right wrist with your left hand carrying the limb away from the body. Stoop and place your head beneath his right arm and hoist him up on to your right shoulder, still retaining hold of his right wrist with your left hand. Pass your right arm between the casualty's thighs and grip his right wrist with your right hand at the same time remove your left hand which becomes free. (*See Figs.* 13*g* & *h*).

Shift the weight of the casualty well on to the centre of your back and rise to the erect position. (*See Fig.* 13*i*).

(iv) *Fireman's Crawl*

If a rescuer finds an unconscious casualty, or one who is unable to help himself, or who is too heavy for one of the above three methods to be applied, the Fireman's Crawl can be used as follows.

Turn the casualty on to his back and tie his wrists together. Kneel astride him facing his head and place your head through the loop thus formed by his arms. By crawling on your hands and knees you can then drag him with you, even though he may be heavier than you are. (*See Fig.* 14).

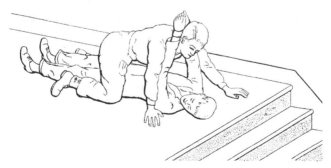

Fig. 14
Fireman's crawl.

29

(v) *Removal downstairs*

To move the casualty downstairs, lay him on his back, head downwards on the stairs, place your hands under his armpits so that his head rests on the crook of your arm and ease him gently downstairs. (*See Fig.* 15).

Fig. 15

Removal downstairs.

27. **Methods suitable for more than one rescuer**

When there is more than one rescuer available, the following emergency methods can be used :—

(i) *The Fore and Aft Method*

The patient is placed on his back. One bearer raises the shoulders and passes his hands under the arms from behind clasping them in front of the chest. The other bearer takes one leg under each arm and they carry him feet first. If a leg is broken, both legs should be tied together, or put in splints and both carried under one arm. (*See Fig.* 16).

(ii) *Two Handed Seat*

Two rescuers face one another on either side of the casualty and stoop. Each rescuer passes his arm nearest the casualty's head under his back just below the shoulders and, if possible, grips his clothing. They raise the casualty's back and slip their other arms under the middle of his thighs, clasping their hands with a hook grip. (*See Fig.* 17). The rescuers rise together and step off with short paces.

Fig. 16

The Fore and Aft Method.

(iii) *Four Handed Seat*

The rescuers face each other and each grasp their own left wrist with their right hand. Their hands are then put together, the free left hand grasping the right wrist of the man opposite. The casualty puts one arm or both arms round the necks of the rescuers. (*See Fig.* 18).

Fig. 17
Two handed seat.

Fig. 18
Four handed seat.

CHAPTER V

METHODS OF RESCUE (Part II)

33. Lightly Trapped Casualties

When you find a person lightly trapped, e.g. a person unable to move because he is pinned down by a beam or piece of furniture, you must be extremely careful how you move the obstruction.

If he is trapped by his clothing being caught in the debris it is advisable to release him by carefully cutting his clothing rather than by attempting to move the debris. In any case there may be other casualties under the debris and unless it is carefully moved there is a possibility of a further fall, which will injure not only the lightly trapped casualty but others who may be underneath.

It is not always necessary to remove the obstacle trapping the casualty, it may be better to pack it up sufficiently for the casualty to be released. (*See Fig.* 19).

Fig. 19
Casualty trapped by fallen beam.

34. Securing to a Stretcher

During rescue operations there is a possibility of the bearers stumbling and of the debris moving, with consequent risk of the casualty being thrown off the stretcher. In some instances the stretcher will have to be turned on to one side, or up-ended, to pass some obstruction, and on these occasions it is necessary for the casualty to be securely fastened to the stretcher. It may be possible to use the stretcher equipment shown in Fig. 20 but if this is not available it will be necessary to improvise.

Fig. 20

The manifold stretcher harness.

A 40 ft. lashing line can be used for the purpose. The only knot used is the clove hitch which is as simple to tie in darkness as in daylight and which will never fail. It is formed by making two loops in the rope, both anti-clockwise, the second loop, which tends to come in front, being placed behind the first. It can also be formed by making a loop on the handle of the stretcher, so that the running end is imprisoned by the standing part, followed by another loop.

Form the first knot on a handle near the head of the casualty, pass the rope down the side of the stretcher, taking a complete turn under the stretcher and back over the casualty's chest, forming a half hitch. At least three turns must be used, two above the knees and one below. The rope is then passed round the casualty's feet, brought up on the opposite side of the stretcher and fastened with a clove hitch. (*See Fig. 21*)

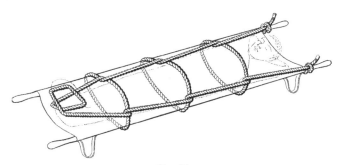

Fig. 21

An improvised lashing.

35. Rescue from Upper Floors

When a casualty is found on an upper floor which is in a dangerous condition, and from which exit is not readily available it is better to make him comfortable and to leave his removal to trained Rescue Section personnel.

If, however, it is *essential* to remove him the "four-point suspension" method should be used.

The casualty is placed on a stretcher and securely fixed by using either the stretcher equipment or a lashing. For raising or lowering, two 40 ft. lashings are used, one at each end of the stretcher. Each end of the lashing is fastened by means of a bowline to one of the "D's" of the stretcher.

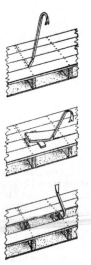

Whilst this is being done other rescuers will cut a hole in the floor, large enough to take the stretcher in a horizontal position. In some cases it may be possible to enlarge an existing hole which has been caused by damage, or to use the well-hole of a damaged staircase.

If it is necessary to make a new hole cut it near the walls and avoid the centre of the floor. Floor boards will have to be taken up, or sawn through, and part of one joist removed leaving a hole of the required size. The removal of the floor boards may be commenced with a wrecking bar. (*See Fig.* 22).

Fig. 22

Uses of a wrecking bar.

The length of the hole must be parallel to the joists, to avoid cutting more than one, as each cut weakens the floor.

With one person to each rope the stretcher is lowered by carefully paying out the ropes so that the stretcher is kept steady. The head of the casualty can readily be kept higher or lower than his feet as his condition demands, though normally the stretcher will be kept in a horizontal position. (*See Fig.* 23).

Two men should be in position on the lower floor to receive the stretcher.

36. Rescue from Basements

This process necessitates the carrying out of the operations described in the previous paragraph, except that the stretcher will be pulled up to the ground floor level instead of being lowered. The casualty should be kept in a safe position while the hole is being cut in the floor.

37. Propping and Strutting

You must take great care not to remove any natural props or struts, such as partly open doors, beams or floor joists which have dropped and are supporting the debris. A wedge should be put under partly open doors to prevent them moving and allowing the debris to collapse. (*See Fig.* 24).

Fig. 23
Lowering stretcher from an upper floor.

Fig. 24
Wedging an open door.

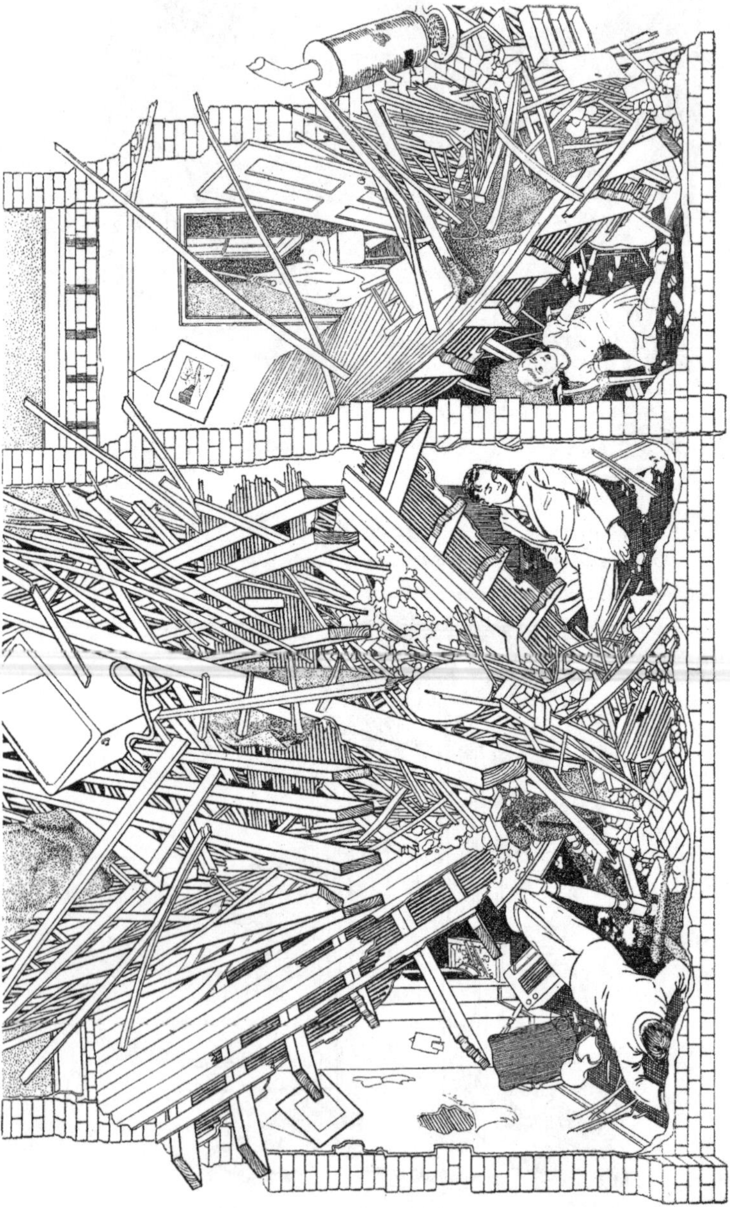

Fig. 25
Typical voids in a collapsed house.

Sometimes a simple prop or strut can be put in to strengthen a floor loaded with debris. It should be put in before any rescue work is attempted above that level. If possible this kind of work should be left to trained Rescue Section personnel but if it has to be done in an emergency great care must be taken to see that the prop or strut is not too long. It is dangerous to attempt to restore a floor to its original level, and the prop is inserted to hold the floor in position, *not to lift it*.

38. Rescue from Voids

When recovering casualties from a void formed by the collapse of floors etc. first see how it is formed and how the debris is supported. (*See Figs*. 6, 11 *and* 25). Only loose material should be removed, never pull out the supports.

If a casualty has to be removed from a very small void you will find a length of board and a 1½ in. lashing very useful. The lashing is attached to the board which is then pushed underneath the casualty, when both board and casualty can be easily drawn out of the void. In some cases the fireman's crawl can be used, but, where voids are large enough, always use a stretcher.

39. Improvised Stretchers

When there is a shortage of stretchers it is better to improvise rather than manhandle the casualty unnecessarily. An old door (*as in Fig.* 26), a sheet of galvanised iron, a blanket, or a short ladder are all examples of improvisation. Another method is to fold a blanket into three,

Fig. 26
Using a door as a stretcher.

44

using six or eight safety pins (three or four on each side) to pin the edges of the blanket together. Two small poles, broom handles etc. are passed through the folds and the improvised stretcher is ready for use. (*See Fig.* 27).

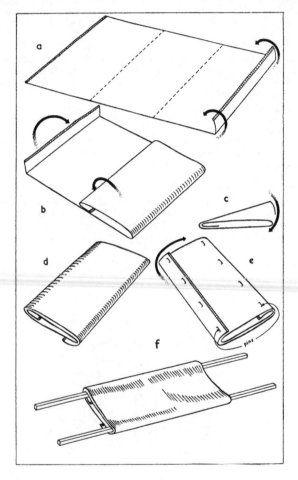

Fig. 27
Another form of improvised stretcher.

When a casualty is being removed from a void, space may not permit of the use of a standard stretcher. In these cases a blanket lift may be used which will be more comfortable for the casualty and easier for the team to handle. It is made by doubling the blanket lengthwise, and rolling the edges in fairly tightly to the side of the casualty, thus forming a hand hold for the bearers. (*See Fig.* 28)

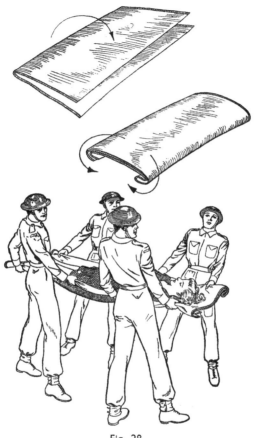

Fig. 28
The blanket lift.

40. Handling a stretcher in difficult situations

A stretcher should, wherever possible, be carried in the horizontal position. There may be times when this is impossible as the casualty may have to be carried over debris and the bearers will have to climb up and down piles of rubble. In such cases four or six bearers are an advantage. If four bearers are available, one should be at the head (No. 1), one at the foot (No. 2) and one at each side (Nos. 3 and 4). When they have to climb over a large heap of debris Nos. 3 and 4 take the full weight of the head of the stretcher while No. 1 climbs up, when the head of the stretcher is lifted for him to grasp. The stretcher is then advanced, Nos. 3 and 4 climb taking the weight of the foot of the stretcher while No. 2 climbs. A similar procedure is adopted when climbing down. (*See Fig*. 29).

Fig. 29
Moving a stretcher over debris.

If only two bearers are available they must lay the stretcher down as each obstruction is reached. As the material on which the casualty is lying is apt to sag, the stretcher, when laid down, must rest on the " D's" with the bed of the stretcher clear of obstructions. Debris is inclined to move under the weight of a human being so that special care is necessary in selecting places for the setting down of the stretcher.

41. Using a Stretcher in a confined space

In confined spaces, if there is sufficient height and the casualty has been secured to the stretcher it may be stood on end and by grasping the sides, can be moved round sharp corners.

Where the height is insufficient to permit of this method being used, as in the case of shelters, a compromise between the horizontal and vertical positions is necessary. The stretcher should be carried feet first as far as the middle of the right angled bend, when the foot is placed on the ground and the head lifted as high as the roof will permit. The stretcher can then be worked round the bend, one bearer easing the feet and another the head.

It should not be turned on its side, or height will be lost and difficulties increased. At the same time there will be a risk of the casualty banging against the inside of the bend.

42. Passing Over a Gap

When taking a casualty out of a damaged building it is often necessary to cross a gap in the floor. A ladder may be used as a bridge providing that the precautions outlined in paragraph 52 of Chapter VI are followed.

Alternatively two or more joists may be laid across the hole as illustrated in Fig. 30. They should be twice as long as the hole so that they rest on the sound joists of the damaged floor.

Fig. 30
Two men carrying a stretcher over a gap.

It is wise to use six bearers as a safety precaution when crossing a pile of debris which contains gaps. Four of them take the handles of the stretcher, while two go across the gap and take the handles as the stretcher is passed forward to them. The two bearers already in the foot position turn inwards and by taking hold of the side runners help to support the stretcher as it goes over, until they relieve bearers at the head. These two bearers cross the gap and take up their original position as the head of the stretcher reaches the far side of the gap. (*See Fig.* 31).

Fig. 31
Passing a stretcher over a gap.

CHAPTER VI

ROPES AND LADDERS

48. Use of Ropes

In rescue work a number of problems are solved by the proper use of ropes. Experience has proved that incidents occur where persons have to be rescued from above or below ground level, and therefore the need for lowering or hoisting will arise.

All persons undertaking these operations should have a sound knowledge of the use of ropes, the tying of knots and their proper application.

Any chafing or rubbing will damage ropes and decrease their strength, therefore they should not be allowed to pass over a sharp or rough edge without some protection, such as sacking or similar material.

49. Care of Ropes

Ropes must be kept in an even atmosphere, and stored as far as possible, in a cool dry place with plenty of ventilation. They should, for preference, be made up into hanks and hung where no artificial heat can effect them. Ropes are not suitable for service until they have been " softened up " and become pliable by handling or use on exercises. All ends of ropes must be securely whipped preferably with waxed twine to prevent the strands untwisting. (*See Fig.* 32).

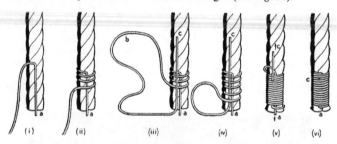

Fig. 32
Method of whipping the end of a rope.

Oil or Grease must not be put on Ropes for the following reasons :—

1. Ropes used by the Rescue Section are made from manilla, hemp or sisal, which produce their own lubrication ;
2. If oil or grease is applied, it prevents air from getting to the fibres ;
3. Dust and grit collect on greasy ropes and damage the fibres, making them more difficult to handle and shortening their life.

50. Terms used in connection with Ropes

Anchored. Fastened to some immovable object such as a large tree, post, or well-driven picket.

Haul. The act of pulling on a rope.

Half-Hitch. A closed loop on a rope, a simple fastening of a rope round some object by winding and crossing one turn over another turn so that one bites on the other without actually knotting the rope. (*See Fig.* 33).

Paying out or Easing. To ease off or slacken a rope.

Rope Sizes. The size of manilla and other fibre ropes is denoted by the circumference of the rope in inches.

Running End. The free end of a rope.

Standing Part. The part of a rope which is taking the load.

Whipping. Binding ends of rope with twine to prevent the strands untwisting.

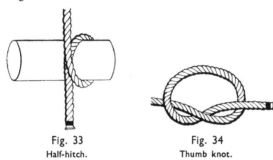

Fig. 33
Half-hitch.

Fig. 34
Thumb knot.

51. Essential Knots

There are five knots which everyone must know how to tie and apply under any conditions. They are :—

  (i)   Thumb Knot
 (ii)   Reef Knot
(iii)   Clove Hitch
 (iv)   Bowline
  (v)   Chair Knot

(i)   *Thumb Knot*

The thumb knot is formed by making a loop and passing one end through it. (*See Fig.* 34).

(ii)   *Reef Knot*

For joining two ropes of equal thickness. This is best described as two thumb knots tied in reverse direction, left over right then right over left. It is quickly untied and is a useful knot for general purposes. (*See Fig.* 35).

Fig. 35
Reef knot.

54

(iii) *Clove Hitch*

This forms the basis of many securing knots and can be used in the end of a rope or in the centre.   To tie at the end of a rope, pass the running end round a pole bringing it out underneath the standing rope. Pass the running end round the pole again above the first half hitch, bringing the running end under itself to tighten, pulling both the running end and the standing rope.   When tied thus in the end of a rope, it is a good anchoring knot and is easily untied.   To tie in the centre of a rope, two loops are formed, one in the left hand (anti-clockwise) and one in the right hand (anti-clockwise) the latter being passed in front of the left hand loop.   Both loops are then passed over the pole and drawn tight.   (*See Fig.* 36)

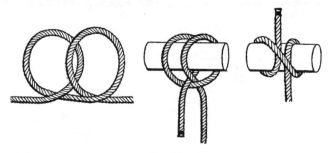

Fig. 36

Method of making a clove hitch.   Left : on a rope or spar.   Centre and right : by means of two locking half-hitches slipped over an object or spar.

(iv) *Bowline*

This forms a non-slip loop at the end of a rope and is a most useful anchoring knot.   It may also be used for lowering or raising purposes and for attaching a rope to a person as a safety line.

To tie this knot take the running end of the rope in the right hand, pull it across the upturned palm of the left hand, lasso the fingers of the left hand, forming a loop, pull loop to required size, pass running end (which is held in the right hand) up through the loop in the left hand, then underneath the standing rope and back down through the loop.   Pull standing rope and running end to tighten.   (*See Fig.* 37).

Fig. 37
Bowline.

55

(v) *Chair Knot*

This knot is very important for emergency rescue work. Its purpose is to form an efficient and quickly made sling in which a person may readily be raised or lowered. The sling formed by this knot gives support to the chest and legs of the person being rescued.

It is formed by grasping the rope, near its centre, in the left hand, palm down. Approximately a yard from the left hand take the rope in the right hand, palm uppermost. Turn the left hand palm upwards forming a loop (anti-clockwise), turn the right hand palm down forming a loop. Pass the standing ropes through the loops of the opposite hand pulling them through thus forming two loops with a knot in the centre. These loops can be adjusted to the required size. A half-hitch is then made on each loop to keep them at their required size.

One loop will be slightly larger than the other to keep the person being raised or lowered in a " chaired " position. (*See Fig.* 38).

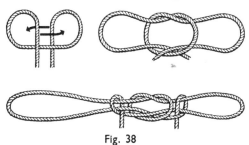

Fig. 38
Method of making a chair knot.

Having learned how to form these knots it is most important that their varied application is thoroughly understood and frequently practised.

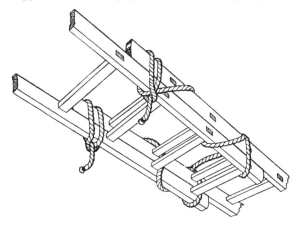

Fig. 39
Lashing two ladders together (showing knots on underside).

52. Use of Ladders

Ladders play an important part in rescue work and it would be advantageous to have two short ladders not less than 8 feet long. These when lashed together with a 1½ inch rope would form a ladder approximately 13 feet long. (*See Fig.* 39).

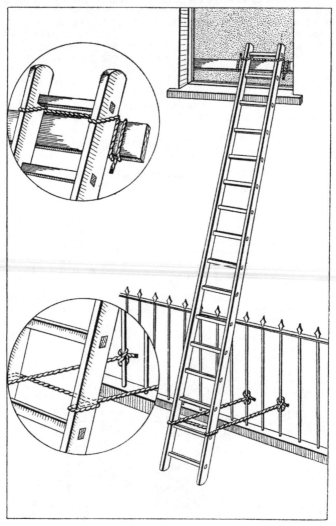

Figs. 40 and 41

Fig. 40 (upper circle).   Securing head of a ladder.
Fig. 41 (lower circle).   Anchoring foot of a ladder.

A ladder of this size would reach the first floor windows of most dwelling houses, and also into basements and would prove valuable when making a reconnaissance.

It would normally take two men to fasten, carry, and erect the ladders. Care must be taken that the reinforcement (if any) of a ladder is always on the underneath side of the load, and that a firm foundation is found for the foot of the ladder.

In some cases it is necessary to tie or anchor the foot of the ladder to stop it slipping. This can be done by using a 15 feet-1½ inch lashing. (*See Fig.* 41).

At other times the head of the ladder may have to be fastened. Again a 15 feet-1½ inch lashing could be used. One man must hold the foot of the ladder until the head has been secured. (*See Fig.* 40).

Short ladders are very useful for getting over obstacles, damaged walls, high fences, and the like. (*See Fig.* 42).

Fig. 42

Passing a ladder over a wall.

They can also be used for bridging a gap, by placing one or both side by side over the opening (reinforcement if any on the underneath side) and putting a board or boards on the rungs of the ladder. Wherever possible, one length of board should be used on one ladder, but if this is not possible, care must be taken to overlap the ends of the boards where they meet. (*See Fig*. 43).

Fig. 43
Bridging a gap

The ladder or ladders must be quite long enough to bridge the gap and give adequate support at either end.

CHAPTER VII

DEBRIS CLEARANCE

58. Methods of Removal

Debris resulting from a collapsed building can be removed in three ways, apart from the obvious moving of debris which is on or near the casualty.

(i) selective clearance, removing debris from a specified part of the site, where casualties are known or suspected.

(ii) systematic clearance of the whole site in order to recover casualties, or bodies, whose exact whereabouts are unknown.

(iii) general clearance, or the complete clearance of the site. This third method is not a rescue operation.

Debris which may be covering victims must not be walked over indiscriminately nor disturbed in any way until a plan of action has been decided upon. It is far from easy to recognise a body in a pile of debris, especially when large quantities of lime and dust are present.

Where it is essential to clear debris from the top downwards, helpers should be stationed in such a position that they can pass timbers and other pieces of debris to one another without having to climb over the debris. (*See Fig.* 44).

59. Selective Clearance

Immediately the known casualties have been dealt with, leaders of teams must try to find any persons still unaccounted for. The most likely position of casualties may be ascertained by collecting information, by deduction, or by a calling and listening period.

The behaviour of floors is a good guide to follow. Try to find what happened to the particular floor on which a missing person was supposed to have been, as this will generally produce a clue to their position.

A few minutes thought at the beginning of the job may save hours of work later.

Always proceed on the assumption that a trapped casualty is alive, therefore :—

Speed is necessary.

Care is essential in moving even the smallest piece of material.

Once located, an endeavour should be made to keep the casualty informed of what is being done for him.

Wherever possible a natural way through the debris should be found. If it becomes necessary to force a way through then great care must be taken. Timber which is not comparatively free must not be removed or pulled out of the debris by force as it may be protecting a casualty, or supporting a section of the debris.

When you get close to a casualty remove the debris by hand rather than by the use of tools. In this case gloves should always be worn. If it is necessary to use a shovel do so with care. For removing dust and small rubble in confined spaces or when working close to a casualty a small fireside shovel is best.

Pointed-nosed shovels, with short handles, prove best when dealing with mixed debris where there is no level bottom for the shovels to work on.

Ordinary square-nosed shovels are used in the more straightforward clearance when there is no restriction of room or movement, and a level foundation can be found to work on. Only persons skilled in rescue work should use picks on debris, and even then only with the greatest care.

60. Systematic Clearance

Should there still be persons missing, and their exact location in the debris is unknown, then systematic debris clearance must be commenced. This should not be confused with general debris clearance to clear a site, a straightforward job usually carried out at a later stage by mechanised means.

Systematic clearance is a rescue operation demanding considerable expedition as well as care to avoid further injury to casualties and mutilation of bodies.

Debris must be removed clear of the operations and segregated, timber on one pile, bricks on another and so on. The practice of moving debris from one part of the site and dumping it on to unsearched debris *must* be avoided.

61. Debris Bins

The actual removal of debris may be done in various ways. If you are working with a regular rescue party they will have debris bins, which when filled, can be manhandled to a vehicle or a selected spot where the debris is to be dumped. They are also issued with barrows in which the debris can be wheeled away.

Debris bins are much better than baskets as they enable small debris and dust to be removed, can be used for getting water out of flooded basements in which casualties are trapped, and are useful for the collection of human remains.

One man can carry a bin—normally on his shoulder—but he needs help to raise or lower it. (*See Fig.* 45).

Unless a regular rescue party is present you may have neither bins nor barrows. It is however quite possible to use a bucket or something similar in lieu of a debris bin.

When removing debris in a confined space or over obstacles it is best to form a human chain. (*See Fig.* 44). The bins, buckets, or whatever you are using are passed from man to man and emptied at points known to be clear of casualties.

Fig. 44
A human chain for the removal of debris.

Fig. 45
Method of lifting and carrying debris bins.

CHAPTER VIII

RECOVERY OF VALUABLES

67. Finding

It frequently falls to the lot of rescue personnel and others assisting them at an incident, to find money and valuables. As a person who improperly retains any such property removed from bombed premises is liable to very severe punishment, it is most important that members of the Civil Defence Corps and the general public should clearly understand their responsibilities and liabilities in this matter.

68. Disposal

Any article of value, however small, found on bombed premises, must be handed over immediately to the team leader who will arrange for it to be given to the Damage Control Officer, or to the senior police officer on duty.

The greatest possible care must be exercised in this direction. Cases occurred in the last war where men quite innocently put money or valuable articles found on the site into their pockets, with the intention of delivering the articles to the authorities, but were unfortunately apprehended by the police before they had been able to carry out their intention. As it is most difficult in such circumstances for any person to prove the innocence of his act and intention, the only safe course is for the finder immediately to declare his find to his colleagues, and, as soon as possible, to hand the articles to a responsible officer, as mentioned in the preceding paragraph, and obtain a receipt for them.

CHAPTER IX

HANDING OVER TO RESCUE PARTY

74. Technical Control

When a Rescue Party arrives at an incident the leader will take charge of all rescue work until relieved by a senior officer of his own Section.

He may, or may not, wish to retain the services of the original team but in either case it will be necessary for the leader of the team which has carried out the initial work to hand over to the leader of the incoming Rescue Party.

The new leader cannot accept responsibility or put his party to work until he has a complete picture of the situation. The original team should have dealt with the surface casualties and possibly the lightly trapped. They may have started on the rescue of those seriously trapped though handicapped to some extent by the limited equipment available.

75. Information Required

The incoming leader will need to know :—

   (i)   The extent of the site on which the team has been working, and what has been accomplished.

  (ii)   The names and addresses if obtainable, of casualties who have left the site, and position from which they have been recovered.

 (iii)   The probable position of those suspected to be trapped, and whether any contact has been made.

 (iv)   Any information already received from wardens, neighbours, etc.

  (v)   Whether there are any known dangers e.g. flooding, escape of coal gas, etc.

 (vi)   Position of temporary mortuary.

 (vii)   Whether any liquid and what amount has been given to casualties still trapped, who are suffering from crush injuries.

(viii)   Whether a doctor is present.

 (ix)   Whether the team from whom he is taking over can remain if required to assist.

If the team can remain, the rescue party leader will probably divide his party into halves, and add to each half a number of the original team. One half would work under the deputy leader of the incoming party and the other under the leader who would co-ordinate the work of both. A composite party of this nature has a big advantage in that it comprises those with an intimate knowledge of the area and an elementary knowledge of rescue and those who are specialists in rescue work.

F.

CHAPTER X

DO'S and DON'TS

DO make a reconnaissance before you start work. The time will not be wasted.

DO examine a casualty before removal and see that you give the correct first aid treatment.

DO free the nose and mouth of a casualty from dust and grit and so ease his breathing.

DO protect a casualty from falling debris and dust by using blankets, tarpaulins, corrugated iron sheets, etc.

DO be careful how you move debris from the vicinity of a casualty.

DO keep a casualty warm and so reduce shock.

DO make sure the stretcher is properly blanketed so that the casualty has the maximum amount of warmth and comfort.

DO learn how to carry a stretcher over debris and obstacles.

DO remember that a stretcher case should be conveyed in an ambulance.

DO remember to keep a list of all casualties dealt with.

DO keep off wreckage as much as possible and leave it undisturbed or the natural voids may be destroyed by further collapses.

DO be careful how you remove debris and obstacles, especially from voids, to prevent further collapse.

DO use gloves when removing debris by hand.

DO remember to exercise great care when using sharp tools in debris.

DO walk as close as possible to the wall when on damaged stairs and upper floors.

DON'T move an injured person without rendering first aid unless he is in immediate danger.

DON'T smoke or strike matches in case there is an escape of coal gas.

DON'T crawl over the debris or disturb parts of the damaged structure unless you are compelled to by circumstances.

DON'T pull timber out of the wreckage indiscriminately or you may cause further collapse.

DON'T enter dangerous places without informing the other members of your team, or if possible, without a companion to help in case of accident.

DON'T touch loose electric wiring.

DON'T throw debris aimlessly on one side—you may have to move it again.

APPENDIX A

TRANSPORT OF CASUALTIES

1. Blanketing a Stretcher

Before a casualty is laid upon a stretcher you must cover it with a blanket folded lengthwise, or an overcoat, so that he does not lie directly upon the canvas. This adds to his comfort and reduces shock. *Remember* that it is more important to put blankets under him than over him. With two layers of blanket underneath and one on top a casualty is better off than with one layer underneath and two on top.

Two blankets only are required to blanket a stretcher properly. The way to do it is as shown in Fig. 46.

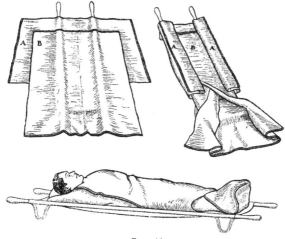

Fig. 46
Blanketing a Stretcher.

(i) Lay one open blanket (A) lengthwise across a stretcher with one side close to the head end, and one end of the blanket having a slightly longer overlap of the stretcher than the other.

(ii) Fold a second blanket (B) in three folds lengthwise and lay it on top of the first blanket (A) along the stretcher with its upper edge about 15 inches below the upper edge of the first blanket (A). There will now be four thicknesses of blanket upon which the casualty will lie.

(iii) Open out the two ends at the foot of blanket (B) for about 2 feet to form two flaps.

(iv) Roll up or pleat in concertina fashion the overhanging ends of blanket (A) and place them on the edges of the stretcher so that they will not drag on the ground when the stretcher is brought close to the patient.

(v) When the patient is laid upon the stretcher wrap the two flaps of blanket (B) round his feet and tuck the ends between them.

Open out the rolled up folds of blanket (A) and wrap first the short then the long end round the patient tucking it well in at one side.

Your casualty will now be warmly blanketed.

To secure blankets as a pack on a stretcher.

(1)   Lay blankets (A) and (B) on the stretcher as described in 1(i) and (ii) above.

(2)   Fold in the two edges of blanket (A) taking the folds to the sides of the stretcher twice, then once again on to the stretcher.

(3)   Place the foot-end of blanket (B) on the stretcher, then fold it over and over with blanket (A) to form a flat pack, in the centre of which a hot-water bottle is placed.   Secure the pack thus formed to the stretcher with a strap passed round it and the stretcher.

2.   Lifting, loading and carrying a stretcher

Loading into ambulance

The placing of an injured person upon a stretcher, carrying him from an incident and loading the stretcher into an ambulance is in accordance with methods which experience has shown to be the most comfortable for the patient.   You should therefore know how to do this properly so that by disturbing him as little as possible you will lessen his discomfort and prevent further shock.   Elaborate drill in carrying out the above is not necessary for you, as any form of drill must of necessity be modified to meet difficult situations.   You should however be capable of efficiently performing the simple exercises depicted below which aim at providing and maintaining concerted action and good team work among those dealing with casualties.

(i)   *Lifting a stretcher*

Four men of approximately the same height are allotted as bearers to carry each stretcher.   For convenience they are numbered 1, 2, 3, and 4, each four men constituting a stretcher squad.   The No. 1 bearer of each squad is the leader and gives all orders.

The position which these bearers take up in relation to a stretcher are :—

> (*a*)   No. 1 on the right of the stretcher with his toes in line with the front end of the right pole.
> (*b*)   No. 2 on the left of the stretcher in line with No. 1.
> (*c*)   No. 3 on the right of the stretcher behind No. 1 and his heels in line with the rear end of the right pole.
> (*d*)   No. 4 on the left of the stretcher in line with No. 3.

These positions are permanent.

On the command " lift stretcher—collect wounded " all four bearers stoop together and lift the stretcher from the ground with the hand nearest to the stretcher.   They then double by the shortest route to the patient and halting three paces from and in line with his head, place the stretcher on the ground and stand up to await further orders.

(ii)   *Loading a stretcher*

On the command " load stretcher " No. 1 bearer goes to the *right* of the patient at his hips, Nos. 2, 3 and 4 to the *left* of the patient at his knees, hips, and shoulders respectively.   All bearers now turn inwards together, kneel on one knee and pass their hands, palms upwards, beneath the body of the patient, No. 2 bearer supporting the legs, Nos. 1 and 3 by joining hands the thighs and hips and No. 4 the shoulders and head.   At a given signal the patient is lifted gently off the ground on to the knees of 2, 3 and 4 bearers, No. 1 disengages and brings the stretcher which he places in front of the bearers ready for the patient to be lowered on to it.   He then takes up his former position and again links hands with No. 3.   On the command " lower " the patient is lowered gently on to the centre of the stretcher, the bearers disengage, rise and resume their permanent positions at the poles of the stretcher.

(iii)   *Loading a stretcher with only two bearers*

The stretcher is again placed in line with the patient as before.   After giving first aid the two bearers stand astride the patient facing the stretcher.   The patient's arms are folded across his chest if he is unconscious but, if not, he may be able to help by grasping the leading bearer round the neck with one or both hands as he bends down, the bearers both bend together, lift the patient by the shoulders and thighs and shuffle forwards straddling the stretcher as they reach it.

(iv)   *Lifting and carrying the loaded stretcher*

On the command " lift stretcher " all bearers stoop together, grasp the stretcher poles and lift the stretcher holding it at the full length of their arms.

At a given signal they step off together with the inner foot, *i.e.*, that nearest the stretcher, so as to be out of step to prevent the stretcher from swinging.

As a rule it does not matter whether a casualty is carried head first or feet first, but when going uphill it is more comfortable for him to be carried head first, unless there is some reason to the contrary.

(v)   *Loading a stretcher into an ambulance*

(1)   The stretcher is brought to the ambulance by the four bearers and lowered to the ground one pace from and in line with the vehicle, the patient's head to the front.

(2)   No. 1 bearer gives the command " load."

(3)   All bearers turn inwards, lift the stretcher together and, taking a side pace to the ambulance, raise the stretcher gently to the level of the berth to be loaded, No. 1 and 2 bearers placing the front runners of the stretcher upon the tracks in the ambulance.   The ambulance attendant enters the ambulance to guide the stretcher and secure it, while Nos. 1 and 2 bearers assist Nos. 3 and 4 to slide it into place.

HOME OFFICE

CIVIL DEFENCE

Manual of Basic Training

VOLUME II

BASIC METHODS
OF PROTECTION AGAINST
HIGH EXPLOSIVE MISSILES

PAMPHLET No. 5

LONDON: HIS MAJESTY'S STATIONERY OFFICE
1949

SIXPENCE NET

GENERAL PREFACE

The series of Civil Defence handbooks and pamphlets is produced under the authority of the Home Secretary by the Civil Defence Department of the Home Office with the assistance of an in co-operation with the Secretary of State for Scotland and other Ministers concerned.

Measures for safeguarding the civil population against the effects of war which these publications describe, have become an essential part of the defensive organisation of this country. The need for them is not related to any belief that war is imminent. It is just as necessary that preparations for Civil Defence should be made in time of peace as it is that preparations should be made for the Armed Forces.

The publications cover, as far as is possible, measures which can be taken to mitigate the effects of all modern forms of attack. Any scheme of Civil Defence, if it is to be efficient, must be up-to-date and must take account of all the various weapons which might become available. The scale of bombing experienced in Great Britain during the 1939–45 war might be considerably exceeded in any future war, and types of weapons and tactics which were not experienced in this country might conceivably be used against it in the future. It does not follow that any one of the weapons, e.g., the atomic bomb, will necessarily be used, and it is most important that a proper balance is held between what is likely and what is possible.

The use of poison gas in war was forbidden by the Geneva Gas Protocol of 1925, to which this country and all the other countries of the Western Union were parties. At the outbreak of a war, His Majesty's Government would try to secure an undertaking from the enemy not to use poison gas. Nevertheless the risk of poison gas being used remains a possibility and cannot be disregarded any more than can certain further developments in other scientific fields.

The publications are designed to describe not only precautionary schemes which experience in the last war proved to be extremely effective in preventing avoidable injury and loss of life, or widespread dislocation of national industries, but also the training, both technical and tactical, which will be required of the personnel of the Civil Defence Corps if they are to be ready effectively to play their part if war should ever break out. The publications aim at giving the best available information on methods of defence against all the various weapons. Information is not complete in respect of some of these weapons and the best methods of countering them, but as results of experimental work and other investigations mature, they will be revised and added to from time to time so that the Civil Defence Corps may be kept up-to-date and their training may be on the most modern and experienced lines.

CONTENTS

NOTE

*The pagination of this pamphlet is not continuous as it
may be necessary to introduce new pages at a later date.*

CHAPTER IV TYPES OF SHELTERS

CHAPTER V METHODS OF PROTECTING DOOR AND WINDOW OPENINGS

CHAPTER VI NOTES ON SOME SPECIAL FACTORY PROBLEMS

BASIC METHODS OF PROTECTION AGAINST HIGH EXPLOSIVE MISSILES

INTRODUCTION

The purpose of this pamphlet is to describe as briefly as possible the effects of high explosive missiles, and to provide an elementary knowledge of the principles of protection against them which is essential to all persons connected with Civil Defence.

The atomic bomb, and also attacks by chemical and/or biological weapons, will provide their own problems which have been dealt with in separate pamphlets.

In the event of another war in which this country was engaged, the scale and weight of attack from the air might be heavier than any previously experienced in this country; but—until atomic or biological weapons are used—the problems presented, including the protection that would be needed, would be of much the same order as were occasioned by World War II.

For the present it is probable that raids would be carried out by piloted aircraft carrying normal bomb loads of high explosive, incendiary bombs, or parachute mines; rockets, or flying bombs. Flying bombs were carried by aircraft for a short period of the last war though their most effective use was from fixed launching sites on the ground. Rockets were, of course, an entirely independent weapon also fired from bases on the ground. Considerable experience was gained of all these types of attack during the last war and the lessons learnt can be applied to meet such attacks if they should arise in future.

Saturation Bombing

Saturation bombing is a form of tactics which can be used with any weapons, and may be defined as a concentrated attack upon a town, part of a town, or other strategic target, with the object of so saturating the target area that the defending forces are temporarily unable to function.

It was this form of bombing which was so highly developed by the United Kingdom and United States Army Air Forces against Germany during the latter part of the late war.

CHAPTER I

TYPES OF HIGH EXPLOSIVE BOMBS AND THEIR EFFECTS

1. ELEMENTARY PRINCIPLES OF EXPLOSION

A high explosive substance is one which is capable of very rapid burning; when this takes place a relatively small amount of high explosive is almost instantaneously converted into a large volume of gas at a very high temperature. This produces a very high pressure. Some high explosives are more effective than others. For example the aluminised explosives developed during the last war were considerably more powerful than T.N.T.

When an explosion occurs above the ground the rapidly expanding gases transmit a considerable shock to the surrounding air and produce what may be termed a *pressure pulse*: this is followed by a *suction wave*. The word *blast* is commonly used to describe both these phenomena.

When an explosion occurs underground, at a moderate depth, the force of the explosion will blow out the earth above it and form a crater. Debris will be scattered, there will be earth shock and some blast though the latter will be less than from a burst above ground.

When an explosion takes place at a greater depth below ground the force of the explosion is used up in making an underground cavity, known as a *camouflet*. The explosive force will be transmitted through the ground as earth shock; there will be no blast above ground. The dangers of a camouflet are two-fold: first, the roof may cave in when traffic passes over it and people may be injured by falling into the cavity; secondly, the cavity will be full of poisonous gases—largely Carbon Monoxide—so that a person falling into the cavity, though not injured, may well die as a result of inhaling Carbon Monoxide.

2. HIGH EXPLOSIVE BOMBS AND FUSES

A high explosive bomb consists of a charge of high explosive contained in a case fitted with a fuse and exploder.

The thickness of the case may vary from a very thin one made of some light alloy to the massive steel case fitted with an armour piercing nose as was used, for example, against the German submarine pens during the last war.

The fuse may be designed to explode the charge:—
    (i) Before reaching the target (proximity fuse)
    (ii) On impact
    (iii) After a period of delay, which may vary from a fraction of a second, up to days

The fuse may be sensitive to mechanical, magnetic or acoustic influences.

3. TYPES OF HIGH EXPLOSIVE BOMBS

Broadly speaking, high explosive bombs can be divided into three main types.

(i) Thin Case Bombs

In this type the ratio of the weight of the charge to the total weight of the bomb (known as the charge weight ratio) is highest. On explosion the case is burst open giving rise to numerous light fragments, but the chief object of this type of bomb is to produce the maximum blast effect.

This type of bomb is usually fitted with an impact fuse: if any other type of fuse is fitted the speed of descent of the bomb must be checked, by the use of a parachute or similar means, to prevent the case breaking-up on impact.

(ii) Medium Case Bombs

This type of bomb produces rather less blast but more fragments than the thin case bomb. Any type of fuse may be fitted to this bomb. If a delay action fuse is fitted and the bomb penetrates the ground the effects of blast and fragmentation decrease with the depth of penetration, but there is a corresponding increase in the effects of earth shock. The charge weight ratio is less than that of the light case bomb.

(iii) Heavy Case Bombs

These bombs usually referred to as armour piercing or semi-armour piercing bombs are used principally against heavily protected targets such as capital ships, important installations protected by massive reinforced concrete, large shelters, submarine pens and the like.

Being fitted with armour piercing noses they have a short delay action fuse to allow the bomb to penetrate the target before exploding. Inside such targets as mentioned above damage is caused by large, heavy fragments and blast. If the bomb penetrates below ground level there is considerable earth shock. This type has a low charge weight ratio.

4. EFFECTS OF HIGH EXPLOSIVE BOMBS

(i) Impact

Any bomb which strikes a target, even though it fails to explode, will cause damage by the force of its impact. The heavier the bomb and the more robust its construction the greater will be the damage done.

If a large bomb just misses a target and is of such a type that it will penetrate the ground, even though it does not explode it may set up enough earth shock to cause damage to the target.

(ii) Blast

Blast from high explosive bombs will break windows and may remove roof coverings over a wide area. Within a more limited area it may cause the collapse of the ordinary brick built house.

(iii) Fragmentation

Fragments from bombs besides inflicting casualties can cause structural damage. The same applies to debris which may be flung violently from craters or damaged buildings.

(iv) Earth Shock

In addition to being produced by the impact and penetration of bombs which fail to explode, more violent earth shock is produced by bombs which explode underground.

5. SPECIAL TYPES OF HIGH EXPLOSIVE BOMBS USED IN THE LAST WAR

(i) Incendiary Bombs

Some of the incendiary bombs dropped were fitted with an explosive attachment: this was done partly to discourage fire fighters and partly to scatter the burning magnesium and so spread the fire.

(ii) Anti-personnel Bombs

Anti-personnel bombs are small fragmentation bombs usually fitted with a device to slow-up their descent so as to prevent penetration of the ground. In order to present the maximum hazard to Civil Defence personnel some were fused to explode on impact, some after a period of delay and others if subjected to vibration or movement.

(iii) Other Aerial Weapons

Parachute Mines, Flying Bombs and Rockets were extensively used against civilian targets. From the nature of the damage produced these weapons may be classified as thin case bombs. The rocket, although fitted with an impact fuse, hit the ground so fast—about 3,000 miles per hour— that a considerable crater was formed. Casualties and damage were caused by blast and earth shock and also by the outflung debris and parts of its own machinery which were blown in all directions and acted as additional missiles.

Whether the fall of a single high explosive bomb, a saturation raid with high explosive bombs or even a raid with atomic bombs is being considered, the fundamental principles underlying their action remain the same, save that the atomic bomb introduces additional hazards peculiar to itself.

6. ATOMIC BOMBS

A special pamphlet is being prepared dealing not only with the effects of an atomic bomb but with the methods by which protection and remedial measures against its various effects can be taken. Attention is drawn to the report of the British Mission to Japan published by H.M. Stationery Office in 1946, which gives valuable information in regard to the effects of the atomic bombs dropped at Hiroshima and Nagasaki.

Although the atomic bomb possesses special properties, i.e. heat flash and gamma rays, it is in many ways essentially a blast weapon of very much greater destructive capability than any ordinary type of bomb. In the form used against Japan the heavy damage is found within half a mile from ground zero (the point directly underneath the point of burst), but damage of varying degrees from blast, fire and radiation extend up to a radius of $2\frac{1}{2}$ miles.

Investigations made so far indicate that protection designed to resist the effects of normal high explosive attack (other than direct hits) will give some measure of protection against the atomic bomb and that the addition of supplementary strengthening will obviously help to increase such protection.

CHAPTER II

PRINCIPLES OF PROTECTION

12. SOME RECOMMENDATIONS

Part of the object of a bombing offensive is greatly to reduce war production and to disrupt the life of the community.

If the enemy is to be prevented from achieving this aim, work must go on until danger is imminent and the ordinary day to day life of the community must be interrupted as little as may be.

Due to the ever increasing speed of aircraft and the rocket-type of missile the interval between the warning and the fall of the bomb will become shorter.

Even in saturation attacks the number of direct hits on buildings is small compared with the number of near misses.

Taking all these considerations into account together with the fact that to get protection one must be *inside* the shelter *before* the bomb bursts, the following recommendations are made.

13. TAKING COVER

(i) In the Open

A bomb or other missile which is going to strike very near to you if audible at all cannot usually be heard for more than a couple of seconds.

If you are exposed in the open during an attack you have not more than a second or two to do what you can to protect yourself.

The worst and most dangerous thing you can do is to run for cover unless, indeed, you are within one jump of it.

Throw yourself flat, wherever you are. Lie face downwards, resting on the elbows, and clasp your hands behind your head. The chest should be very slightly raised off the ground so as to prevent internal injury from earth shock.

Blast, splinters and debris tend to fly outwards and *UPWARDS*. Therefore, if you can manage to roll into the gutter, do so, as the camber of the road and the kerb both tend to protect you.

In open country it is sometimes possible to roll into a fold of the ground, or into a ditch.

(ii) When very near to buildings or other cover

A wall, archway, doorway or narrow alley may give protection. It must be remembered, however, whether indoors or out, that shock is transmitted through walls, etc., so that it is dangerous to lean directly against any part of a building. Your head is the most vulnerable part from this point of view.

(iii) When inside a building

It is better to be near an inside wall than an outside one.

Avoid being in a direct line with an outside door or a window.

Remember the extreme danger from flying glass. Even interior glass can become a deadly missile.

One of the safest parts of a normal room is in the angle of the chimney breast and the wall. Chimney breasts are less liable to collapse than any other part of a building.

(iv) General

It cannot be too strongly emphasised that it is most important, from the point of view of reducing casualties as a whole, for everyone in an area under attack to make use of any shelter that is available. Recent research has shown that there would be less fatal casualties if everyone were in relatively poor shelter than if half the population were in shelter twice as good and the other half remained in the open.

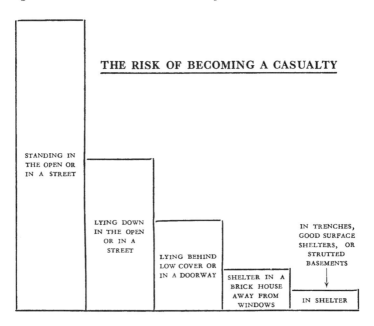

CHAPTER III

STANDARDS OF PROTECTION AGAINST HIGH EXPLOSIVE AND OTHER BOMBS

19. GENERAL INFORMATION

The following information in regard to protection afforded by different materials and conditions is given to afford a general background knowledge of the effects of High Explosive missiles. The information is of general interest to everyone concerned with Civil Defence.

20. SURFACE SHELTERS

Properly constructed surface shelters having walls of 12 in. of reinforced concrete or 13½ in. of reinforced brickwork (Quetta Bond) and a 6 in. reinforced concrete roof tied to the walls will provide full protection against the effect of a 500 lb. medium case bomb exploding 15 ft. away from a shelter wall, and will be capable of resisting light incendiary bombs and any normal debris load.

21. PROTECTION AGAINST BLAST AND SPLINTERS

Protection against blast and splinters from a 500 lb. medium case bomb exploding 50 ft. away will be afforded by the following materials of the thickness indicated:—

Lateral protection

(i)	Mild steel plate ...	...	1½	inches
(ii)	Reinforced concrete	...	12	,,
(iii)	Brickwork or masonry	...	13½	,,
(iv)	Unreinforced concrete	...	15	,,
(v)	Ballast or broken stone	...	24	,,
(vi)	Earth or sand ...	...	30	,,
(vii)	Solidly stacked timber	...	36	,,

Overhead protection

(i)	Mild steel plate ...	...	5/16	inch
(ii)	Reinforced concrete	...	6	inches
(iii)	Efficient brick arching	...	9	,,
(iv)	Earth, sand or ballast	...	18	,,

(v) The inside of an existing substantial building having a roof and not less than two storey floors overhead, provided that the floor above the protected space is supported to enable it to resist the debris load.

22. DEBRIS LOAD

The strength of the roof of a shelter should also be sufficient to withstand any debris load which might fall on it on the collapse of adjacent buildings.

23. EARTH SHOCK

A shelter should be designed as a complete box to enable it to resist earth shock.

24. MINES AND ROCKETS

Shelters constructed to the above requirements will also provide whole or partial protection against the effects of mines and rockets depending on their situation in relation to the point of burst. As a rough guide it may be stated that complete protection can be obtained at a distance of 70–120 ft. from the centre of the explosion, though this distance will vary with the weight of the explosive charge.

25. BOMB RESISTING STRUCTURES

To resist a direct hit from a 500 lb. medium case bomb, a shelter will require a reinforced concrete roof 4 ft. 6 in. thick. The walls above ground should be of the same thickness and below ground they should be 7 ft. thick.

Tunnels or caves 60 ft. below ground or 40 ft. in solid rock would provide equal protection. The standards quoted above would also provide protection against a direct hit by a 1,000 lb. medium case bomb, though some damage might be caused in the compartment below the point of impact.

Shelters providing protection against medium case type bombs also provide a measure of protection against the atomic bomb. They can generally be so constructed as to be capable of being strengthened at a later step, if necessary, to provide a higher degree of protection.

CHAPTER IV

TYPES OF SHELTERS

31. BROAD CLASSIFICATION

In this chapter a brief description is given of the various types of shelters used successfully in the last war. This information is again intended as a general background of interest in helping to understand the basic principles of protection against High Explosive missiles.

Shelters were given a broad classification by types as follows:—

(i) Domestic Shelters (for household use)

(*a*) ANDERSON SHELTER. This shelter was designed for erection outside the house. It consisted of 14 gauge corrugated steel sheets, steel angles, ties and channel irons. It was normally sunk about 3 ft. into the ground and covered over with earth to a minimum depth of 15 in., which, with the 14 gauge corrugated sheet gives the equivalent of 18 in. of earth.

The standard shelter was 6 ft. 6 in. by 4 ft. 6 in. by 6 ft. high. It was designed to shelter six persons, but was capable of being lengthened to accommodate eight, ten or twelve persons; or of being shortened to accommodate four persons.

Unless the entrance was screened (within 15 ft.) by a building or existing wall, a screen wall had to be provided. Trouble was sometimes experienced due to flooding by subsoil water in which case the below ground portion was tanked by a lining of cement concrete.

The shelter was, on occasions, erected on the surface, which involved casing it in cement concrete. The result was efficient but expensive.

(*b*) MORRISON SHELTER. This shelter was designed for use in a house and its chief function was to protect the occupants from being crushed by the collapse of the building. Protection against blast and fragments was provided by the walls of the house, which were sometimes specially thickened for this purpose.

It consisted of a steel table measuring 6 ft. 4 in. long by 3 ft. 10½ in. wide. It provided sleeping accommodation for two adults and a child, or a considerable number of small children in a sitting position, when used as a school classroom shelter.

(*c*) STRUTTED REFUGE ROOM—STRUTTED BASEMENT. The object of this form of shelter was the same as the Morrison shelter, i.e. to provide strutting to prevent the collapse of the room and to use the walls as protection against blast and fragments. Strutting was either steel or wood and the design and strength suited to the weight to be supported.

(*d*) SMALL TRENCH OR SMALL SURFACE SHELTER IN GARDEN. This type of shelter needs no special comment.

(ii) Communal or Communal Domestic Shelter

This type of shelter was designed for the joint use of the occupants of two or more houses or flats in cases where it was impracticable to provide shelter for individual households.

Various kinds of shelter were used to suit local conditions, of which the principal were:—

(*a*) TRENCHES. Trench shelters were trenches dug in the ground with a suitable lining to the sides, floor and roof and provided with entrances and emergency exits. They were constructed either wholly or partly below ground. Any part above ground was protected by earth cover (18 in. of earth) or 6 in. of reinforced concrete.

Trench linings found best by experience consisted of reinforced concrete cast in situ; but timber, steel sheeting or precast concrete units were also used.

An important consideration was found to be the effect of earth shock on the sides of the trench which would cause the roof to collapse unless the design was such as to prevent this contingency.

Normally trenches were 4 ft. 9 in. or 7 ft. clear width with a height of not less than 6 ft. They were constructed in separate 50-person units, or divided into sections by changes in direction at right angles or by baffle walls so that each section would accommodate not more than 50 persons.

Seating or bunking was provided in accordance with the needs of the situation.

(*b*) SURFACE SHELTERS. This type of shelter, as its name implies, was constructed entirely above ground. Walls were of structural concrete not less than 12 in. thick, or reinforced brickwork not less than $13\frac{1}{2}$ in. thick. The roof was of reinforced concrete not less than 6 in. thick. The structure was also designed to resist earth shock.

If the shelter was designed to hold more than 50 persons it was divided into compartments each holding a maximum of 50 persons.

All such shelters were provided with one or more entrances screened against blast and fragments, and a suitable number of emergency exits spaced as far apart as possible.

Any shelter sited nearer to a building than half the height of that building, had the roof designed to take the debris load from the building if it should collapse.

(*c*) STRUTTED BASEMENTS—VAULTS OR COAL CELLARS. No special comment is needed on these two types of shelter, both of which were extensively used. In the case of vaults and coal cellars, means of intercommunication were made where possible so as to provide emergency exits, especially in rows of houses in typical London streets.

The strutting was designed to carry any normal weight that might collapse on the roof of the shelter.

(iii) Public Shelters

Public shelters were constructed or adapted as circumstances required. The principal types were:—

(*a*) TRENCHES—SURFACE SHELTERS—BASEMENT SHELTERS.
Descriptions of these types of shelter have already been given in the immediately preceding sections.

(*b*) RAILWAY ARCHES. Good shelter was provided by railway arches by closing the ends by reinforced brick or concrete screen walls to a height of not less than 8 ft. Because railway communications are especially liable to attack however, care had always to be taken not to concentrate too many people in any one archway.

(*c*) TUNNELS AND CAVES. Tunnels with 40 ft. or more overhead cover were used as shelters, as also were caves where they existed, e.g. London Transport Tube Stations and the Chislehurst Caves. Some tunnel shelters were specially constructed. As with all types of shelters, entrances had to be adequately protected by screen walls. In cases where the top cover fell below the general standard, baffle walls were provided to limit the number of persons in any one compartment.

(*d*) OTHER SHELTER REQUIREMENTS. Shelters of suitable type were also provided for schools, factories and commercial buildings. Normally they conformed to those already described, and many of them were made available to the public outside working hours.

(*e*) ADDITIONAL POINTS OF INTEREST. A few tools such as picks, shovels and crowbars were always kept in shelters to help the occupants to force a way out if they were trapped by debris.

Originally all shelters were provided with gas-proofing equipment, though this practice was later abandoned.

CHAPTER V

METHODS OF PROTECTING DOOR AND WINDOW OPENINGS

37. SIMPLE METHODS

Large numbers of casualties were caused by glass during the last war, and particular attention was directed towards reducing this risk and also to the dangers of open doorways through which blast and splinters might travel.

The methods employed were simple. Door openings or windows were screened by baffle or screen walls of any suitable materials of a thickness equivalent to $13\frac{1}{2}$ in. of brickwork built up to a height 6 ft. above the floor level of the room to be protected. Sandbags were also used for this purpose.

The danger from flying glass was further reduced by fixing wire netting of not more than $\frac{1}{2}$ in. mesh on the inside of the window frame or over the whole of the window opening; or by pasting a fabric, such as cheese cloth or curtain net, on the inside so as to cover completely the glass and frame. The most satisfactory adhesive was found to be flour paste with a small quantity of borax ($\frac{1}{4}$ oz. to 1 pint of paste) added to prevent mildew.

CHAPTER VI

NOTES ON SOME SPECIAL
FACTORY PROBLEMS

Bombing experience showed that factories presented certain problems which had to be given special consideration and treatment. The position varied naturally with different types of industry, but the notes in this Chapter cover points of interest which were, in the main, common factors in industry.

43. LOCATION OF PROTECTION

It was found essential, in the interests of production to try and provide shelter or emergency protection as close to the actual place of work as possible. Since factories were instructed normally to ignore the public warning siren and work to an emergency alarm provided by roof spotters or other means, the siting of the protection had to be carefully chosen and many methods improvised, sometimes using stacks of solid raw materials in shops, adapting trenches used for running heating pipes and so on.

44. CAUSES OF CASUALTIES

Casualties in factories were caused by glass splinters, bomb fragments and blast as is normal with High Explosive bombing. In addition, however, it was found that casualties were also caused by the blast hurling tools, raw materials and other things found loose in most factories and special precautions had to be taken to reduce this risk. Most factories have also a considerable roof space and even if the roof itself survived, parts of it were liable to be dislodged and cause injury to personnel.

In other words it was found that, apart from the usual hazards caused by the explosion of a High Explosive missile, most factories provided a number of additional potential missiles which blast might hurl about and thus increase generally the risk of casualties, unless practical steps were taken to reduce this possibility to a minimum.

45. PROTECTION OF PLANT

The importance of giving special protection to important plant and vital points in factories, against blast and splinters, was very fully demonstrated during the war. Comparatively trivial damage might easily suspend production for days or even weeks. The most important services, where such special protection was required were water, electricity and gas; and essential machinery required special care in some cases.

The most usual form of protection was the provision of blast or traverse walls and substantial overhead cover, and, in addition, where practicable, of the duplication of supplies and services.

It is of interest to note that machine tools were found, on the whole, the most difficult to destroy by bombing; and even though the factory buildings were collapsed or badly damaged, production could be started up again provided the necessary services could be restored, in a surprisingly short time.

HOME OFFICE

CIVIL DEFENCE

Manual of Basic Training

VOLUME II

ATOMIC WARFARE

PAMPHLET No. 6

LONDON: HIS MAJESTY'S STATIONERY OFFICE
1950

TWO SHILLINGS NET

GENERAL PREFACE

The series of Civil Defence handbooks and pamphlets is produced under the authority of the Home Secretary by the Civil Defence Department of the Home Office with the assistance of and in co-operation with the Secretary of State for Scotland and other Ministers concerned.

Measures for safeguarding the civil population against the effects of war which these publications describe, have become an essential part of the defensive organisation of this country. The need for them is not related to any belief that war is imminent. It is just as necessary that preparations for Civil Defence should be made in time of peace as it is that preparations should be made for the Armed Forces.

The publications cover, as far as is possible, measures which can be taken to mitigate the effects of all modern forms of attack. Any scheme of Civil Defence, if it is to be efficient, must be up-to-date and must take account of all the various weapons which might become available. The scale of bombing experienced in Great Britain during the 1939-45 war might be considerably exceeded in any future war, and types of weapons and tactics which were not experienced in this country might conceivably be used against it in the future. It does not follow that any one of the weapons, e.g., the atomic bomb, will necessarily be used, and it is most important that a proper balance is held between what is likely and what is possible.

The use of poison gas in war was forbidden by the Geneva Gas Protocol of 1925, to which this country and all the other countries of the Western Union were parties. At the outbreak of a war, His Majesty's Government would try to secure an undertaking from the enemy not to use poison gas. Nevertheless the risk of poison gas being used remains a possibility and cannot be disregarded any more than can certain further developments in other scientific fields.

The publications are designed to describe not only precautionary schemes which experience in the last war proved to be extremely effective in preventing avoidable injury and loss of life, or widespread dislocation of national industries, but also the training, both technical and tactical, which will be required of the personnel of the Civil Defence Corps if they are to be ready effectively to play their part if war should ever break out. The publications aim at giving the best available information on methods of defence against all the various weapons. Information is not complete in respect of some of these weapons and the best methods of countering them, but as results of experimental work and other investigations mature, they will be revised and added to from time to time so that the Civil Defence Corps may be kept up-to-date and training may be on the most modern and experienced lines.

Binders for Manual of Basic Training are available from H.M. Stationery Office, price 1s. 0d. net

This picture shows the mushrooming of the column of smoke which rose 60,000 feet into the air over the Japanese port and industrial centre of Nagasaki.

68054

This picture shows the upper portion of the cloud from the burst of the atomic bomb over the warships assembled in the lagoon at Bikini Island.

CONTENTS

NOTE

The pagination of this pamphlet is not continuous as it
may be necessary to introduce new pages at a later date.

1

APPENDIX II GLOSSARY OF TERMS

FOREWORD BY THE PRIME MINISTER

The object of this pamphlet is to provide all members of the Civil Defence Corps and other Services associated with Civil Defence with a short manual of practical information about the atomic bomb and its effects. It is, of course, our earnest hope that we shall never have to experience the horrors of an atomic attack. The tremendous force of atomic power should be used for industrial and humanitarian purposes and not for mass destruction. Ever since the Washington Declaration, which I signed with the President of the United States and the Prime Minister of Canada in November 1945, the United Kingdom has pressed for international agreement to ensure that atomic energy should be used only for peaceful purposes. But any such agreement would be illusory without the most rigorous system of international control. Although nearly two years ago nine out of the eleven members of the United Nations Atomic Energy Commission agreed on what they considered to be a really effective plan for the control of atomic energy and although this plan was subsequently approved by the overwhelming majority of the General Assembly of the United Nations, the Soviet Union has so far refused to accept it, and has instead put forward counter-proposals which were rejected in the Commission by a nine to two vote on the ground that they did not provide an adequate basis for effective international control. We shall not, however, abandon our hope that an effective system of international control may ultimately be adopted by the United Nations, and we for our part will certainly do all in our power to make such an agreement possible. In the meantime we must proceed with our Civil Defence preparations on the basis that, in the event of war, we might be subjected to atomic attack and with the object of minimising the casualties which must inevitably accompany such an attack.

June, 1950.

3

ATOMIC WARFARE

INTRODUCTION

This pamphlet is based on the known effects of the type of bombs used against the two Japanese cities of Hiroshima and Nagasaki.

Many people must have said to themselves, and, indeed, must still be saying: "What is the good of doing anything against this weapon? There can be no defence against the atomic bomb." No complete defence can be provided against any weapon of war, but just as it proved possible to devise means of mitigating the consequences of other forms of attack in the last war, so it is certain that means can be found of mitigating the consequences of atomic warfare. It is one of the aims of this pamphlet to try and put the whole matter into proper perspective and to show, as is indeed the truth, that there are to-day a great many practical steps that will greatly reduce the casualty producing power of this bomb. And it is confidently hoped, as time goes on and knowledge increases, that the defence can be steadily improved. The introduction of the atomic bomb into warfare represented a great and unparalleled jump in the power of a single offensive weapon. It is the business of defence to catch up, as it has always caught up ; and great efforts have been and are being directed to this end. Of the three major effects produced when an atomic bomb explodes, two—blast and flash-burn—are not new although they have their own special characteristics. The third—radiological effect—is novel in character and in its results, and there will, therefore, be a natural tendency to give it special prominence. But it is most important that a correct balance should be maintained, a point which instructors should specially note. **Some of the radiological effects, although they must be taken into account, will not normally be experienced ; nor should they necessarily prove a serious hazard to operations if they were encountered.**

There are many problems to which, at present, only imperfect or partial solutions can be given. As knowledge increases, so will these gaps gradually be filled. And while the situation that might be created by the use of atomic bombs would be of the utmost severity, involving many casualties and heavy destruction to property, it can be said with confidence that the defensive measures which are being and will continue to be gradually developed, backed up by sound teaching and good training will enable the effects to be greatly reduced.

It would be outside the scope of this pamphlet to deal with the general Civil Defence measures which might provide protection against or mitigation of the consequences of an atomic bomb. The measures which proved effective in the last war, such as the warning system, the provision of shelters, schemes of dispersal and measures for preventing the spread of fire, would undoubtedly reduce casualties and damage under conditions of atomic warfare.

Appendix I deals briefly with the elements of nuclear physics, and is included in the hope that it will help all concerned to a better understanding of the practical problems which this new weapon has produced. For those who may wish to study further the science of nuclear physics many publications already exist. But such studies are not essential for ordinary Civil Defence purposes, and the aim has been to describe, in this pamphlet, only the major results experienced when an atomic bomb is burst, and the counter-measures which may be taken against them.

CHAPTER I

FEATURES OF ATOMIC EXPLOSION

1. Methods of Attack

Atomic bombs might be exploded on the ground, under water, low in the air, or high in the air.

With the high air burst bomb, the material damage on the target area is the most widespread. With the low air burst bomb the area affected would be smaller but the material damage more intense. With an under water burst, the maximum area of contamination would be experienced.

There is little doubt that the high air burst bomb is the most effective against a normal target, i.e. a well built up area, since the maximum blast effect will be experienced. There may be special circumstances, connected with a particular target, which would merit a variation of these tactics, but they would be the exception rather than the rule.

2. General Description of Explosion

When an atomic bomb explodes in the air, a ball of fire several hundred feet in diameter results. From this a dazzling flash of light, intense heat, and various forms of radioactivity shoot out in all directions, followed by blast and sound waves. The light, heat and radioactive effects begin to arrive at the target area on the ground some seconds before the slower moving blast and sound waves, while the radioactive " fission " products, into which the material of the bomb breaks up on explosion, arrive still later, if at all.

The ball of fire, quickly losing brilliance, rises up in the air, with the ascending hot gases produced by the explosion, in a column, first multicoloured and then white, of swirling gas and particles. This column rises to a height of many thousands of feet and billows out giving the appearance of a huge mushroom on its stalk. On the ground below, where the blast has hit, the scene is obscured by a cloud of dust and smoke.

3. Dangers Resulting from Explosion

The enormous energy released from the explosion of an atomic bomb takes three main forms capable of causing damage to materials and danger to persons. These are Heat, Radioactivity and Blast.

Heat flash and blast, though much more intense and of much greater range in the case of the atomic bomb, are already known in warfare in connection with high explosive weapons ; but radioactivity is a new effect peculiar to the atomic weapon and produces an immediate danger at the time of explosion. It might also, under suitable circumstances, subsequently give rise to persisting danger from contamination or irradiation of ground or materials.

Taking these forms of effect in the order of their arrival on the target, a brief description is given of each and is followed in succeeding chapters by a detailed consideration of the damage and danger they may cause to property and persons, and some of the problems they will create for Civil Defence.

(i) *Heat Flash :* On the explosion of the bomb a wave of intense heat called " heat flash " radiates in all directions. The rays travel in straight lines at the speed of light (186,000 miles per second) and are so intense that the surface of objects just underneath the ball of fire are raised in temperature by many thousands of degrees. Even at distances of five miles, the flash is sufficiently intense to produce a feeling of bodily warmth. This heat flash lasts only about a second and has no great penetrating power.

The heat flash, however, is capable of directly igniting inflammable material such as dark cloth, paper, and dry rotted wood (as it did in Japan), thereby starting immediately many fires simultaneously over a wide area. Isolated instances of the starting of such primary fires were reported at distances of nearly two miles from the centre of damage (ground zero) and many buildings near to the centre, which survived the blast effect, were gutted by fires started by the heat flash which entered through windows and open doors and ignited inflammable contents. The surface of many materials which do not normally show visible signs of heat was affected, roof tiles were blistered, polished granite roughened, and concrete reddened at distances varying from half to one mile from ground zero.

These details are given to emphasize the range and degree of heat flash, but it will be appreciated that in a country like ours, where the great majority of buildings are of brick, stone or concrete, the risk of large numbers of fires being started by heat flash is much less than it was in Japanese cities.

When to the fire-raising dangers of the heat flash are added those of secondary fires which normally occur following the collapse of buildings on domestic fires, the breaking of gas mains, and the damage to electricity communications resulting from blast, it will be seen that the atomic bomb is a potent fire-raising weapon. And it will be necessary to increase precautions against fire, particularly as regards the inflammable contents of otherwise fire resisting buildings.

(ii) *Radioactivity (Immediate Danger) :* When an atomic bomb explodes radioactivity is given off in all directions in the form of radiation called " gamma " rays and as particles called " neutrons ". The bomb material itself also splits up into radioactive dust known as " fission products ".

(a) *Gamma Rays :* These rays travel at the speed of light and are scattered in the air and reflected from nearby objects in much the same way as are light rays. Thus, although the most intense beam of gamma rays is the direct one from the ball of fire, there is nevertheless some gamma radiation from every other part of the sky, just as in strong sunlight a room which faces north still receives light from the visible sky and by reflection from other objects. Most of the gamma rays are emitted in the first few seconds. The intensity decreases rapidly as time goes on and as the emitting material moves away by rising in the ball of fire. After one minute there is little danger from gamma rays. Judging from experience

8

of high air burst bombs in Japan (i.e. those causing the most widespread damage) the effective danger range from these bombs appeared to be about one and a quarter to one and a half miles from the centre of damage.

Gamma rays have very great powers of penetration and will go through considerable thicknesses of building and other materials. They will readily enter the human body and are very damaging to it. They do not, however, render radioactive the materials which they penetrate, and their intensity is reduced in the process. So far as is known at present, no form of clothing will give protection against gamma rays, but a large measure of immunity can be obtained by structural precautions of a conventional character. This is more fully discussed in Chapter III.

Unprotected persons within half a mile of ground zero would receive a fatal dose of radiation and, at about three quarters of a mile, half might die. Beyond this range the intensity of the rays falls off and there should be relatively few deaths ; but lesser effects of radiation, such as loss of hair, might be expected up to one and a half miles. In Japan 15-20 per cent. of fatal casualties were attributed to gamma rays, but the percentage might have been higher had the casualties survived other injuries. (See Fig. 1.)

The figures set out in the preceding paragraph are those given as an estimate by the British Mission from the experience of the high air burst bombs used in Japan and under similar conditions would apply to persons in a British city. *It must be stressed however that they apply to persons caught in the open with no warning or suitable shelter,* and that even ordinary houses will give some degree of protection by lessening the intensity of the rays that penetrate them.

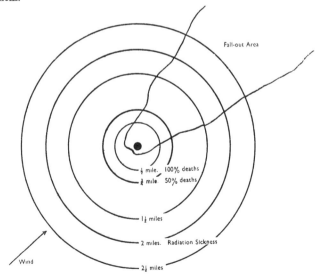

Fall-out Area

¼ mile. 100% deaths
¾ mile. 50% deaths
1½ miles
2 miles. Radiation Sickness
2½ miles

Wind

FIG. 1.   Radii of Gamma Flash.

9

(b) *Neutrons :* These are the other form of penetrating radiation producing immediate danger at the time of explosion. They are minute particles emitted from the split nuclei of the atoms at the time of explosion, and they travel at great speed in all directions reaching the ground, if near enough to it, almost at once. The duration of their emission is short, probably not more than a few seconds. Their lethal range too is much shorter than that of gamma rays, and it is probable that the dangers associated with them will come only with the other forms of atomic attack, rather than from high air burst bombs.

Neutrons have great powers of penetration both of materials and of the human body to which they are injurious, but at the time they are not felt. They differ from gamma rays in that they render radioactive many materials which they penetrate. This form of radioactivity is called " induced " and can persist for considerable periods depending on the material irradiated.

The casualties likely to occur from neutrons alone are difficult to estimate but except close underneath an air burst bomb the thickness of concrete sufficient to give protection against gamma rays would also give protection against neutrons. It must be remembered that probably the most important factors in causing fatal casualties within the neutron range are from the effects of blast, i.e. collapse of buildings, heat flash and gamma ray flash. It is possible, however, that there might be danger from some induced and persisting radioactivity which neutrons produce in other materials.

(iii) *Radioactivity (Delayed Danger) :* In the preceding paragraphs some mention has been made of " fission products " and of neutrons causing " induced " radioactivity in materials which they penetrate. These two forms of radioactivity produce " delayed " danger from the penetrating gamma rays they give off and from actual radioactive particles getting on the body or being breathed or swallowed.

(a) *Fission Products :* These are the intensely radioactive particles resulting from atomic fission. **The likelihood of these products being deposited in dangerous amounts on the target area from high air burst bombs is small.** They are carried up in the column of smoke and ascending hot gases to a very considerable height and are there dispersed by the winds and eventually become harmless. It might be possible, while they are still fairly concentrated, for a dangerous deposit to be brought to earth down wind of the target by a rainstorm. If this did happen, the area contaminated would not normally be very great and it might easily occur in open country where very little harm might result. The probability of this happening is not very great, though it cannot be ignored, and is something for which a watch should be kept.

With low air bursts or ground bursts these products will create a danger from radioactivity as they will be deposited on the ground and in the crater and may drift along with the wind, falling out as they go and creating a fan shaped area of contamination of sufficient intensity to cause danger for a number of miles down wind.

In underwater explosions the fission products will be present in the water and mist thrown up and can contaminate persons and objects over several square miles.

Areas contaminated by fission products or induced radioactivity will remain radioactive after the explosion, emitting penetrating gamma rays and giving rise to danger from actual radioactive particles getting on to the body or being breathed or swallowed. Exposure to atmospheric conditions, heat, chemical treatment, etc., will have no effect in destroying them. If an element is radioactive it will decay normally according to its specific " half life " which may be a few seconds or many years. " Half life " is the term used to indicate the length of time it takes for a radioactive element to lose half its radioactivity by natural decay.

As many different elements with different half lives may be involved in causing radioactive contamination, and as the intensity of the danger will also vary with many factors such as height of explosion, climatic and meteorological conditions, the nature and composition of the ground, etc., it is not possible to say in advance how long a contaminated area will remain dangerous ; but in exceptional circumstances it may be some time before it could be safely re-occupied.

The high initial intensity, however, will fall very quickly and allow rescue parties, fire fighters and other Civil Defence workers to enter contaminated areas and carry out essential work normally without any special protective clothing though the time they stay there may have to be limited in accordance with a certain maximum permissible radiation dose, which is now being investigated and will be announced in due course.

Though radioactivity is unseen and unfelt, its presence can be detected and its intensity measured by instruments which are described in a later chapter ; as is also the outfit which would be worn to prevent fission products getting on the body.

(b) *Induced Radioactivity:* This is caused by the neutrons given off from the nuclei of the split atoms penetrating materials and rendering certain of them radioactive and dangerous. As with fission products the danger only occurs with low air or ground bursts, and will, in effect, increase by a small proportion the radioactive danger caused by the fission products. This induced radioactivity is also found in underwater bursts ; but the induced radioactivity is usually masked by the enormous radioactivity of the fission products.

(iv) *Blast :* The difference between the blast from an atomic bomb and that from a high explosive bomb is that, at a distance from each at which the *pressures* are equal, the *duration* of the blast from the atomic bomb is a hundred or more times longer than that from the high explosive bomb. This results in the mechanism of damage from the atomic bomb being quite different from that from the high explosive bomb.

Figure 2 shows a typical pressure-time curve from a medium sized high explosive bomb at a distance at which fairly severe structural damage would be caused. It will be seen that the pressure rises to a value of 15 lb./sq. in. (over 2,000 lb./sq. ft.) which is much more than the *static* load which any normal structure could withstand. However, this pressure only lasts for a very short time (1/10 sec.) and it is therefore much more in the nature of a blow suddenly delivered to the structure than a static load. The ability of a suddenly applied blow to cause damage is determined both by the pressure and by the time for which it acts. In fact it is the product of these two (known as the " impulse ") which measures the damaging ability of the blast from a normal high explosive bomb. This point can easily be demonstrated on an ordinary door. If the door is unlatched it can be pushed open by a force of a few ounces applied somewhat slowly by the little finger. However, if the door is struck quite a hard sharp blow with the fist it will not move very far, even though the instantaneous force between the fist and the door (corresponding to the blast pressure) may have been many pounds. In fact if the door is hit hard enough it is quite likely to be torn off its hinges, and this, of course, is just what high explosive blast does. It gives things a hard sharp blow rather than a gentle push, and many of the so-called freaks of blast can quite easily be explained once this point is fully appreciated.

Again it will be seen from Figure 2 that the pressure, or positive, phase of the blast is followed by a negative or suction phase. Although the suction in this negative phase is only about $\frac{1}{3}$ of the pressure in the positive phase, the duration is about 3 times as long, and therefore the *impulses* in the two phases are approximately equal. Hence their potential abilities to cause damage are also approximately equal. However, since the suction phase occurs last, there is a tendency for its effects to be the more noticeable. For example, the wall of a building may be badly cracked in the pressure phase and may then collapse outwards in the suction phase.

If the impulse criterion were applied to the atomic bomb it would be expected to demolish 9-inch brick walls to a distance of over 10 miles. However, at this distance from the atomic bomb the peak pressure is only about 0.1 lb./sq. in. which is very much less than the static strength of the wall, and consequently, however long this pressure is applied, it cannot hurt the wall. It will thus be seen that the impulse criterion breaks down for the atomic bomb. The position is that the blast impulse is only the criterion of damage so long as the maximum blast pressure is substantially greater than the static strength of the target, and this is not the case at the limits of damage to normal structures with an atomic bomb. With the atomic bomb, therefore, blast pressure rather than impulse tends to be the criterion of damage. If the effective blast pressure exceeds the static strength of the structure failure must be expected, whereas if it is less no failure can occur however long the duration of the blast. In fact, atomic bomb blast is more like strong wind than the sudden blow which represents the effects of high explosive blast, and many of the failures observed at Hiroshima and Nagasaki resembled closely the kind of damage that might be done to buildings by a very strong wind.

The reason for the absence of suction damage at Hiroshima and Nagasaki should now be clear. As stated earlier the *impulses* in the positive and negative phases are about equal, so that if blast impulse is the criterion of damage many cases of suction failure must be expected. However, the *pressure* in the positive phase is 3 or 4 times as great as in the negative, so that when pressure is the criterion of failure, few, if any, suction failures are to be expected. If a building does not fail under the pressure phase it is rather unlikely to fail under the much lower pressures in the suction phase.

The blast damage from an atomic bomb (and also from a large high explosive bomb) can be increased by bursting the bomb above ground level. The pressure wave from the bomb is then reflected by the ground and, since the reflected wave is travelling through air that has been compressed and heated by the direct wave, it tends to travel faster than, and to catch up with, the direct wave. Where the reflected wave catches up with the direct wave the two coalesce to form what is called a Mach wave and it is the formation of this wave which accounts for the increase in damage due to the air burst.

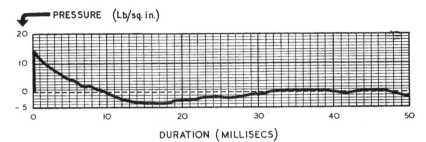

DURATION (MILLISECS)

Fig. 2.

4. Casualty Considerations

The causes of casualties from the atomic explosion would be flash burns, radioactivity, ordinary fire burns and mechanical injuries from falling masonry and flying debris. Estimates of the percentage causes of death as assessed on experience in Japan is:—Heat Flash 20-30 per cent., Gamma Rays 15-20 per cent., and Mechanical Injuries and Burns 50-60 per cent.

5. Estimates of Casualties in a British City

If the people in our cities were caught, as were the Japanese, without warning, before any evacuation had taken place, and with no suitable shelters, the casualties caused by a high air burst bomb would be formidable. The British Mission to Japan estimated that *under these circumstances* as many as 50,000 people might lose their lives in a typical British city with a population density of 45 persons to the acre. Much can be done, however, to mitigate the effects of the bomb and to save life, and it is certain that with adequate advance preparations, including the provision of suitable shelters and with good Civil Defence services, the lives lost could be reduced to a fraction of the number estimated by the British Mission.

13

CHAPTER II

HEAT FLASH

10. Effects on Persons

The effects of heat flash on unprotected people will be severe. The nearer to ground zero the greater the danger ; those at ground zero would be killed. Severe third degree burns would result up to about 1 mile and burns of lesser intensity up to $2\frac{1}{2}$ miles. In Japan 20-30 per cent. of fatal casualties were attributed to flash burn. A similar proportion is to be expected in Britain if there is no warning and people are caught in the streets. (See Fig. 3.) If, however, there is enough warning for the population to take cover and they do so, the number of fatal casualties from flash burn should be relatively small.

The duration of the heat flash is very short, probably not more than about a second or two. Moreover the rays attributed to travel in straight lines. Protection is therefore relatively easy and will be given by any form of building ; while even clothing, though it may itself become ignited, affords some degree of protection for the skin underneath, particularly if not in close contact with the body, and especially if of a light rather than a dark colour. This colour differentiation only applies, however, at distances where the heat intensity has fallen below that which would fire the fabric as a whole. Fog and mist reduce the distances to which flashburn is experienced.

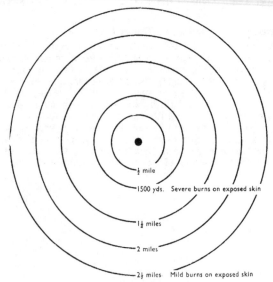

FIG. 3.   Radii of Heat Flash.

11. Effects on Material

It is difficult to estimate from experience in Japan the fire danger which might result in Britain. In this country house construction and siting gives rise to a lesser fire risk. Moreover, our Fire Services and equipment are much better. In Hiroshima 4 square miles of the centre of the city were burnt out and in Nagasaki about 1½ square miles. An American estimate for a possible burnout area of one of their cities is about 2 square miles from a considerably more powerful and improved bomb, if such can be produced.

With a low air burst explosion the heat effects would be more intense but concentrated over a much smaller area ; with a ground burst they would be mostly dissipated in the crater area ; and with an underwater burst the heat would be largely absorbed in converting water into steam.

12. Problems of a Fire Storm

In the Hiroshima attack a fire storm was reported though this phenomenon was not experienced in Nagasaki. The production of a fire storm, either by an atomic bomb or a heavy saturation attack by a combination of high explosive and incendiary bombs, is a problem which is being scientifically studied. Nothing was known of this effect of certain methods of bombing until after the war, when it was found to have occurred in Hamburg, and possibly also in several other German cities.

The risk of a fire storm being caused by a high or low air burst atomic bomb must be taken into account, though there will clearly be certain areas which will be much more susceptible to the raising of a fire storm than others. The features of a fire storm are the intense heat caused, together with the high winds which make the task of fire fighting and rescue much more difficult. A fire storm does not, however, start at once, and there will certainly be a number of preventive or mitigating measures which can be instituted beforehand and which will be made known in due course. One of the most important problems to study in this connection will be the recognition of symptoms that a fire storm may be in process of developing and the necessity of taking the most urgent possible steps to evacuate any personnel in the area wherever they may be. The time lag between the actual bombing and the development of the fire storm may be long or short, but in either case will demand the most urgent and immediate action if people in the area are to be saved. As further data become available training will be given not only in appreciating the situation but, also, in any preventive steps that may be devised.

CHAPTER III

RADIOACTIVITY

The effects of radiation in man may be: —

(a) *Immediate :* At the time of the explosion, through entry into the body of gamma rays and neutrons.

(b) *Delayed :* Subsequent to the explosion, through exposure of the person to the radioactive products of atomic fission ; or to materials on the target which may have been rendered radioactive by neutrons (induced radioactivity).

Although the entry of the gamma flash into the body is immediate, it must be remembered that the physiological results are delayed.

17. Immediate Effects

The main radiation hazard arises from direct exposure of the person to gamma rays and neutrons at the moment of explosion. Because of their great powers of penetration, however, both these agents may affect, in varying degrees of intensity, people within their range who are protected by buildings from other effects of atomic explosion.

Gamma rays and neutrons do not produce any sensatory reaction, and the victim may not realise at the time the danger that he has incurred.

The onset of the resulting symptoms (" radiation sickness ") is early or late according to the dose of radiation received ; this will vary with the distance from the explosion and the degree of protection, if any, at the time it occurred.

In high air bursts, however, possibly the whole of the injury can be attributed to gamma rays, since the range of effectiveness of the neutrons is very much more limited.

18. Protection against Immediate Effects

Against attacks by certain types of war gases various other protective devices are available, such as protective clothing and preventive or curative ointments. It is emphasised that measures of this kind have no value against these " immediate " effects, i.e., gamma rays and neutrons, though the position is not quite the same as regards " delayed effects " as is shown in paragraph 20.

It is, however, satisfactory to know that in the design of shelters protection against the lethal results of radioactivity is a practical proposition.

The principle is that of " screening ". Although gamma rays are extremely penetrating there is a limit to their powers in this direction. When passing through matter they expend a proportion of their energy which is directly related to the total density of the material penetrated. Even air reduces their intensity somewhat. The denser the screening material the greater its power of reducing the intensity of the gamma rays in a given thickness. For example, building

25

materials such as brick and concrete have a greater stopping power than has wood for a given thickness, and lead greater than either on account of its greater density.

The walls of ordinary dwelling houses and surface shelters of last-war type would afford a definite though limited degree of protection, depending upon the distance from the point of explosion. Really thick masonry could remove the danger from gamma rays altogether, even close to ground zero, whilst a moderate thickness of earth affords excellent protection ; and only a few feet of earth overhead would afford complete immunity from the effects of gamma rays. The thickness of all ordinary materials which will afford complete immunity from the effects of gamma rays will be notified in due course.

Shelters of the last-war type, such as the Anderson, the surface shelter, tunnels and caves, trench shelters and the like, would provide a very substantial degree of protection, which could be made complete with extra thickening.

19. Delayed Effects

Delayed radiation risks are not considered likely to be serious with air burst atomic bombs. If experienced they will be mainly due to the agency of fission products and, more rarely, of induced radioactivity ; a remote possibility may arise from the employment by an enemy of certain radioactive by-products.

Fission Products : As stated in Chapter I it is unlikely that fission products in high concentration will be found on a target area unless the explosion has occurred at a low height, underground, or underwater in close proximity to the target. Under these conditions the initial contamination may present such a serious hazard that the affected area may have to be evacuated for some time. On the other hand, any area experiencing heavy contamination from a low air burst bomb will almost certainly be completely pulverised by blast and unless there were people trapped in shelters in this area there might be no immediate need for any Civil Defence or other personnel to enter it.

Apart from their external radiation effects, fission products are dangerous if they gain entrance into the body by inhalation, by contamination of broken skin, or through contaminated food or drink ("radioactive poisoning").

Induced Radioactivity : In a low air burst, many elements and their compounds in materials in the central zone may be rendered artificially radioactive through bombardment by neutrons released by the explosion.

Although the intensity of induced radioactivity may rapidly wane, prolonged exposure of the body to the radiations evolved may constitute a definite hazard to man.

Radioactive by-products : In the manufacture of fissile elements and in the operation of atomic piles, certain highly radioactive materials of varying half-lives are produced which may, theoretically, be used in war in the form of radioactive dusts or clouds. The quantities so produced, however, are not likely to be so great as to create a serious menace ; moreover, their progressive decline in activity, coupled with difficulties in storage, carriage, handling and loading, make their possible employment in war still more problematical.

20. **Protection against Delayed Effects**

There are six principles of protection against the effects of delayed radioactivity. They are:—

    (i) Detection (Radiation Metering).
    (ii) Suitable Clothing and Equipment.
    (iii) Avoidance of Heavily Contaminated Areas.
    (iv) Personal Cleansing.
    (v) Decontamination.
    (vi) Periodical Medical Examination and Rules Governing Exposure.

(i) *Detection (Radiation Metering)*

Means of immediate detection of the presence of radioactivity already exist in the shape of radiation meters. These are instruments which record the total radiation dose received at the spot where the instrument is, or, in some cases, the rate at which that dose is being received. Since gamma rays travel quite long distances in air, these instruments average up the effects of fission products from a considerable area, just as the body would do. Other instruments, in their turn, will indicate the slightest trace of radioactive contamination on clothing or skin, resulting from dust or water contaminated by fission products. These meters will be more fully discussed later in this chapter. In this connection, however, it is important to remember that gamma rays of themselves are incapable of contaminating anything, or of rendering any material radioactive.* Gamma rays depend, for their effects, entirely on causing casualties from radiation sickness.

Although scientific knowledge is not needed in the use of meters, a certain amount of training is necessary and will be given to selected individuals. Ability to manipulate and read instruments is not in itself enough. Training is needed in the interpretation of the readings taken.

Three types of meter have been recommended for use in the Civil Defence Corps and ancillary Services. They are as follows :—

    (*a*) Individual Dosimeter.
    (*b*) Portable Dose-rate Meter.
    (*c*) Contamination Meter.

Individual Dosimeter: This is a small instrument which can be easily carried on the person. The type at present recommended for Civil Defence is known as the Quartz-Fibre Electroscope. It is about the size of, and similar in appearance to, a fountain pen, and has a clip by which it can be fastened in the breast pocket ; other types are under development.

The total dose is recorded and the wearer can from time to time take a reading, and thus keep a constant check upon his own safety. The reading is taken by applying one end of the instrument to the eye and reading the dose on the scale which will be visible against the light. (See Fig. 4.)

Portable Dose-Rate Meter: There is an important difference between this type of instrument and that just described, in that instead of reading the total dose which has accumulated up to the

---

* Scientists can detect slight activity following bombardment by gamma rays, but it is of no significance for the present purpose.

FIG. 4.   Individual Dosimeter.

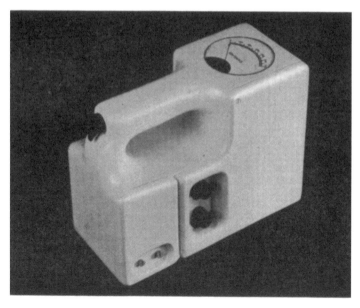

FIG. 5.   Portable Dose-Rate Meter.

28

Photos Nos. 1 and 2. H I R O S H I M A . General views looking across the centre of damage, the approximate position of which is marked with an arrow. It will be seen that some of the framed buildings quite near the centre remained standing. The tall building in Photo No. 1 is the same as that seen in Photo No. 7. The foreground illustrates the remnants of Japanese dwellings, razed to the ground.

Photo No. 3. N A G A S A K I . A general view of the area near the centre of damage, which is to the left in the picture, only 300 yds. away from the bridge. Note the little that remains (in the foreground) of blasted and burnt Japanese dwellings. For a view of such houses, undamaged, see Photo No. 19.

Photo No. 4. N A G A S A K I . A general view showing some of the industrial buildings. That in the foreground was a gutted woodworking plant, just over a mile from the centre of damage, which was beyond the group of chimneys of the Mitsubishi Steel Works, seen in the middle distance.

Photo No. 5. NAGASAKI. Reinforced concrete school with a timber roof, 500 yds. from the centre of damage, which is to the right of the photograph. The upper part of the long wall further from the explosion has been bent over, partly by a thrust through the roof from the other long wall and partly by wind suction. This is a typical case of "mass distortion."

Photo No. 6. NAGASAKI. Mass distortion of steel framed shed buildings about half a mile from the centre of damage, which was to the right of the buildings in the photograph. It will be seen that the entire main frame is seriously distorted away from the explosion.

Photo No. 7.   H I R O S H I M A .   Reinforced concrete building about 300 yds. from the centre of damage, which is to the left of the photograph. There was no serious structural damage, although a roof panel was depressed and some internal party walls were deflected.   Designed for earthquake resistance, this building has a composite reinforced concrete and steel frame.

Photo No. 8.   H I R O S H I M A .   Reinforced concrete building 200 yds. from the centre of damage, which is to the right. The blast from the bomb forced the roof slab down, the slab shearing round the column heads, leaving the internal columns projecting through the debris. Few concrete buildings failed in this way.

Photo No. 9. H I R O S H I M A . Reinforced concrete school 500 yds. from the centre of damage, which is to the right. The frame of this building was of special design (portal) and resisted the lateral forces. The outside walls were of continuous reinforced concrete, and although they were deflected, as seen, they did not fail.

Photo No. 10. N A G A S A K I . Reinforced concrete single storey factory rather less than a mile from the centre of damage, which is to the right. The arched reinforced concrete roof failed, the side nearer the explosion being forced inwards and the far side forced upwards.

Photo No. 11. H I R O S H I M A . Small steel framed shed ¼ mile from the centre of damage, showing the distortion of the entire framework, with the building leaning away from the explosion.

Photo No. 12. N A G A S A K I . Large steel framed shed in the Mitsubishi Steel Works, ¾ mile from the centre of damage. The steel stanchions have been bent (away from the explosion) and the roof trusses on both sides of these stanchions have collapsed.

Photo No. 13. NAGASAKI. ½ mile from centre of damage. Typical damaged machines in one of the many timber workshops destroyed by blast and fire. Some machines were overturned by movement of the buildings, some destroyed by fire alone; others damaged by exposure to the weather.

Photo No. 14. NAGASAKI. Blast effect on a gasholder ½ mile from centre of damage. Note the way in which the whole framework has been bent away from the explosion.

Photo No. 15. HIROSHIMA. Three storey bank building with load bearing brick walls of strong construction and comparable with British standards. This degree of damage to such buildings extends to a radius of ½ mile from centre of damage. Compare with the behaviour of the reinforced concrete framed building in the background.

Photo No. 16. NAGASAKI. The Roman Catholic Cathedral 600 yds. from centre of damage. The walls were of heavy load-bearing brick construction. Most of the damage is attributable to blast, although fire subsequently consumed all combustible debris. Note in the foreground the huts erected by the Japanese for temporary living quarters after the atomic bomb raid.

Photo No. 17. H I R O S H I M A . Typical, part below ground, earth-covered, timber framed shelter 300 yds. from the centre of damage, which is to the right. In common with similar but fully sunk shelters, none appeared to hav been structurally damaged by the blast. Exposed woodwork was liable to "flashburn." Internal blast probably threw the occupants about, and gamma rays may have caused casualties.

Photo No. 18. N A G A S A K I . Typical small earth-covered back yard shelter with crude wooden frame, less than 100 yds. from the centre of damage, which is to the right. There was a large number of such shelters, but whereas nearly all those as close as this one had their roofs forced in, only half were damaged at 300 yds., and practically none at half a mile from the centre of damage.

Photo No. 19. NAGASAKI. Typical Japanese houses in a street screened from damage by the surrounding hills. Buildings of similar construction formed the main proportion of buildings in Nagasaki and Hiroshima.

Photo No. 20. NAGASAKI. A room in the concrete hospital, ½ mile from the centre of damage. The building was structurally undamaged, and one of the few of its type to escape internal fire damage. The collapse of suspended ceilings, partitions, etc., caused many casualties; fire would have increased their plight.

Photo No. 21. HIROSHIMA. Roughening of polished granite by "flash" heat effect at 200 yds. from the centre of damage. The polish remains only where shielded by (a) a man seated on the steps, (b) a man leaning against the corner of the plinth adjoining the steps and (c) in the "shadows" of the plinth mouldings.

Photo No. 22. NAGASAKI. Timber framing scorched by heat radiation at ¾ mile from the centre of damage. The surface is unscorched where it is shielded by the uprights.

Photo No. 23. HIROSHIMA. Shadow cast by valve-wheel on side of gasholder 1¼ miles from the centre of damage. The bituminous coating on the steel plates was affected by heat radiation except where shielded by the wheel and spindle.

Photo. No. 24. NAGASAKI. Section of ridge tile and part of pantile recovered from the centre of damage, showing the " bubbling " effect produced by the intense heat radiation. Note the gradations on the half round tile; also the unscorched section of the pantile where the tile has been protected by the overlap of the adjacent tile.

moment, they measure the rate at which that dose is being received per hour. Portable meters are battery-operated and are likely to be supplied for Civil Defence use in a stout, felt-lined case with a shoulder sling. A dial reading can be taken at any time by turning a switch. (See Fig. 5.)

These meters are for measuring dose rate contours around the heavily contaminated central zone at ground zero, so that safe working times can be calculated from previously prepared tables. The process is analogous to the use of the pocket vapour and ground detectors for blister gas.

Contamination Meter : This is a very sensitive instrument for the purpose of detecting any trace of radioactive contamination on the skin or clothing of individuals.

Contamination meters are for installation in hospitals, cleansing stations, and other places where personal cleansing is necessary. By walking past the instrument it is possible to tell whether an individual is contaminated or not, as the increasing meter reading and rising stridency of the incorporated loud-speaker will give immediate evidence of the fact. The contaminated can thus be segregated from the uncontaminated, and the former recalled and subjected to a detailed " frisking " by going over them with the probe of the instrument held close to but not touching their skin and clothing. This will indicate with accuracy the exact location and area of the contamination. (See Fig. 6.)

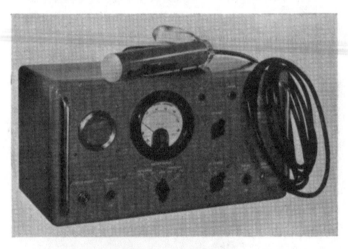

Fig. 6. Contamination Meter.

(ii) *Clothing and Equipment :* Though no form of clothing exists which will protect the wearer against gamma flash, or the gamma rays emanating from fission products and from materials in which radioactivity has been induced, it is quite easy to protect the individual from the alpha and beta particles which are likely to be given off, since they have both a very short range and practically no powers of penetration, as explained in the following paragraphs.

Alpha particles have an extreme range of only a couple of inches in air, and have no powers of penetration. The danger lies in the possibility of their being emitted by material which has been inhaled, or swallowed, or absorbed into the body through broken skin (e.g., wounds). The likelihood of exposure of this sort is regarded as small.

Beta particles have a range of several yards in air, and poor powers of penetration. Like the alpha particles they are extremely dangerous if they are emitted by material which has gained access to the interior of the body and, in addition, they can cause severe skin injuries if contact of such material with the bare skin is prolonged. Any ordinary clothing of reasonably close weave suffices to keep beta active material from contact with the skin, provided that openings at wrist and ankle can be kept closed in one way or another. The wearing of the respirator will protect against inhalation or swallowing.

It will, also, be necessary to keep contaminated dust, and the like, out of the hair. This can be done by any suitable type of hood or cap, nor need the latter be non-porous.

From the foregoing emerges a picture of suitable clothing and equipment for those who have to pass through or work in a heavily contaminated area, namely :—

   (a) Respirator.

   (b) Denim Overalls (example).

   (c) Gloves (preferably of rubber or fabric).

   (d) Gumboots or strong leather boots as used in the Rescue Section.

(iii) *Avoidance of Heavily Contaminated Areas :* It should be a rule that no person is allowed to enter or remain in a heavily contaminated area unless his duty compels him to do so. Members of the public normally need to be evacuated in a planned and orderly manner. Reconnaissance personnel with their meters will know the extent of the area, and their advice must be followed.

Certain precautions must be enforced in the case of persons who have to stay and work in the area. No food, drink, sweets, smoking materials, etc., must be carried, owing to the danger of their contamination by fission products. If the work in the area is going to take longer than an hour or two it will be necessary to provide food and drink. This could be done by mobile canteens bringing the necessary supplies from outside to the upwind perimeter of the area, in airtight containers, and allowing no persons to partake until their hands have been thoroughly washed and scrubbed (particular attention being paid to the parts under the nails). Nor, once gloves have been removed, must the hands be allowed to touch clothing or equipment.

(iv) *Personal Cleansing :* There are numbers of protective measures common to both atomic and chemical warfare. The arrangements for cleansing contaminated personnel are an example, and an almost identical procedure will serve those contaminated by fission products as well as those contaminated by chemical warfare agents.

It has been stated earlier in this chapter that there is no need to make use of non-porous protective clothing, unless chemical warfare agents are also present in the radioactive area. None the less care will be needed in undressing so as to prevent the spread and inhalation of radio-contaminated dust. During the process of undressing care must be taken not to shake particles of clothing as they are removed, since this would tend to make dust particles fly, and so spread the contamination. A light spraying with water is definitely valuable and should be the rule. Each article when removed must be placed in an ordinary bin to await disposal or decontamination.

Washing procedure will have to be very thorough, use being made of scrubbing brushes ; and it will be of advantage if hand-basins and nail brushes can also be provided, since the angle of skin and nail needs careful attention. After washing, the person should again be metered. If contamination still remains the washing will have to be repeated until the meter records a negative result.

(v) *Decontamination :* It is important to realise that radioactivity, unlike chemical warfare agents, cannot be destroyed. It can be removed and taken to a place where it can do no harm, or it can be left to decay by natural means, which in some cases is a very long process and in others relatively short. There is at present no other method of decontamination suitable for use in Civil Defence.

(a) *Clothing :* If clothing is badly contaminated it will probably be better to dispose of it altogether. More lightly contaminated clothing can be rendered safe by more or less normal laundry methods, or by dry cleaning.

(b) *Other Materials :* If decontamination can be taken in hand before the contamination has had time to be absorbed into the material, removal by methods similar to those used for removal of persistent gas contamination can be undertaken.

(c) *Streets and Public Places :* There is at present no known method of achieving complete decontamination, though hosing down will certainly help to aid dispersion provided it can be done without creating a further hazard with the water thus used: i.e., the disposal of such water must be carefully watched. If conditions permit the area can be left to the process of natural radioactive decay.

(d) *Food :* Gamma rays have no harmful effects upon foodstuffs. Foods which were within very close range of neutrons when the bomb exploded are likely to be irradiated and would have to be disposed of irrespective of whether they were in airtight containers or not. The depositing of fission products upon unprotected foodstuffs constitutes the greatest danger, which would be obviated by storing of food in airtight containers.

(vi) *Periodical Medical Examination and Rules Governing Exposure :* It will be necessary to keep a careful check upon the health of Civil Defence personnel whose work carries them into radioactive areas. Meters of one kind or another will indicate the amount of dose received on any one occasion and will warn the individual when it is no longer safe to expose him or herself.

Linked with this problem is that of the dose which may not be exceeded. This maximum permissible dose is now under active investigation and will be notified in due course. It depends to some extent on the time over which it is accumulated. It can be said now, however, that there will have to be a number of different scales laid down to meet the varying conditions of operations. For example, there will be a scale required for the general public, another scale for Civil Defence Corps personnel and the personnel of associated Services such as the Police and the Fire, and a further scale for special emergency work such as the rescue of trapped shelter occupants. These scales, when finally decided, must be known to all holding positions of responsibility so that they can take operational decisions, and also to those concerned with medical and first aid work. The general object will be to ensure, as far as practical, that exposure is under careful control, and if exceptional risks have to be taken at least they will not be ordered blindfold.

A radioactive dose is measured in units known as roentgens. Radiation meters for Civil Defence, such as the individual dose meter, measure either roentgens or roentgens per hour depending on whether they measure the total radiation dose or the radiation dose rate. The exception is the Contamination Meter, which gives an indication of small traces of radioactivity, and is concerned with measuring the amount of radioactivity contamination. This is measured in curies (or milli-curies or micro-curies as the case may be).

21. **Radiation Syndrome**

(i) *Acute :* Radiation sickness is seen in its most characteristic form in individuals who have been exposed to external body radiation at the moment of explosion. Acute symptoms are unlikely to arise from exposure to fission products unless the area is highly contaminated and exposure is early and sufficiently lengthy.

The most severe cases develop symptoms and signs of deep shock, with extreme weakness and vomiting, within a few hours of exposure. With a lesser dose the onset of symptoms may not be apparent for some days ; varying degrees of shock are then noted, with vomiting, rising fever and marked weakness. Those who survive for some time may later show signs of damage to the blood system, gastric and intestinal disturbances supervene, and infection is common.

The least severe cases may not develop symptoms until after the third week, and in these recovery is the rule; similarly, patients who survive to the sixth week have a good chance of recovery. One of the most characteristic signs of radiation sickness seen in these cases, as well as in victims who survive for ten days or longer, is falling out of the hair, usually confined to the scalp but sometimes affecting the eyebrows or beard ; re-growth of hair occurs in three or four months.

Some of the more serious complications of radiation sickness are due to damage to the bone marrow, from which most of the normal constituents of the blood originate. This damage affects the production of both white and red blood cells, with a resulting diminution of their numbers in the circulation. As the white blood cells play a vital part in the defence of the body against bacteria, their absence or diminution in the circulation enables these bacteria to gain the upper hand, and infection may be widespread. Similarly, the diminution in the number of red blood cells gives rise, very often, to severe anaemia or bloodlessness—a condition which is aggravated by the tendency to bleeding which is a common feature of the disease. The cause of death is usually a combination of infection, loss of blood and anaemia.

(ii) *Chronic :* As at present defined, for peace time occupations, the maximum permissible dose rate for repeated exposures, is 0.1 roentgen per 8-hour day, or 0.5 roentgen per week.* (For a definition of roentgen which is the unit of measurement for a radioactive dose, see Appendix II.)

Repeated exposures, over long continuous periods, to daily dose rates considerably in excess of those quoted above may result in symptoms of chronic radiation sickness as shown by gastro-intestinal discomfort, increasing weakness, and blood changes of varying degrees of severity. Repeated exposures to doses of 25 roentgens and above may give rise to sickness.

Under peace time conditions, as described in the preceding sub-paragraph, there is no risk of sterility occurring. Under war time conditions, where increased risks may have to be taken in the course of urgent operations, a risk of temporary sterility may arise. It should be noted, however, that the close investigations which have been, and are, in fact, still being conducted in the two Japanese cities of Hiroshima and Nagasaki, show clearly that this is a purely temporary phase.

Chronic skin conditions may also arise if radioactive material is left in contact with the skin or is otherwise carried on the person for prolonged periods.

First aid Treatment : Treatment for shock is most important, as well as for any other injuries sustained. Complete physical and mental rest are of the greatest importance together with careful control of environmental temperatures to prevent chilling, and scrupulous care to prevent infection through any wounds. Many casualties will be suffering from radiation sickness and external wounds ; and a reduced blood formation lays the body open to wound infection. The skin of radiation victims is very susceptible to heat and great care will be necessary in the use of hot water bottles and other sources of heat. If radioactive contamination is suspected, cleansing will be necessary before admission to a First Aid Post or Hospital.

Chronic conditions are soon recognised if the cause is known or suspected. These cases should be referred to appropriate medical centres ; treatment of the condition and avoidance of further exposure are usually followed by a steady recovery, but periodical medical examinations may be necessary in certain cases. Reference is made only to first aid treatment in this pamphlet. There is much that can be done on the medical side to cure and mitigate the effects which are described. These measures will be made known in the most appropriate way to all those who require this medical and technical knowledge.

---

* *Note :*—A dose rate of 0.5 roentgen per week represents the dose which can be tolerated, without ill effect, for a period of at least 60 years assuming an exposure of the whole body.

22. Radioactivity Poisoning

This term is used to describe the results that may follow the introduction of radioactive materials into the body, where they will act as local or systemic poisons due to the emission of damaging radiations. These radioactive materials may gain entrance into the body in various ways ; e.g. :—

(a) By inhalation in the absence of a respirator.

(b) By ingestion, or entrance by the mouth through contaminated food, water, pipes, cigarettes, etc.

(c) By injection, or entrance into the circulation through contaminated wounds, abrasions or otherwise damaged skin.

The symptoms that may follow the entrance of radioactive material into the body may be of rapid onset if the dose is very large ; more often it is slow and subtle in development, possibly extending over a period of months or even years. The effects may be localised to one part of the body (e.g., lungs, skin, etc.) or they may become systemic and give rise to general constitutional disturbances.

As these radioactive materials are effective in extremely minute quantities, prevention is obviously the only line to adopt. This is effected by a well-fitting respirator, hood, and adequate protective clothing ; and by the avoidance of all food, drink or smoking while in a contaminated condition, and the observance of a strict working and cleansing discipline.

First aid is only applicable to personnel who may sustain cuts or wounds while working under contaminated conditions ; when this occurs, the damaged skin should be flushed freely with running water and encouraged to bleed.

CHAPTER IV

BLAST

27. Effects on Persons

The direct effects of blast from high air burst bombs on persons is less than might be expected and serious internal injury is rare. The bulk of the casualties will be secondary due to injuries from falling masonry and flying debris. Such injuries would occur up to $1\frac{1}{4}$-2 miles and to a lesser extent from glass and other flying debris at greater distances. The greatest number of indirect injuries and of deaths is likely to be caused by collapse of buildings due to blast with the survivors possibly trapped and exposed to fire dangers. It has been estimated that 70 per cent. of all casualties would suffer from physical injury of some sort.

Protection against blast would not present an insoluble problem. Japanese air raid shelters, even of poor construction, stood up well and underground shelters were a complete protection. Shelters could be constructed to resist both blast and gamma rays.

28. Effects on Material

From air burst bombs the blast wave is from above downwards and strikes roofs first, and near the centre of the damaged area buildings are collapsed or, with specially strong buildings, roofs are crushed in or dished even where the walls remain standing. Further away, where the blast wave is becoming more horizontal, buildings are pushed over or distorted.

The type of building and the distance from ground zero are the factors influencing reaction to blast. Unframed buildings like ordinary dwelling houses suffer more severe damage than framed buildings, whether of reinforced concrete or steel, and buildings of earthquake-resisting construction remain practically undamaged at 2,000 feet from ground zero. Bridges, which are built to withstand vertical pressure, stand up to the blast much better than ordinary houses, which are not so constructed, though reflection from roads, rivers, etc., may cause displacement on the underside and is a point to be carefully watched.

The British Mission estimated that from a high air burst bomb such as was used in Japan, an ordinary British city with 15 houses and 45 persons to the acre would suffer damage to dwelling houses to a distance of 2 to $2\frac{1}{2}$ miles from ground zero on the following scale:—

Nature of Damage	Average Radius from Ground Zero and Number of Houses Involved
Demolished or requiring demolition	1 mile 30,000 houses
Uninhabitable and requiring major repairs	$1-1\frac{1}{2}$ miles 35,000 houses
Temporarily uninhabitable but requiring only minor repairs	$1\frac{1}{2}$ miles—2 to $2\frac{1}{2}$ miles 50,000—100,000 houses

39

This damage would affect the dwellings of 400,000 people and, even allowing for those who might be casualties and those who could return after minor repairs to their houses had been completed, or who did not have to leave their houses at all, some 100,000 persons would need rehousing, creating a very big Civil Defence problem. (See Fig. 7.)

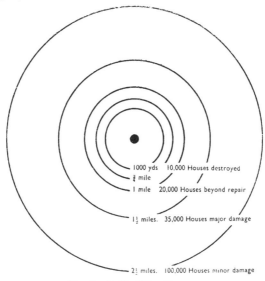

1000 yds   10,000 Houses destroyed
¾ mile
1 mile   20,000 Houses beyond repair
1½ miles.   35,000 Houses major damage
2½ miles.   100,000 Houses minor damage

FIG. 7.   Radii of Blast Damage.

29. Effects on Public Utility Services

The effects of the high air burst bomb on public utility services would be confined to damage above ground. Gas and water mains would be undamaged except possibly where they are carried over bridges. Sewers, too, should be all right. Over-ground installations such as gas holders, water pumping stations, electricity sub-stations, overhead electricity, tramway, telephone and telegraph cables, trams, buses and motor cars would be damaged more or less severely up to one mile or so from ground zero and would present a big problem of repair to the utility services. Railway and tramway tracks would probably remain intact but be affected by debris, adjacent fires, overturned rolling stock, etc. Ground burst or low air burst bombs would produce a cratering effect and earth shock involving considerable areas of underground damage, but the ground area affected would be much smaller. Delayed danger from induced radioactivity and fission products might, if present, also considerably complicate the work of repair.

30. Rescue Problems

Apart from fire one of the major problems would be rescue work, and it must be accepted that the effect of blast, as indeed was discovered during the last war, will inevitably produce large quantities of rubble and debris which will complicate the rescue problem.

Rescue work, as always, requires high discipline and technique, and it is clearly important that in any area the design and location of shelters should be carefully mapped beforehand and made available for rescue parties. The rescue parties should also familiarise themselves with the use of these maps, since after an explosion the ordinary landmarks may not be available and approach to any such shelters would almost certainly be difficult owing to the rubble and debris.

It will be of first importance to initiate some action with the greatest possible speed, even though full operations will take time to develop. Rescue parties with light equipment might be able, for example, to go straight in over the rubble and begin a preliminary reconnaissance and start rescue operations while the main force follows up. This force may require mechanical equipment to clear a path for their heavy vehicles, and the sooner people trapped in shelters have some evidence that help is arriving the better. In certain cases where conditions are suitable, it may be possible to make the quickest approach by water, and in studying this problem all these possibilities must be taken into account and training will be initiated in due course so as to prepare rescue parties and others to operate under conditions which may be quite unfamiliar at present.

APPENDIX I

ELEMENTARY ATOMIC PHYSICS

1. The Structure of Matter in Relation to the Size of the Atom

In order to understand the way in which matter is built-up it must be realised that substances which we think of as solids in fact are not ; in other words matter is not continuous. From our point of view a very thin piece of steel, such as a safety razor blade, is solid ; from the point of view of the atom it is more akin to a piece of rabbit wire.

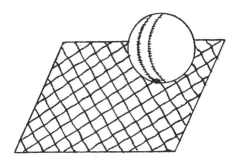

Wire stops ball as if it were solid.

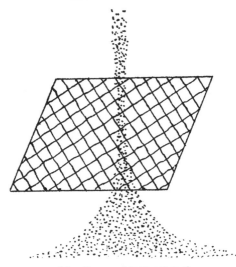

Wire allows sand to pass through.

Fig. 8.

Now let us think about a piece of 1-inch mesh rabbit wire, first from the point of view of a cricket ball, and secondly from the point of view of a handful of dry sand. If a cricket ball falls on to the sheet of wire it will be stopped, and the cricket ball could scarcely be blamed if it said that the sheet of wire was a solid sheet. On the other hand if a handful of sand was dropped the grains of sand would fall through the sheet of wire ; true there would be collisions between the grains of sand and the wire, but none the less the sand would go through the wire, and the sand would not consider the wire sheet as being solid or continuous matter. (See Fig. 8.)

2. Structure of the Atom

The atom is composed of a " nucleus ' and circling round it there are a number of small very light particles known as electrons each of which carries a negative electric charge. This set-up may be likened to our solar system with the sun as the counterpart of the nucleus and the earth, and other planets which revolve round it taking the place of the electrons. (See Fig. 9.)

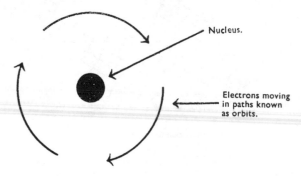

Nucleus.

Electrons moving in paths known as orbits.

Fig. 9.

The nucleus is not just a solid lump but is composed of two kinds of particles held very strongly bunched together. (See Fig. 10.) One kind of particle carries a positive electric charge and is called a proton, and the other carries no electric charge and is called a neutron. Protons and neutrons are practically the same weight and both are very much heavier than the electron. The number of protons and electrons is such that as a whole the atom is electrically neutral.

Fig. 10. Nucleus.

48

When atoms combine to form substances the nucleus of each atom remains unchanged but the orbits link-up. This is not unlike the situation caused when people link arms, having done so they have become a group having its own characteristics, yet the characteristics of each person remain unchanged. (See Figs. 11 and 12.)

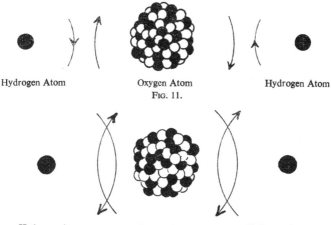

Hydrogen Atom   Oxygen Atom   Hydrogen Atom

FIG. 11.

Hydrogen Atom   Oxygen Atom   Hydrogen Atom

Linked-up (combined chemically) to form water.

FIG. 12.

Chemical reactions IN NO WAY AFFECT the nuclei of the atoms; they are brought about by the linking-up—or the unlinking —of electron orbits.

3. Radioactivity

It has long been known that some of the heavier elements emit radiations; such elements are said to be radioactive. The radiations come from the nuclei of the atoms and may be fast moving charged particles (alpha particles and electrons) and penetrating radiation similar to X-rays (gamma rays).

The radioactivity continues through many intermediate stages until finally all the atomic nuclei have changed into atoms which are quite stable. Thus radium—which is radioactive—ultimately becomes lead which is stable.

The time taken for this to happen depends on the element in question; for example—after 1,600 years half of a piece of radium will have become lead, after another 1,600 years only a quarter of the original amount will remain as radium and so on. This time is known as the " half-life "—for radium it is 1,600 years, for some elements it is only a fraction of a second whereas for others it may be millions of years. Under certain circumstances any element can become radioactive.

4. Neutrons

Because matter is not continuous and because the neutron is not electrically charged it can travel a long way in matter and, indeed, may pass right through it.

5. Fission

Some neutrons when passing through matter will collide with a nucleus and when this takes places one of two things may happen: it may either bounce off and continue its journey, or it may be captured by the nucleus, that is, it may enter, and become part of, the nucleus.

The added mass and energy of the captured neutron causes the nucleus to become unstable (radioactive) and to restore its equilibrium may do one of two things ; it may either emit radiations with or without neutrons, or with heavy elements, it may break in two and emit one or more neutrons ; this process is known as fission. (See Figs. 13, 14 and 15.)

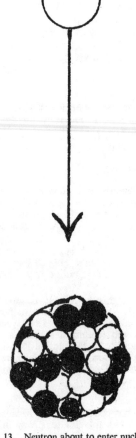

FIG. 13.   Neutron about to enter nucleus.

When fission takes place the energy released is enormous—if a pound of fissionable material could all be fissioned it would release as much energy as the explosion of 8,000 tons of T.N.T.

Some substances, after capturing a neutron, fission more easily than others: Uranium 235 and Plutonium markedly so. Fission is only observed in the heaviest elements.

FIG. 14. Nucleus after neutron capture. Excess energy causes distortion; emission of radiations may restore equilibrium or the nucleus may fission.

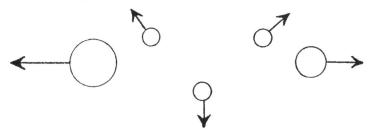

FIG. 15. After fission: the two fission fragments move apart, in this instance there are 3 fission neutrons.

6. Explosive Requirements

If this enormous energy release is to be used as an explosive the following requirements must be satisfied: —

(a) The fission process must be capable of being initiated without the use of bulky and heavy apparatus.

(b) The fissioning of one nucleus must be capable of producing sufficient neutrons to propagate the process throughout the mass of fissionable material—that is to say it must start a chain reaction.

(c) The chain reaction must progress throughout the whole mass at such a speed that not only does it give rise to a rapid release of energy—a sine qua non of an explosion —but so rapidly that the mass of fissionable material is neither melted nor blown asunder before the bulk of it has had time to fission.

Below a certain size (the CRITICAL SIZE) a chain reaction cannot take place ; above this size nothing can prevent it taking place. The existence of a critical size is due to the decreasing ratio of surface-volume as the size increases ; by decreasing the mass of fissionable material the ratio surface-volume is increased and there is a greater possibility of neutron escape at the surface.

By using a sufficient mass of Uranium 235 or Plutonium, enough of the neutrons produced in fission will be utilised in producing further fissions to propagate the process throughout the mass of material; moreover, the process will proceed in such a small time that the result is an explosion. This time is of the order of a few micro-seconds—and a micro-second is one-millionth of a second. (See Fig. 16.)

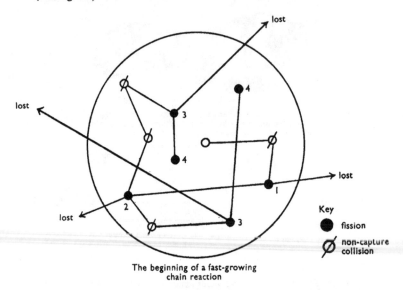

The beginning of a fast-growing
chain reaction

FIG. 16.

The figure gives a representation of the paths of neutrons in the initial stages of a chain reaction.

The chain started with fission 1 brought about by a neutron which started at 0 in the centre of the material. This fission gave two neutrons one of which was lost, the other causing fission 2. This fission gave rise to three neutrons one of which was lost, the other two causing fissions numbered 3, and so on. It can be seen that non-capture collisions are frequent as shown at ∅. By the use of a reflector the build-up of the reaction would have been enhanced as some of the neutrons shown as lost might well have been reflected back into the mass.

7. The Atomic Bomb

From the above it follows that in principle the bomb may be made up as follows: The material used may be pure or reasonably pure Uranium 235 or Plutonium. It may be made up into two or more pieces each of which is sub-critical in size yet, when brought together are well above the critical mass—for the more material that is assembled together the less the proportional leakage of neutrons out of the mass and, therefore, the greater the increase of neutron intensity per generation and the more rapid the whole process.

With two sub-critical masses suitably apart no self-sustaining chain reaction can start; when they are brought together nothing can prevent it starting. If they are brought together slowly the reaction will start as they approach each other and long before the whole mass has fissioned the material will have melted; instead of an explosion comparable to that of thousands of tons of T.N.T. there will merely be an energy release sufficient to melt the assembly.

The whole should be encased in some dense material which will delay the expansion of the mass sufficiently to permit additional generations of fission before the process is brought to a stop by increasing size. (See Fig. 17.)

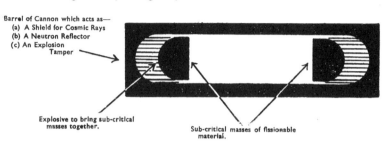

Barrel of Cannon which acts as—
  (a) A Shield for Cosmic Rays
  (b) A Neutron Reflector
  (c) An Explosion
       Tamper

Explosive to bring sub-critical masses together.

Sub-critical masses of fissionable material.

FIG. 17. Diagram illustrating Principle of Atomic Bomb.

APPENDIX II

GLOSSARY

ALPHA PARTICLE.—A helium nucleus (positively charged) travelling at high speed. Given out when atoms of Uranium, Radium and some other substances undergo spontaneous radioactive breakdown. Very short range and negligible penetrating power, e.g., stopped by a sheet of paper. Dangerous if emitted within the body, i.e., if Uranium or Radium, etc., is inhaled, swallowed or obtains entrance to the body through wounds.

ATOM.—Smallest unit of an element that retains the characteristics of that element.

BETA PARTICLES.—Fast electrons emitted when certain atoms undergo radioactive breakdown. Beta emitting substances can cause severe skin burns and are dangerous if they gain entrance to the body as with alpha emitters.

CHAIN REACTION.—Self-sustaining process in which some neutrons from one splitting atom are able to split more atoms, setting free still more neutrons which carry on the reaction indefinitely.

COSMIC RAYS.—Penetrating radiation coming to the earth from outer space.

CRITICAL SIZE.—The size of a piece of Uranium 235 or Plutonium which is just large enough to support a chain reaction within itself.

CURIE.—A unit of radioactivity approximately that associated with 1 gram of Radium.

DOSE.—The amount of radiation energy absorbed by a person. Measured in roentgens.

DOSE RATE.—The rate at which radiation is received. Measured in roentgens per hour.

ELECTRON.—The lightest known particle. A constituent of all atoms, around whose nuclei they revolve in orbits not unlike those of planets round the sun.

ELEMENT.—One of the basic substances which cannot be further decomposed into any other more basic substance by chemical means. Ninety-two elements are found naturally on the earth.

FALL-OUT.—The fall-out of fission products from the airborne cloud of radioactive material from a bomb resulting in the deposition of fission products on the ground.

FISSION.—The splitting of an atomic nucleus into two more or less equal fragments and a number of neutrons, with the liberation of a large amount of energy.

FISSION PRODUCTS.—Fragments produced when atoms undergo fission.

FIRE STORM.—A condition which may develop in a large area fire, if the uplift of the hot gases over the area is concentrated and powerful enough to produce a violent wind at the periphery; this restricts the spread of fire outwards but intensifies the extent of combustion in the burning area.

FRISKING.—The passing of the probe of a Contamination Meter over the skin and clothing of a person. This will indicate the presence or absence of radioactive contamination.

GAMMA FLASH.—A phrase coined to distinguish the intense emission of gamma rays from an atomic explosion from the gamma rays given off by natural and induced radioactive substances and by fission products.

GAMMA RAYS.—Extremely penetrating radiation of very short wavelength. Can destroy living tissues and produce a number of physical effects, e.g., fluorescence, and chemical effects. X-rays are exactly the same radiation as low energy gamma rays, but are produced from special electrical machines.

GROUND ZERO.—That point at ground level vertically beneath the point of explosion of an atomic bomb. The greatest damage of all kinds is to be found here.

HALF LIFE.—The time taken for half the nuclei in a radioactive substance to disintegrate spontaneously—always constant for nuclei of the same sort. Varies from a few millionths of a second in the case of some materials to 10,000 million years for various types of nuclei.

HEAT FLASH.—The intense heat radiation emitted by an atomic bomb at the moment of explosion. Causes burns and primary fires over a wide area.

HOT AREA.—The area in which residual radioactivity may be detected after the explosion of an atomic bomb.

INDUCED RADIOACTIVITY.—Radioactivity induced in many materials by neutron bombardment as from the explosion of the atomic bomb.

NEUTRON.—One of the particles composing the nucleus of an atom. Approximately the same mass as a proton, but is electrically neutral. Has the property of penetration of all materials, and the rendering of many of them radioactive. Damages the human tissues.

NUCLEUS.—The " core " of an atom, where nearly all the mass is concentrated. Composed of protons and neutrons.

PERMISSIBLE DOSE.—The maximum total dose of radiation over any given period which is believed to cause no permanent ill effect to the body.

PLUTONIUM.—A metal of high atomic weight made by bombarding atoms of Uranium with neutrons. Can undergo fission and has replaced Uranium 235 in the later atomic bombs. Is a man-made element and was not found in nature until after it had been made artificially.

PROTON.—A positively charged particle found in the nuclei of all atoms.

RADIATION.—Energy in the form of electro-magnetic waves. May also be applied to beams of alpha particles, beta particles and neutrons.

RADIATION METERS.—Instruments of various kinds whose purpose is to detect radioactivity, and to measure radiation dose and radiation dose rate. Some record the total dose received up to any given moment; others record the rate at which that dose is being received per hour.

RADIATION SYNDROME.—A medical condition which follows any considerable amount of tissue damage caused by X or gamma rays, etc. Symptoms not usually perceptible until the passage of a few hours, or even of some days.

RADIOACTIVE POISONING.—The results which may follow the introduction of radioactive materials into the body.

RADIOACTIVITY.—The production of alpha or beta particles and gamma rays by the spontaneous breakdown of atomic nuclei; also as a result of the explosion of an atomic bomb.

ROENTGEN.—The measuring unit of radiation dose.

SCREENING.—Radiations are reduced in intensity on passing through matter. This phenomenon is known as screening.

SHIELDING.—See Screening.

URANIUM.—A heavy metal derived from naturally occurring ores, usually pitchblende. Normally the surface is a dark-yellowish brown colour. It has the highest atomic weight of the elements found in nature. Is mildly radioactive and contains 0.75 per cent. of Uranium 235.